A HISTORY OF
MODERN
POLAND

A HISTORY OF
MODERN
POLAND

FROM
THE FOUNDATION OF THE STATE
IN THE FIRST WORLD WAR
TO THE PRESENT DAY

∷

By **Hans Roos**

Translated from the German by
J. R. FOSTER

ALFRED A. KNOPF · NEW YORK · 1966

Library of Congress Catalog Card Number: 65-11131

:·:

THIS IS A BORZOI BOOK
PUBLISHED BY ALFRED A. KNOPF, INC.

:·:

First American Edition

Originally published in Germany as *Geschichte der Polnischen Nation,* © 1961 by W. Kohlhammer GmbH., Stuttgart

Preface

A history of the Polish nation which tries to portray the period from the refounding of the republic in the First World War to the present day can hardly conform to the criteria of the conventional national history. The pages that follow attempt to depict not only the political and diplomatic history of Poland, but also the pattern of Polish society and the political ideas associated with it. In addition, I have tried at least to touch upon the academic and literary concepts which in the case of the Poles in particular have had such a profound effect on political attitudes. The text of the book is largely based on the many monographs and other works by Polish historiographers both in Poland itself and in exile and also to some extent on my own researches. In view of the difficulties involved in reading Polish books in the original, I have made no attempt to quote sources; the bibliography, which consists mainly of books in Western languages, will provide something of a substitute and will also facilitate deeper studies of individual subjects. The absence of references has not absolved me from the duty of dealing carefully and critically with the material; although the unfamiliarity of most Western readers with the subject as a whole lends the facts themselves a special value, and has made it desirable to put them in the foreground, importance has also been attached to making judgements.

Such were the conditions and assumptions on which the book was undertaken; it is the first to deal with the history of Poland in this particular period.

HANS ROOS

Contents

Contents

Maps

A map showing the nineteenth century partition of Poland will be found immediately following the introduction

Abbreviations

Some groups and political parties with their abbreviations and approximate English equivalents

AK   (*Armia Krajowa*) – Home Army. [Polish Underground.]

BBWR   (*Bezpartyjny Blok Wspolpracy z Rzadem*) – Non-party block for co-operation with the [Pilsudski's] Government.

BNR   (*Biloruska Narodna Rada*) – White Russian [or Belorussian] National Council.[1]

KPP   (*Komunistyczna Partia Polski*) – Communist Party of Poland.

KRN   (*Krajowa Rada Narodowa*) – National Council of Poland. [Communist controlled.]

ONR   (*Oboz Narodowo-Radykalny*) – National Radical Movement (lit. 'Camp'). [Right-wing organization.]

OWP   (*Oboz Wielkiej Polski*) – 'Camp of Great Poland'. [Right-wing organization.]

PAN   (*Polska Akademia Nauk*) – Polish Academy of Sciences.

POW   (*Polska Organizaya Wojskowa*) – Underground military organization founded by Pilsudski in the First World War.

PPR   (*Polska Partia Robotnicza*) – Polish Workers' Party. [The new name given to the reconstructed Polish Communist Party in 1942.]

PPS   (*Polska Partia Socjalistyczna*) – Polish Socialist Party.

[1] In the text the old form 'White Russian' has been used throughout. In addition, throughout the book Polish names have been anglicized to the extent of omission of all Polish diacritical signs.

Abbreviations

PSL   (*Polskie Stronnictwo Ludowe*) – Polish Populist or Peasant Party.[1]

PZPR   (*Polska Zjednoczona Partia Robotnicza*) – Polish United Workers' Party. [The result of the 1948 merger of PPR and PPS.]

SDKPiL (*Socjaldemokracja Krolestwa Polskiego i Litwy*) – Social Democratic Party of the Kingdom of Poland and Lithuania.

SD   (*Stronnictwo Demokratyczne*) – Democratic Party.

SL   (*Stronnictwo Ludowe*) – Populist or Peasant Party. [Pro-Communist wing.]

SP   (*Stronnictwo Pracy*) – Labour Party.

UNR   (*Ukrainska Naridna Rada*) – Ukranian National Council.

ZSL   (*Zjednoczone Stronnictwo Ludowe*) – United Peasant Party. [Formed by merger, under Communist pressure, of PSL and SL in 1947.]

ZMP   (*Zwiazek Mlodziezy Polskiej*) – Union of Polish Youth.

ZMS   (*Zwiazek Mlodziezy Socjalistycznej*) – Union of Socialist Youth.

---

[1] The Polish adjective *ludowy* = popular, rustic. (*Trans.*)

A HISTORY OF
MODERN
POLAND

POLAND·1772

CONGRESS
POLAND·1815

PRUSSIA

AUSTRIAN
EMPIRE

COURLAND

Ri

Libau

Schauler

Memel

SAMOGITI

Wilkom

Königsberg

K

Gdynia

Goldlap

LIT

Danzig

Suwalki

Gro

Marienwerder

Allenstein

ERMLAND

MASURIA

POMERANIA

POMORZE

P R U S S I A

Lomza

Wolkowys

Ostroleka

Bialysto

Netze

Byagoszcz

Thorn

Vistula

Modlin

P

BERLIN

POSEN

WARSAW

Br

Posen

Warta

Lit

Oder

P O L A N D

SILESIA

Breslau

Lodz

Deblin

Elbe

Lublin

Chelm

Kielce

Zam

Katowice

San

Prague

Cracow

Przemysl

Lwo
(Lemb

BOHEMIA

Teschen

EASTERN GA

Drohobycz

A U S T R I A N   E M P I

RUTHEN

VIENNA

HUNGAR

Danube

NIA

Miles

0 100 200

MOSCOW ⊚

RUSSO-POLISH FRONTIER 1667

Düna

Dünaburg
(Dvinsk)

Polozk

•Vitebsk

•Smolensk

WHITE

•Borisow

ANIA

Minsk•

RUSSIA

•Mogilev

ilna

ida

nen

Sluzk•

Bobruisk•

Beresina

Dnieper

S   S   I   A

Pripet

ESIA

Pinsk•

Goryn

Ubort

RUSSO-POLISH FRONTIER 1772

OLHYNIA

•Luck

Styr

Słuch

Zhitomir

Kiev

•

Bila Zerkwa•

•Kanev

Poltava •

el

Tarnopol

U   K   R   A   I   N   E

Dnieper

A

PODOLIA

Zbrucz

•Husiatyn

Bar•

Bug

anisławow•

Dniester

BUKOWINA

Pruth

W. Bromage

Introduction

Before the First World War the Polish people occupied a special position among the stateless peoples and races of Eastern Central Europe in that it formed a 'historical nation' and felt itself as one. Unlike peasant peoples such as the Esthonians, Letts, Lithuanians, White Russians and Ukrainians, the Poles had preserved their own aristocracy and converted foreign ones, especially those of the Lithuanians and White Russians, to Polish culture and the Polish language. Before partition the Polish aristocratic republic had been the constitutional channel through which the Polish or naturalized Polish aristocracy had been enabled to rule over a subject peasantry of Polish, Lithuanian or White Russian stock. After it had been partitioned the Polish nation developed through this very aristocracy a passionate national consciousness, which also spread to the middle and working classes in the second half of the nineteenth century. It was largely the sense of belonging together, of a common culture and history, that saved the Poles in all the partitioned zones from losing their Polish inheritance to any substantial extent. In spite of its official incorporation in the empires of Germany, Austria and Russia, Polish 'society', as the Poles called the totality of organizations intended to replace the State of which they had been deprived, felt itself to be the heir and guardian of the lost national community. It is true that in the period before the First World War this society no longer corresponded to the aristocratic nation of the eighteenth and early nineteenth centuries. Particularly after the revolt of 1863–4 and the ensuing liberation of the peasants in the Russian zone the process of democratization and 'Polonization' had penetrated deep into all social classes.

Admittedly it had not gone equally deep in all zones. In Prussian

Poland, especially in the province of Posen, Polish national feeling had a well-developed middle class of the Central European kind and a strong farming class upon which to exert itself; the farmers and townspeople, who had emancipated themselves in the favourable conditions provided by the Prussian State and were also good businessmen, had created a network of societies and economic organizations which almost amounted to a sort of substitute state. Since 1871 the Prussian Government had tried to Germanize the Polish zone by making German the language of instruction in the schools and by settling Germans on the land, but the administrative achievements of the Poles enabled them to offer considerable resistance to these attempts. A very curious interplay of national and cultural interests was observable: the great mass of the Polish middle classes, farmers and workers gladly made use of the tested institutions of the Prussian army and the Prussian administration and were also loyal to the State, but inwardly they rejected it. Only a few families belonging to the landed aristocracy had any real ties with the Prussian crown.

In the Austrian zone, that is in the crown territory of Galicia and the duchy of Teschen, the process of industrialization and of the creation of a middle class had not gone so far as it had in Posen. Most of the population consisted of small farmers over whom the landowning aristocracy maintained a clear social and political ascendancy. In the towns a kind of middle class was formed by the Jews, who had not been assimilated as they had in the Prussian zone; the very existence of this Jewish middle class hindered the creation of a Polish one. Since 1867 Galicia had enjoyed an autonomous administration which used Polish as its official language and was run mainly by Poles; indeed, in comparison with the mainly peasant Ukrainian population of eastern Galicia the Poles well-nigh occupied the position of a master race. Thus Polish society in Galicia was one of the props of the Austrian Empire precisely because the denationalizing tendencies usual in the German and Russian empires were absent. The political supremacy of the native landed nobility was not assailed until 1907, when a liberal measure giving the vote to the middle classes and the workers was introduced; from then onwards the farmers too began to form their own political organizations.

The part of Poland incorporated in Russia was divided into two politically and juridically different administrative areas. In the 'Kingdom of Poland' or 'Congress Poland' set up in 1815, which was populated mainly by Poles and contained only small minorities of Germans, Jews, Lithuanians and Ukrainians, relics of Polish autonomy were preserved in the Civil Code; the extreme policy of Russification in force since 1886 had been toned down since the revolution of 1905 to the extent that Polish was again permitted as the language of education and as the official language at the lower levels of administration. The 'historical Eastern Marches' of the old Polish realm, officially known as the 'Western Territory of the Russian Empire', had a peasant population which was predominantly Lithuanian, White Russian and Ukrainian; the Poles, who were either landed aristocrats or townspeople, formed a minority, though an autochthonous one. In these territories too the official policy of persecuting all things Polish, pursued since 1864, had had to be abandoned in favour of a certain degree of toleration. It was the Polish claim to these territories, regarded by the St Petersburg Government as essentially Russian and ruled accordingly, that until 1905 had wrecked every attempt at Russo–Polish reconciliation, especially during the rebellions of 1830–31 and 1863. While in the autonomous administration of these frontier areas the Polish nobility still held a favoured position, in the Kingdom it had largely lost its influence as a result of the unsuccessful revolts and of Russian agrarian policy. Here industrialization, which was concentrated particularly in Warsaw, Lodz and the region of Dabrowa, had created a middle class and a powerful industrial proletariat. Thus the social conditions for the formation of political parties were far more favourable in Congress Poland than in Galicia, even though party activities were restricted by the Russian censorship and police and most of the numerous Jews settled there founded their own Jewish party organizations. At any rate Congress Poland produced political impulses which had a considerable effect not only on the frontier territories in the east but also on the Austrian and Prussian areas.

In fact Congress Poland was the home of the two most important political schools of thought produced in Poland since the rebellion of 1863. The oldest and most influential political tendency, that of National Democracy, went back to the secret society known as the Polish League, which in turn linked up with the still older National Liberal ideas of the 'Democratic Society' that had been so powerful before the rebellion. Colonel Zygmunt Milkowski, one of the last 'centralizers' of the Democratic Society, had founded the League in 1886 with the object of overcoming the prevailing positivism and the political indifference of the decades after the rebellion, and also to oppose the merciless Russification policies of men like Michail Katkow and Osip Hurko. The League was reorganized in 1891–2 by Roman Dmowski, who was twenty-eight at the time, transformed into the 'National League', and freed from the domination of the old men round Milkowski. In opposition to the liberal ideas of the older democrats, Dmowski and his friends gradually secured the ascendency of an impatient, racially tinged nationalism and a worship of force which in an extreme form had hitherto been alien to Polish political thinking. More or less at the same time as the League, a broad socialist movement split into various individual groups grew up; at first it largely rejected the idea of national independence and cherished anarchistic, cosmopolitan ideas. However, round about 1890, under the influence of Marx, Engels, and Lassalle, and also that of the League – some of its leaders, such as Zygmunt Balicki, were at the same time socialists – most of the socialist leaders were gradually converted to patriotism. In 1892 almost all the socialist groups in the Kingdom and in exile abroad united under the leadership of Boleslaw Limanowski, an old disciple of Lassalle, and at the instigation of Stanislaw Mendelson, who had been close to Engels, to form the Polish Socialist Party (PPS). The ideology of the PPS was based not so much on the economic ideas of Marx and Engels about the class struggle as on their political theories. The leader of the PPS admired the

6

unyielding attitude of Marx and Engels towards Tsarism and their championship of Polish independence. The effective leader of the PPS at the time of its foundation was Jozef Pilsudski, a young country squire from Vilna. He was a thorough enemy of the Russians, and he developed methods of underground conspiracy which were at least as effective as those of the League. Thus although the two secret parties, the PPS and the League, both sprang from the older aristocratic democracy of the nineteenth century, and although they both represented an anti-Russian and nationalist ideal, for social reasons their paths diverged more and more. The League came to represent middle-class democracy, while the PPS demanded moderate social democracy in the name of the workers.

The Russo-Japanese War of 1904–5 and the resulting revolution in Russia finally crystallized the differences between the two camps, which had been visible since 1900. The PPS, at that time a secret organization with some 50,000 members and a yearly income of about a million roubles (thus far stronger than either wing of the Russian Social Democratic Movement), took up the struggle against the Russian State by means of mass strikes and partisan activity to such purpose that during the war a Russian army some 300,000 strong and consisting mainly of front-line troops had to be stationed in Congress Poland. Pilsudski travelled to Tokyo to conclude a Polish–Japanese alliance against the Russian empire. But this struggle, which grew between 1906 and 1908 into a guerrilla war between Poland and Russia, also led to a reversal in the fortunes of the PPS. In 1906 there was a split inside the PPS between the older 'Right' and the younger 'Left'; the latter rejected the nationalistic anti-Russian policy of the 'Right' and decided to support a purely economic struggle against Tsarism to be conducted in alliance with the Russian Social Democrats. The Left drew ideologically nearer to the 'Social Democratic Movement of the Kingdom of Poland and Lithuania' (SDKPiL), which had existed as early as 1893–6 as an ephemeral group under the spiritual leadership of Rosa Luxemburg, but since 1900 had been built up by Feliks Dzierzynski into an effective, properly organized

7

party. Thus the right wing of the PPS under Pilsudski had to fight inside the revolutionary camp against the left wing of the PPS, the SPKPiC, both wings of the Russian Social Democrats and the 'General Jewish Workers' League (Bund) in Poland and Russia', since all these parties rejected the idea of a politically independent Poland and possessed followers in the territory which had once been Poland. It was true that the PPS Right could point to the enthusiastic support of Marx and Engels for Polish independence, thus collecting most of the Polish workers under its standard and inheriting the position of the old PPS. It also commanded the unconditional support of the 'Polish Social Democratic Party in Galicia and Silesia' (PPSDGiS), which under the leadership of Ignacy Daszynski, an energetic agitator and parliamentarian, passionately opposed the anti-nationalistic and cosmopolitan tendency, and had great importance within the Austrian Social Democratic Movement as a whole. Nevertheless, the new PPS never attained the power of the old. This was mainly because, thanks to the activities of Rosa Luxemburg, the powerful Social Democratic Movement of Germany gradually withdrew the support it had previously given. Among the German Social Democrats, too, a younger, Russophil tendency was replacing the older friendship for Poland displayed by men like Engels, Bebel and Liebknecht.

However, the real antagonist of the PPS in Polish society was the League. Its secret central office had decided about 1902 to regard Germany as the chief adversary of Polish culture and had therefore worked since then quite logically for a reconciliation with the Russian State on a Pan-Slav basis. The League was also hostile to the Jewish community, on the grounds that it formed an obstacle to the formation of a powerful Polish middle class. The final decision in favour of an anti-German and pro-Russian policy was made at the time of the revolution. The property-owning *bourgeoisie*, frightened by strikes, socialistic solutions and the slogans of the PPS condemning the private ownership of the means of production, henceforward tended to lean for support on the Russian authorities. The nationalist programme was reduced to the demand for autonomy for Congress Poland; the League gave up claims to the Eastern Marches in the hope that the Poles' higher standard of civilization would gain leading positions for them in the Russian empire as a whole. Thus the national interest was largely defeated by economic interests. The other side of the coin was the demand that all the eastern parts of Germany which could conceivably be claimed for the Poles should be annexed to a future autonomous Poland within the Russian empire. This particular demand made the League's programme by far the most popular one in Posen, although the cultural conditions and general level of civilization in the Prussian zone were incomparably better than those in Congress Poland. The primary reason for this development was the Prussian policy of Germanization, especially the expropriation law of 1908. Dmowski's prognosis seemed to be confirmed when the drastic changes of the revolutionary period brought a marked reduction in Russification and the League was able to build up a legal National Democratic Party – known by Poles as the 'Endecja' – which achieved great successes in the first elections for the Duma. However, when reactionary tendencies gained the upper hand in Russia, the hoped-for autonomy failed to materialize and some of the measures granting toleration were revoked, numerous groups which insisted on the policy of independence broke away from the National Democrats. One of these consisted of the followers of the Germanophil publicist Wladyslaw Studnicki. This gave Pilsudski the opportunity to move outside the framework of the PPS and to incorporate middle-class politicians in the camp of national independence. Thus in the years before the First World War the political situation became much clearer: an anti-Russian camp was confronted by an anti-German one; a socialist intelligentsia by a *bourgeois* group; a group aiming at independence by one aiming at autonomy; a revolutionary one by one favouring legal methods.

In Galicia the fundamental political questions were different, in so far as the nationalist problem was satisfactorily settled by the already existing autonomy. Of course, here too national democracy and socialism confronted each other, but there were also older and more influential political traditions which had been created by the conservatives of the so-called 'Cracow school'. This party had been founded after the revolt of 1863 by a number of influential men, including Stanislaw Tarnowski, the founder of the Cracow Academy of Sciences; and in Michal Bobrzynski, governor of Galicia from 1907 to 1911, it possessed a gifted leader. Its policy was based on the reconciliation with the Austrian State effected by Count Agenor Goluchowski in 1863, which not only guaranteed the Poles of Galicia a Polish provincial Government but also gave them considerable influence with the Government in Vienna. This successful piece of co-operation coloured the thinking of the Cracow school and worked in two directions. The older tendency represented the concept of 'threefold loyalty', according to which the Poles in Germany and Russia were to seek a reconciliation on the Galician model with their respective Governments. The obstacle to this policy was the attitude of the Governments in Berlin and St Petersburg, and as a result the only people who supported it in the years before the First World War were the extreme aristocratic party in Congress Poland and eastern princes like the Radziwills, the Potockis and the Sanguszkos. In these circumstances, ever since the Bosnian annexation crisis of 1908 and the consequent Russo–Austrian tension, the Poles in Galicia had begun to wonder more and more whether in view of the coming war Galicia could not be made into a 'Polish Piedmont', and an independent Poland built up round Galicia as Italy had been built up round the Kingdom of Sardinia.

It said a good deal for the force and logic of such ideas that they spread to other parties with a very different social background. The great champion of the notion of achieving Polish independence through a Galician Piedmont was the Germanophil Jewish publicist Wilhelm Feldman. In 1912, during the crisis caused by the Balkan wars and Russo-Austrian tension, the leaders of the Cracow Convention united in Cracow with the leaders of the Galician left and centre parties to form the 'Provisional Commission of the United Independence Parties'. Its adherents included not only the Galician PPSDGis and the PPS, some of whose leaders were in exile in Galicia, but also a large group of the 'Polish People's Party', which was headed by Wincenty Witos and represented the peasants. Most of the middle-class National Democrats, some of the conservatives, especially those of eastern Galicia, and the Ukrainian groups stood aloof. An indication of the amazing power of the idea of independence was its capacity to unite the conservative aristocracy and the socialist workers in one block. From 1911 onwards, with the approval of the Austrian General Staff, Pilsudski was able to organize shooting clubs which brought together Galicians and Poles from the Russian zone; by the outbreak of war they had 7,000 members. This nucleus of a future Polish army was supported by the Provisional Commission, although Daszynski did not like this 'game with tin soldiers' and disapproved of Pilsudski's gradual transition from the socialist camp to the 'independence' camp.

Thus before the First World War Poland possessed an abundance of political talent and political parties. In the Kingdom of Poland the main responsibility was carried by Roman Dmowski, who was President of the Polish Club in the Russian Duma, although since 1908 he had secretly renounced the idea of playing the part of an Agenor Goluchowski in the Russian zone and had sunk into political quietism. The model which he and his 'Pan-Poles' secretly admired was the power-drunk ideology of the Pan-Germans. How inconspicuous compared to Dmowski was a man like Wladyslaw Studnicki, a minor nobleman from Dünaburg (Dvinsk), who was incapable of forming a party – he had no followers – yet as 'champion of the one great idea' of independence unleashed powerful spiritual forces in the whole people. Four-fifths of Poland, he kept declaring, was subject to Russia, and therefore the idea of Polish independence could only be directed against the Russians. In his stories, which found their way into literally every cottage, the novelist and Nobel prize winner Henryk Sienkiewicz portrayed the days of Poland's past in bright, romantic colours. His Poland was the medieval empire of the Jagellons, and it included Ruthenians, Cossacks, Tartars and Karaites as well as Prussian knights, Masurians, Samogitians and Goralians. It was thanks to him that the egalitarian national state projected by men like Napoleon III, Dmowski and Woodrow Wilson was invested in the eyes of the Poles with such a legendary quality. If Sienkiewicz's work put a sort of spiritual frame round the Poland which had disappeared and now had to be created afresh, the aristocracy of Warsaw, Minsk and Vilna continued to pursue that old mode of Polish life in which politics were regarded more as a kind of artistic or charitable activity than as a business. Prince Zdzislaw Lubomirski, subsequently mayor of Warsaw, and his colleague at Minsk, the famous numismatist Count Emeryk Czapski, were the very incarnation of the rich, gay, aristocratic, liberal Poland of the eighteenth century. The world of the socialists looked very different. There was the real founder of the PPS, the rich Warsaw banker's son Stanislaw Mendelson, who had turned from the cosmopolitan anarchism of his youth to patriotic socialism, and finally ended up as an orthodox Zionist. There was Maria Jankowska-Zaleska, the daughter of a rich man from the frontier district, who had left her husband, her children and her Ukrainian estates to forward the cause of socialism with Mendelson. Finally, there were those unyielding champions of a national and socialist Poland who had not graduated from large-scale terrorist activities in the revolutionary period. The fighting organization of those days had united men as different as Tomasz Arciszewski, the trade unionist and leader of the metal workers of Congress Poland, Aleksander Prystor, a nobleman from Vilna, and Walery Slawek, the student and terrorist. Slawek, the son of a Polish prince and a Ukrainian woman, was an idealist who, undeterred by having his face horribly mutilated by a bomb he had made himself, continued to struggle with the greatest unselfishness for Polish independence. The distance between this kind of attitude and the almost exaggerated cosmopolitanism of a Rosa Luxemburg seemed nearly unbridgeable. The Lublin banker's daughter had nobly devoted her life to the liberation of the working class throughout the world, and therefore completely rejected the most modest expression of patriotic enthusiasm. For all her

splendid literary gifts she was not free from that doctrinaire
rigidity which made old August Bebel call her a 'rose-coloured
bed-bug'. Her colleague, Feliks Dzierzynski, who came, like
Pilsudski (who was ten years older) from the landed aristocracy
of Vilna, already displayed, in a manner almost reminiscent of
Robespierre, the characteristics of the puritanical theorist. Compared with the success of orthodox socialism and of world
revolution human life meant little to him; it was this tendency to
fanaticism which enabled the soft and pampered son of a
Lithuanian nobleman to become the creator of the Cheka.

Compared with the variety of the political scene in the Kingdom
of Poland, political life in the Prussian zone was sober. The same
Poles who had refused to be 'Polish-speaking Prussians' had
unwittingly become, after a century of Prussian domination,
'Prussian Poles'. Among the great majority of those Poles in
Posen, West Prussia and Ermland who were conscious of their
nationality, the National Democratic view was so universal and
so powerful that the other modes of thought represented were
little more than functions of their correlatives in Congress Poland.
It is true that Polish opposition to Prussia never assumed revolutionary characteristics; it was restricted to parliamentary and
publicist activities, but it was largely directed by the secret central
committee of the League. Nevertheless, for many landed families,
class and feudal interests came before patriotism. Loyalty to the
reigning dynasty, as practised by the Cracow conservatives, was
just as binding for the Prussian branch of the Radziwills, who
were closely related to the Hohenzollerns, as it was for Count
Bohdan Hutten-Czapski, who was the scion of a Polish senatorial
family and the son of an officer in the rebel army of 1830, yet
proudly confessed, 'I was always a Prussian'. In these circumstances, political life in Galicia seemed to offer the best hope for
achieving Polish independence. The curious tactical alliance of
Polish–Austrian noblemen and privy councillors such as Apolinary
Jaworski, Leon Bilinski and Michal Bobrzynski with the Lithuanian revolutionary Pilsudski was somewhat reminiscent of the
relationship of Cavour to Garibaldi. None of the imperial

Austrian dignitaries – and here they were in agreement with the politicians of all Poland – believed in the possibility of a restoration of Poland by revolutionary means. A diplomatic solution seemed the only possible one. Pilsudski was quite alone in his faith in the resurrection of Poland through its own strength. Rosa Luxemburg laughed at such a conviction as springing from 'the over-heated imagination of a coffee-house politician'. Pilsudski rejected Lenin, who was in Cracow at this time, as too doctrinaire; but when the latter said he was willing to grant Poland the independence of a purely communist State, Pilsudski reckoned on the unique chance of a war which would put the three partitioning powers on different sides. As early as June 1914 he saw clearly what the course of the coming world war would be; he explained that in such a war the Central Powers would first destroy the Russian empire, but would then in turn be defeated by the Western Powers. The champions of a Polish state should therefore first ally themselves with the Central Powers, and then, when the change in fortunes occurred, go over to the West. This was in fact the programme which Pilsudski followed during the First World War. For him August 1914 was the answer to the prayer which the famous poet Adam Mickiewicz – for whose work Pilsudski otherwise had no particular sympathy – had once addressed to God for a universal war to free the oppressed Poles.

CHAPTER I

The Struggle for Polish Independence in the First World War (1914-1919)

THE OCCUPATION OF POLAND BY THE CENTRAL POWERS

When the First World War broke out neither the German nor the Russian Governments had any very clear idea how to deal with the Polish question. In August 1914 the Berlin Cabinet under Theobald von Bethmann-Hollweg produced a plan for a Polish State covering the area of Congress Poland, but the plan was indefinite and by no means carefully thought out. The future State was to have close political, economic and military ties with Germany. Nevertheless, vaguely as these aims were formulated, they were not unopposed. Because of Posen, which in any case was to go on being subjected to the old policy, the German right-wing parties distrusted any attempt to open up the Polish question. The agreeable habit of looking at the Polish problem only from the point of view of German home affairs had caused Bismarck's statesmanlike far-sightedness to be forgotten. In spite of his fundamental refusal to accept the idea of a Polish national state Bismarck had been prepared, if war with Russia was unavoidable, to 'make Poland rise'. The Tsarist Government, for its part, was just as unwilling to make Dmowski's aims its own and to call into being an autonomous Poland eventually to be enlarged by the inclusion of the German eastern provinces and Galicia. Sergiusz Sasonow, the Foreign Minister, had plans for Polish autonomy, but they were defeated by the traditional policy of unification which had been pursued since 1886 and never fundamentally reversed. So the St Petersburg Government, like that of Berlin, at first handled the Polish question in a dilatory fashion, although on 15 August 1914 the Russian generalissimo, Grand Duke

Nicholas, made a few promises to the Poles in an elegantly phrased proclamation.

The only Government which had a clearly defined policy for the Poles was the Austro-Hungarian. Congress Poland was to be united with Galicia and made into a crown land within the Habsburg monarchy; the Poles were to be given the same sort of autonomy as Hungary enjoyed. However, at the wish of the Hungarian Cabinet the plan for an Austro-Hungarian-Polish triple constitution was soon given up in favour of a 'subdualistic' conception following the pattern of Galician self-government. In spite of occasional tactical retreats before the demands of its German ally, the Vienna Government was to cling firmly to this 'Austro-Polish' concept all through the war. The adoption of this Polish policy was largely due to the efforts of the imperial adviser Bobrzynski and the Cracow School; the Galician conservatives had come to realize that, situated as it was between the two stronger neighbouring States of Germany and Russia, Poland had to seek support in the south. Austro-Polish ties in the sixteenth and seventeenth centuries were recalled; people remembered the dynastic link between Poland and Hungary under the Jagellons and the great war in which Stefan Batory, King of Poland, Lithuania and Transylvania, had driven Tzar Ivan the Terrible out of Lithuania and the Baltic lands. The subsequently famous historian Oskar Halecki, son of an imperial Austrian field-marshal, began at this time to preach the topicality of the 'Jagellonian concept', which implied a wide eastward extension of Poland into the Tzardom of Moscow and hence an Austro-Polish alliance. In an atmosphere created by hopes and wishes of this sort, the Provisional Commission united on 16 August 1914 in Cracow with representatives of moderate National Democracy and a number of like-minded politicians to form the Supreme National Committee (NKN). The NKN claimed to be the nucleus of a future Polish National Government and represented the idea, hardly modified by the National Democratic group, that Galicia was called to be the 'Polish Piedmont'. Hence the committee was regarded as the spiritual progeny of the Cracow school, although many of its officials – Professor Stanislaw Kot, for example, the head of the Propaganda Section, and Wladyslaw Sikorski, its military leader, once an engineer and rifle-club president, now a colonel – represented democratic rather than conservative views.

Jozef Pilsudski did not share the Austro–Polish conception inasmuch as he was absolutely convinced, almost to the point of dogmatism, that Poland had to contribute to her restoration through her own strength. In his view only the sacrifice of blood and a national insurrection could give Poland the moral right to independence. So he carried on the tradition of 1830 and 1863 by publicly announcing on 3 August 1914 the existence of a national organization in Congress Poland and the constitution of a – purely fictitious – national government in Warsaw. Soon afterwards, on 6 August 1914, he crossed the border to the north of Cracow with a small free corps – the so-called 'Cadre Company', consisting of Galicians and volunteers from Russian Poland – and thus strengthened his claim to be waging his own war against Russia in the name of Poland. For ten days he and his volunteers held a few districts round Kieke, then he was called upon in an ultimatum from the Austrian General Staff, drawn up on 13 August 1914, to put himself under the orders of the Cracow NKN and thus avoid the threatened dissolution of his free corps. On 20 August the NKN called for the formation of a 'Polish Legion', in which Pilsudski incorporated his free corps. The 'eastern' or Lemberg (Lwow) legion was disbanded in September 1914, after the Russian armies had occupied Lemberg and eastern Galicia; the capture of Lemberg also caused the National Democratic group to withdraw from the NKN on 20 October 1914. The 'western' legion, on the other hand, which was organized in Cracow, swiftly grew to three brigades, the first of which was commanded by Pilsudski. The unquestionably important military achievements of this brigade in the winter and spring of 1915 quickly gave rise to a myth which awoke recollections of Polish military glory in past centuries. In these battles Brigadier Pilsudski, who was called just 'Commander', won a moral ascendancy which enabled him, in spite of his dependence on the Cracow committee,

17

to make his officers into a guard of convinced fighters for Polish independence. He soon become the most popular figure in any part of Poland.

The Austro–German offensives in the summer of 1915 completely altered the political presuppositions of a solution to the Polish question. In June 1915 the Austrian armies reconquered eastern Galicia and Lwow, and 1 July saw the start of the offensive which forced the Russian troops to evacuate Congress Poland. On 5 August 1915 German units entered Warsaw, and on 20 August they stormed the fortress of Modlin, thus capturing the centre of the Russian defence line along the Vistula. The German and Austrian Governments divided the conquered country into two occupation zones; the northern part of Congress Poland, except for the separately administered region of Suwalki, became the 'Imperial German General Government of Warsaw' under General Hans Hartwig von Beseler, while the southern part became the 'Imperial Austrian Military General Government of Kieke', under General Baron Erich Diller. On 1 October 1915 the administrative centre of the Austrian zone was shifted to Lublin. In this zone a purely military administration was set up at first, while the German zone was subject to a civil administrator under the governor of Kries. But the decisive factor in German occupation policy was still the attitude of Governor-General von Beseler, who had proved himself a worthy, gifted and cultivated officer, but unlike Diller possessed neither administrative experience nor a knowledge of the Polish question. However, he certainly had the will to do what he could to secure a harmonious solution to the Germano–Polish question, and this 'gigantic task' attracted him.

The reactions of the various political groups in the country to the occupying powers corresponded to their traditional views. The attitude of the National Democratic middle class remained cool, both to the occupation authorities and to the Polish Legion allied to them. Walery Slawek, who was a colonel in the Legion at that time, heard a Warsaw lady say to her little daughter, 'Look, there's one of the gentlemen who want to kill your papa!' Among

18

the farmers too, recruitment for the Legion met resistance and reservations. In September 1915 the National Democratic Movement united with allied groups to form the 'Inter-party Club', which rejected all attempts to create an independent State on an anti-Russian basis and was therefore described as the 'passivist' camp. Secret contacts were maintained across the battle-front with Petrograd, whither the National Democratic Party leaders had emigrated, with Dmowski at their head. However, as early as 5 August 1915 the smaller middle-class independence parties approached the Central Powers with a public offer of alliance and demanded a separate Polish army to fight against Russia for Polish freedom. But at first both Berlin and Vienna shrank from prejudicing the Polish question by coming to an irreversible agreement with the independence movement. Moreover, during the first few months of his régime Beseler was concerned mainly with down-to-earth administrative problems and the assertion of German authority. For this reason in September 1915 he dissolved the Central Committee, with its comprehensive Polish self-governing organization, which had come into being spontaneously when Russian power collapsed, and also the Polish law courts. At this period even recruiting for the Legion was forbidden.

To Pilsudski, who had hastened to Warsaw in August 1915, this attitude on the part of the Central Powers was an indication that they looked at the Polish question purely from the point of view of their own military problems. He induced the smaller independence parties to withdraw on 1 September their offer of 5 August. In addition, he steered volunteers who wanted to fight for freedom, and who had hitherto joined the Legion, more and more to his own military underground movement, the 'Polish Military Organization' (POW), which he had founded through his officers Adam Koc and Tadeusz Zulinski in the autumn of 1914 in Warsaw, still occupied at that time by the Russians. He thus had at his disposal, besides his brigade of the Legion, an organization which was trained for partisan warfare and at the right moment would provide the framework for a

Polish army. The Austro–German policy of half-measures, which Pilsudski and the independence parties of the Left with similar views neither helped nor hindered, had thus led to failures right from the start.

It was not until the Berlin conversations of 10–11 November 1915, in which Bethmann-Hollweg and Count Burian, the Austrian Foreign Minister, discussed future solutions, that the Polish question came into the foreground. On the advice of Count Hutten-Czapski, Beseler showed himself ready to make concessions. On 15 November 1915 the university, which had been brought into line with Russian policies in 1869, and the Technical High School in Warsaw were re-opened as Polish institutions. The beginnings of municipal self-government were granted and Warsaw obtained a militia in the uniform of Polish Uhlans. Now the big independence parties, the PPS, the Populist (i.e. Peasant), Party and the National Workers' Alliance, abandoned their reserve; on 17 December 1915 they united to form the 'Central National Committee', with Pilsudski in the background as mentor. This Committee drew up the 'Declaration of the Hundred' of 22 February 1916, which was signed even by National Democratic politicians and which described the aim of the Polish nation as 'the attainment of an independent state protected by its own armed forces'. After this the groups in favour of independence were known as the 'Activist' camp as opposed to the 'Inter-party Club'. The hope of gaining the support of the Activists stimulated not only Beseler's Polish policy but also those of Falkenhayn, the chief of the general staff – who was chiefly concerned to obtain Polish divisions – and the German trade associations. The German chancellor finally gave way to the representations of the latter and turned away from the Austro–Polish conception. On 14–15 April 1916 Bethmann-Hollweg finally rejected the idea of annexing Congress Poland to Austria, and on the 12 August 1916 the two Heads of Government of the Central Powers agreed that the creation of a Polish State should be proclaimed. The Austrians were forced to agree by their difficult military situation, which necessitated German assistance; on the German side, after the fall of Falkenhayn, Ludendorff and Beseler pressed the plan for the proclamation of the State on a still hesitating Bethmann-Hollweg.

On 5 November 1916 the two governor-generals in Warsaw and Lublin proclaimed, in the name of their monarchs, the creation of a 'Kingdom of Poland', which was to be a 'State with a hereditary monarchy and a written constitution'. The future State was to be 'linked to the two allied powers'; the question of its frontiers was left open. Only four days later, at the insistence of Hindenburg and Ludendorff, an appeal was issued calling upon all Poles to enlist in a Polish army and to take up the fight against Russia under German leadership. In spite of this psychologically clumsy combination of the questions of a State and an army, which made the purposes of the German General Staff quite clear to the Polish public, the proclamation of a State created a powerful impression. Wladyslaw Studnicki, who was Beseler's adviser, Michal Lempicki, a former member of the Duma, and Count Adam Ronikier, with their small Germanophil independence groups, reached the zenith of their influence. A few individual politicians like Jan Stecki turned away from the National Democratic Movement, which naturally objected to this way of setting up a State. Even Pilsudski had to admit publicly later on: 'The empty enthusiasm over the proclamation of 5 November and the possibility that a so-called Polish army and a Polish Government could be set up was so immense that a large section of Polish youth was infected by it.' In Germany too the idea of an independent Poland gained ground. Wilhelm Feldmann, who on 1 October 1915 had founded a journal called *Polnische Blätter*, was given favourable treatment by the censorship authorities and gained a hearing in the German Press. Consequently, in spite of the silent reservations of many Poles and in spite of the German right-wing parties, which opposed the policy because of Posen and the swiftly perceptible failure of the attempt to woo the Poles, the new Polish policy could be taken further. Beseler convoked a 'Provisional Council' with advisory functions, which met in Warsaw on 14 January 1917. This committee consisted of twenty-five members appointed by the two governor-generals – fifteen from the German zone and ten from the Austrian zone – who either belonged to the independence parties or as non-party notabilities had some influence on Polish society. The 'crown marshal' of the council was Waclaw Niemojowski, who as a grandson of the leader of the liberals of 1830 symbolized the anti-Russian tradition, while the German Emperor's commissioner was Count Hutten-Czapski. These first steps towards a Polish State put Pilsudski and the left-wing independence parties with similar views in a difficult position. Pilsudski had always striven to preserve the Legion's independence; he had even resigned his command when on 19 September 1916 the Legion was converted into the 'Polish Auxiliary Corps' of the Central Powers. He knew that this step could only increase his moral authority with the legionaries. In fact they developed such an insubordinate mood that at the end of October 1916 the new commander of the corps, the Austrian Colonel Count Stanislaw Szeptycki, had to use stern measures to restore discipline. In November 1916 the corps, which now had a strength of 1,000 officers and 20,000 men, was moved to Congress Poland, to be amalgamated with the new volunteer army. This plan was just as contrary to Pilsudski's aims as it was to those of the Central National Committee, whose slogan was 'No Polish army without a Polish Government'. Pilsudski feared the 'iron organization' of the Germans, who 'with their frightful war machine' would press all able-bodied Poles into their own service. However, in face of the general jubilation at the foundation of a Polish State he had to make up his mind to bow to events, since even 'his own instrument', as he put it, the Legion, was threatening to slip through his fingers. So 'with a sad heart' and against his own inclination he renewed his contacts with Governor-Generals Karl Kuk and Beseler. Although in his view Germany displayed a 'clearly perceptible contempt for all forces stemming from Poland itself', he was ready to take a command in the new Germano–Polish army so long as he obtained an independent position. But this was just what Beseler refused him on 12 December 1916, since he regarded him as 'a military dilettante and demagogue, personally brave but unruly and quite devoid of professional knowledge', a man who was acting almost 'treasonably' towards the German authorities, 'the legitimate rulers of the country'. Nevertheless in January 1917, at the instigation of the Austrians, Pilsudski joined the State Council and even took over the portfolio of military affairs. He quite deliberately 'chose to lose this round, so as to be able to win another', that of national revolutionary Poland. In the inward antagonism between the 'socialistic basis' and 'conspiratorial character', as an Austrian directive of the time put it, of the independence group led by Pilsudski on the one hand, and the conservative tendency of the monarchies on the other, there were grounds for conflict which broke up only too soon the alliance between the two unequal partners.

GERMAN–POLISH CONFLICTS AND THE GRADUAL CREATION OF A POLISH GOVERNMENT

The subordinate position into which Pilsudski and the independence group had been manoeuvred by the proclamation of the Kingdom of Poland was to be cancelled out a few months later. The Polish question was thrown into the melting-pot again by the Russian revolution of February 1917, which produced a curious diarchy in Petrograd with a workers' and soldiers' soviet functioning alongside the provisional Government under Prince Georgii Lvov. On 14–27 March 1917 the Petrograd Soviet issued an appeal to the Polish proletariat which spoke out, in the name of the 'Democracy of Russia', for the 'political self-determination of peoples' and declared that Poland was entitled to be completely independent from a constitutional and international point of view. Then, on 17–30 March, following the advice of the Moscow lawyer Aleksander Lednicki, a Polish democrat who was a friend of Prince Lvov, the provisional Government itself issued a Polish manifesto. This offered the 'Polish sister people', in the interests of the common struggle 'against the quarrelsome Germans', the creation of 'an independent Polish State' consisting of all the territories with Polish majorities; this State was to be 'linked to

A History of Modern Poland

Russia by a free military union'. Both appeals promised more than the Central Powers had in their proclamation of 5 November 1916. Moreover, the Polish question, which so far had been tackled only by Berlin and Vienna, now moved into the wider field of international discussion.

In the early summer of 1917 the Russian Cabinet started in earnest to federalize the Russian empire, a move which was calculated to underline the sincerity of their ideas about Poland in the eyes of the Poles in Russia. Russian troops of foreign (i.e. non-Great Russian) nationality were united everywhere in national corps within the framework of the Russian forces as a whole. Polish members of the army held a general congress in Petrograd from 8 to 21 June 1917, and as a result on 14 July a 'Supreme Polish Army Committee' was set up under the presidency of Wladyslaw Raczkiewicz, a member of the Minsk gentry. In the White Russian provinces a '1st Polish Corps' was even formed; command of it was assumed by General Jozef Dowbor-Musnicki. Cadres for two further Polish army corps were formed in the Ukraine. The creation of these new army corps caused a political split among the Poles in Russia. The National Democrats supported them enthusiastically as Entente troops, while the PPS and Lednicki's Democratic Committee recognized the Polish State on the other side of the battle-front, that is, the State Council and Pilsudski with his legionaries.

The February Revolution also gave the Polish question renewed topicality in the West. Already in January 1916 Roman Dmowski had migrated from Petrograd to London to work for the creation of a National Democratic Poland favourable to the Entente Powers. However, for the time being the British Government still hung back on the Polish question, since the Foreign Secretary, Lord Balfour, shrank from the dismemberment of Austria–Hungary and the severance of the German eastern provinces recommended by Dmowski in his memorandum of April 1917. In the United States the famous Polish pianist Jan Ignacy Paderewski, whose brother had in fact died fighting the Russians as a member of the Legion, did his best to influence President

The Struggle for Polish Independence (1914–1919)

Wilson and his advisers on foreign affairs, Edward House and Robert Lansing, in the same direction. Paderewski's influence became all the more significant when on 6 April 1917 the United States declared war on Germany and thus joined the Entente powers. Like the Germans, the French tried to derive military advantage from the Polish question; on 4 July 1917 the French Cabinet issued a decree dealing with the formation of a Polish army on French soil, but it did not achieve much success. Meanwhile, on 15 August 1917, the representatives of the National Democratic Party and related groups founded in Lausanne a 'Polish National Committee' (KNP) which claimed to be the Government in exile of the restored Polish State. Under the leadership of Dmowski, the KNP showed itself decidedly friendly to the Western Allies. It soon moved to Paris, and through its diplomatic agents – Erazm Piltz in Paris, Wladyslaw Sobanski in London and Paderewski in Washington – won not only *de facto* recognition from the Allied Governments but also political control of the Polish army being formed in France, which only from then onwards acquired any significant strength. Finally, it brought the National Democratic organizations in Russia, the Kingdom of Poland, Galicia and Posen under its control. Thus a serious rival to the Warsaw State had come into being, and the Central Powers' conception of Poland was confronted with that of the Allies.

This unexpected growth of Polish possibilities and hopes could not but provoke a strong response in Polish circles in the Kingdom and Galicia, even if they had previously had 'Activist' tendencies. The Petrograd proclamation in particular made a deep impression. It is true that on 1 May 1917, under German pressure, the Warsaw State Council rejected the advances of the Russian provisional Government, but it demanded at the same time the immediate formation of a Polish Government and the appointment of a regent. On 2–3 May, led by the PPS and the POW, the radical independence parties went into opposition, while students and workers – their enthusiasm kindled by the national holiday on 3 May – demonstrated in all the big towns. The guiding spirit of the opposition was Pilsudski. His secret emissaries – especially his 'foreign minister', Michal Sokolnicki – had kept him well informed about the new opportunities which had arisen for the Poles outside the Austro–German sphere of influence. Another important factor was the Congress of Stockholm (16–20 May 1917), at which Polish politicians of all shades of opinion and from both sides of the battle-front had met. Pilsudski also drew moral support from the decline of the Austro–Polish concept and the growth of the desire for complete independence. The Cracow conservatives had to give up the leadership of the Polish Club in the Vienna Parliament; a meeting of all Polish deputies from Galicia in Cracow on 28 May 1917 adopted the resolution proposed by Wlodzimierz Tetmajer, a member of the Populist (i.e. Peasant) Party, which demanded the creation of a powerful Polish State with access to the sea and emphasized the international character of the Polish question. The internationalization of the Polish problem, the entry of the United States into the war and the powerful offensives mounted by the Allied armies in the summer of 1917 in Flanders, Champagne and on the Isonzo all confirmed in Pilsudski's view the rightness of the prognosis he had made in July 1914. The moment for a final break with the Central Powers, and perhaps even for moving over to the side of the Allies, now seemed to him to have arrived.

Pilsudski's decision was made easier by the policy of the Berlin Government, which on 8 June 1917 certainly gave up its futile attempts to recruit Polish volunteers, but was not induced by this failure to make any concessions in the matter of a state and a government, as its note of 8 June showed. As a result, at its conference of 16–20 June 1917, the PPS decided to change over to open opposition to the occupying powers. On 18 June 1917 Pilsudski united his own small group of direct supporters with the PPS and the peasant People's Party in a 'Democratic Union', which opted for a republic. The Activist camp, that is, the party which supported the idea of a kingdom friendly to Germany, now consisted only of the small and uninfluential clubs centred round Studnicki, Lempicki and Ronikier. Finally, on 24 July 1917, Pilsudski resigned his seat on the State Council and recommended the legionaries of the Auxiliary Corps, who were devoted to him, to refuse to swear the prescribed oath of allegiance to the German Emperor. There had been discussions between Germany and Austria about the formulation of this oath since December 1916. His instructions were disseminated by agitators of the PPS and POW, and they were obeyed; on 9 July 1917 164 out of 275 officers and 4,019 out of 6,500 legionaries refused to take the oath and followed Colonel Slawek into German internment camps. In these weeks of open rupture with the German and Austrian authorities Pilsudski formed the most desperate plans. His first idea was to seize the fortress of Iwangorod (Deblin) on the Vistula and to hold it by force of arms, but he gave this plan up owing to the loss of his most reliable regiment. The formation of the Polish Army Committee in the Russian army (14 July 1917) gave him the notion of breaking through the front with the help of the POW and his squadron of Uhlans and building up his own army out of the scattered Polish units. However, he gave up this well-prepared plan too, since it seemed to him dishonourable to leave his interned legionaries in the lurch. He disclosed his attitude and activities quite openly to Beseler, who had him arrested on 22 July 1917. The imprisonment which Pilsudski, as a 'Polish general', now had to endure in the Prussian fortresses of Wesel and Magdeburg prevented him from exerting any direct influence on the political development of the Poles for a year and a half. Yet in the last analysis this period of captivity increased his influence, for it made such an impression in Poland that even the State Council dared to express its regret. That Pilsudski should now be championing the cause of complete independence against the Germans as he had previously championed it against the Russians, even at the price of his own personal freedom, won the hearts of many of his opponents. This imprisonment finally made him into a national hero; it was this factor which had made the governor-general, who was anxious for an honourable understanding, hesitate for a long time before arresting him. The POW, though weakened by a number of raids, remained in existence as an underground movement. It set up a new headquarters in the form of a 'convention' under Edward Rydz-Smigly and Boguslaw Miedzynski. So thanks to its lack of flexibility the Austro–German occupation policy had lost the support of the Polish left-wing parties without winning that of the right wing; the inevitable economic hardships of wartime did the rest. In these circumstances the State Council, already weakened by numerous individual withdrawals, resigned on 25 August 1917, just ten days after the constitution of the Lausanne Committee under Dmowski.

This serious crisis provoked the Governments of the Central Powers to adopt a more reasonable attitude. The Vienna Cabinet made use of the fact that the conflict between Beseler and Pilsudski was particularly damaging to the reputation of the Germans to whip up fresh popularity for the Austro–Polish concept. It found an excellent supporter in the man who had been military governor-general in Lublin since 1 May 1917, Colonel Count Szeptycki, a Galician aristocrat who as both a Polish nationalist and an officer loyal to the emperor was anxious to secure an Austro–Polish understanding. Szeptycki sought to lighten the burdens imposed by the war and gradually filled the administration under his control with Polish officials. In the summer and autumn of 1917 the Austrian Foreign Minister, Count Czernin, supported by the German ambassador, Count Wedel, was negotiating with the German Government for the cession of Congress Poland to Austria. The two Governments came to an agreement on the lines suggested by Czernin, but the agreement was rendered ineffective by the energetic intervention of Ludendorff.

At the end of July 1917 the Berlin and Vienna Cabinets agreed to give the Kingdom of Poland a Head of State in the form of a regency council. The decision was ratified by the two emperors on 12 September 1917. Legislation, the administration of justice and the management of affairs were to pass, within certain limits, into Polish hands, 'so that from now onwards the authority of the State will rest for the main part in the hands of a national government'. In fact, the law courts were put under Polish control on 1 September and the educational system, which had been considerably improved by the occupation authorities, on 1 October. The

28

regency council, consisting of Aleksander Kakowski, the Archbishop of Warsaw, Prince Zdzislaw Lubomirski, the Mayor of Warsaw, and Count Jozef Ostrowski, assumed office ceremonially on 27 October 1917. Finally, on 7 December 1917, a council of ministers met under the presidency of the well-known historian, Professor Jan Kucharzewski.

During these weeks relations between the Austro–German occupation authorities and the Poles improved. This was not due solely to the granting of a government. For the second time this year an upheaval inside Russia caused a change in the political attitude of the Poles. The Bolshevik revolution of 25 October and 7 November 1917 not only nullified in practice the Petrograd proclamations of March; it also destroyed any prospect of Russia's continuing to fight on the side of the Allies and thus of an eventual reconquest of Congress Poland by Russian forces. This weakened severely the political position of the Passivists united in the Inter-Party Club, especially that of the Endecja. Economic considerations also came into play. The splitting up of estates and the nationalization of many industries by the Bolsheviks affected Polish property-owners in the Eastern Marches on the other side of the Russian front. The region which suffered most was eastern Lithuania round Minsk, Bobruisk and Mogilew, an area which had contained the lines of communication of the former Russian western front and now testified, with its desecrated churches, plundered estates and terrorized towns, to the disintegration of the Russian armies. In this very region the Poles, as landowners and townspeople, formed the leading section in society, and here too the 1st Polish Corps was stationed under General Dowbor-Musnicki, with three disciplined divisions. On 25 January 1918 this corps began fighting the Bolsheviks to protect the local Polish population; it captured the fortress of Bobruisk, with its huge supplies of war material, and on 25 February the town of Minsk as well. By virtue of their common action against the Bolsheviks the German Eastern Command and Dowbor-Musnicki's command became more or less allies. Similarly, on the other side of the battle-front, in the Kingdom, numerous members of the property-owning classes sought support from the Germans. The first sign of this change was the assumption of the post of Minister for Home Affairs in Kucharzewski's Cabinet by the leading National Democrat Jan Stecki. If the February revolution had alienated the Polish left-wing parties from the policy of the Central Powers, the October revolution brought considerable numbers of the right-wing closer to the occupation authorities and the Government set up by them. Consequently, in the last month or two of 1917 and the opening months of 1918, there were fresh prospects for the realization of the conception underlying the proclamation of 5 November 1916.

THE LAST YEAR OF THE WAR

The peace treaties of Brest-Litovsk did considerable damage to the moral conquests which the Austro–German occupation policy had made among the Poles during the October revolution. On 9 February 1918 the diplomatic representatives of the Central Powers concluded with the 'Ukrainian People's Republic' – which had been set up on 22 January 1918 as an independent State in the territory of the former Tzarist provincial administration of Little Russia – a peace which gave the UNR all the predominantly Ukrainian parts of the old kingdom of Poland together with the province of Chelm (Cholm). A secret clause, which soon became known to the Poles, laid down that eastern Galicia was to lose its Polish provincial administration and be given a new autonomous constitution with a Ukrainian bias in preparation for its eventual incorporation in the UNR. The main reason why the Governments of the Central Powers made such enormous concessions to gain this 'bread peace' was that they could reasonably expect large deliveries of food from the rich Ukraine for their hungry peoples. On 3 March 1918 the Soviet Russian delegation under Trotsky had to give up Russian sovereignty over the territory of the UNR, Poland, Lithuania and Courland – a peace of renunciation which Lenin forced through against strong internal opposition in Russia in order to save the Red revolution. The Berlin Cabinet made preparations for the creation of a number of small Baltic

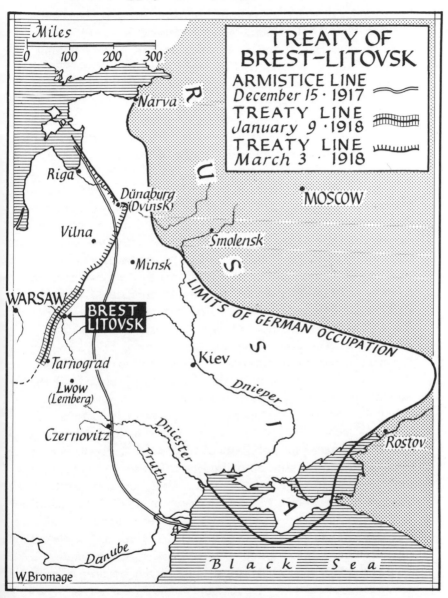

MAP I

States under German protection; on 16 February 1918 an independent State of Lithuania was proclaimed by a Lithuanian 'parliament' (*taryba*) summoned by the German military administration of the Eastern High Command. This new Kingdom of Lithuania was formally recognized by the German Reichstag on 23 March 1918.

This policy of agglomerating independent States along the eastern frontiers of the Polish kingdom, that is, of cutting down the size of Poland, caused considerable bitterness in the Polish public. It was the unanimous conviction of all Poles that the territories which the Germans had disposed of were the Eastern Marches of the Jagellonian empire, and it was in this very region that the three Polish army corps were stationed; these troops had parted company with the Russian forces after the October revolution and in the Polish view had become a national army. The loss of western and central Lithuania to the newly formed Kingdom of Lithuania seemed intolerable, especially as both the Activist and Passivist parties had declared, as early as May 1917, that they favoured the restoration of the historical Polish-Lithuanian union. The occupation authorities caused resentment by encouraging the Lithuanian educational system and often hindered the Polish one; also because they occasionally played off the Lithuanian peasants against their Polish 'masters', and pursued a policy that caused the temporary imprisonment in Germany of the Vilna scholar Waclaw Studnicki, brother of the well-known Warsaw Germanophil politician. Behind all this, people sensed the basically hostile attitude of Ludendorff, who was annoyed at the exclusion of Congress Poland from his eastern command and was now trying to create his own 'dynasty' among the Lithuanians. As long ago as August 1915 Ludendorff had written to Undersecretary of State Zimmerman: 'Now that Poland has been taken away from me, I must found another kingdom in Lithuania and Courland.' The pro-Lithuanian attitude of the German military government was certainly justified in Samogitia, the northern part of the province of Suwalki and the western half of the province of Vilna, since in these areas Lithuanians formed an absolute

majority; but on the other hand the German census of 1916 had
shown that the population of the capital city of Vilna was only
2·6 per cent Lithuanian and 50·1 per cent Polish, and that 58 per
cent of the population of central Lithuania in the regions round
Suwalki, Grodno and Vilna (which formed the eastern part of the
new kingdom) regarded itself as Polish, even though the mother-
tongue of the majority was White Russian. If Polish indignation
about the Lithuanian question was thus directed predominantly
against Germany, the pro-Ukrainian decisions of Brest-Litovsk
were attributed mainly to Austria. The loss of the three provinces
of Volhynia, Podolia and Kiev – the erstwhile 'Polish Ukraine' –
could be swallowed, since their population was almost purely
Ukrainian even if the Polish nobility owned almost half the cultivable land, but it seemed quite impossible to renounce all claims to
eastern Galicia, which had belonged to the Polish crown since
1366 and contained a mixed Ukrainian-Polish population. Lwow
was just as much a Polish city as Vilna. The sacrifice of the Chelm
region, which had been a part of Congress Poland from 1815 to
1915, seemed equally unacceptable, though it is true that it was
not easy to settle the national affiliations of its inhabitants, in spite
of the fact that Ukrainian was the dominant language. Even the
expert advice of the famous geographer Albrecht Penck was
unable to provide a decisive answer.

The Poles gave vent to their outraged national feelings in
strikes, demonstrations and resolutions condemning 'perfidious
Prussia' and 'treacherous Austria'. The Regency Council protested
on 14 February 1918 against this 'new partition of Poland', which
it described as illegal and an infringement of the right of every
people to self-determination; one of the regents, Prince Lubomirski, headed a demonstration in the streets of Warsaw and
broke through the cordon of German police. The Kucharzewski
Cabinet resigned. Count Szeptycki, the governor-general in
Lublin, also resigned, and this was the end of Austro–Polish
reconciliation in his administrative area. Even the Cracow conservatives were furious with Emperor Charles; Baron Goetz, the
leader of the Polish club in the Austrian Parliament, made it clear

A History of Modern Poland

to the head of the Austrian Government that from now on 'the whole Polish people, from the lord of the manor to the humblest workman' was opposed to the monarchy. An indication of the general mood was the attempt by the Legion under the Austrian Colonel Jozef Haller to break through the front in eastern Galicia on the night of 15–16 February 1918 and to join the Polish corps in the Ukraine. A small body of troops, including Haller, succeeded in breaking through and joined the 2nd Polish Corps. This was the end of the notion of the Legion, which had once allied itself to the Central Powers. The man who suffered most in the wreck of the reconciliation policy was Governor-General Beseler. During this period he felt that he was helplessly caught between two fires, 'a fantastic, demanding, not to say shameless, Polish nationalism' on the one side, and on the other 'a prejudiced Germanism' which, in his view, seemed to be bent on 'crippling and oppressing this newly liberated people'.

Just as German politicians underestimated Polish national pride, so they overestimated the ability of the Ukrainians to build their own State. In fact the Government of the UNR lost its capital, Kiev, and most of its territory to Bolshevik troops as early as February 1918; German and Austrian units had to drive the Red guards out of the Ukraine back to Rostov and Taganrog in order to safeguard the 'bread peace'. At the same time German troops forced the Bolsheviks out of Estonia, Livonia and eastern Lithuania, that is the White Russian provinces round Minsk, Mogilev and Bobruisk. This new advance brought the German eastern army into contact with the three Polish corps. The German army command demanded their demobilization, to which General Dowbor-Musnicki consented on 27 March 1918 in the name of the 1st Corps (which had had to hand over Minsk to the German army and was now defending the region of Bobruisk against the Bolsheviks with 20,000 men) so long as the Regency Council should be allowed to participate in any decisions concerning the Polish army. Dowbor-Musnicki, a good strategist who had passed out top of his class from the St Petersburg staff college, saw the impossibility of fighting both the Bolsheviks and the German

34

army and therefore put himself under the orders of the Regency Council. However, the demobilization of his corps did not proceed very far, for the 2nd Corps under General Eugeninsz de Hennig Michaelis and Colonel Haller refused to demobilize at all. The 2nd Corps was surrounded by German troops and forced to capitulate on 13 May 1918 near Kanev on the Dnieper, after three days of violent fighting. A small section escaped under the leadership of Colonel Haller, who travelled via Murmansk to France and took command of the Polish army garrisoned there. After this, German troops encircled the 1st Corps as well and forced them too to lay down their arms on 12 May 1918, although some units tried to resist at the instigation of Barthel de Weydenthal, the emissary of the POW. This liquidation of the Polish forces in the east put the fiasco of the Germans' Polish policy in a clear light. Certainly the fears of the German army command, that 'pro-Allied' sentiment was widespread in the corps, were amply confirmed; but this hardly justified such drastic action, which could only do further damage to the Germans' reputation in the kingdom.

Nevertheless, in spite of the treaties of Brest-Litovsk and the demobilization of the army corps, 4 April saw the formation in Warsaw of a Government which worked hard and tirelessly for a reconciliation between Germany and Poland. Apart from the Prime Minister (Jan Steczkowski, a banker from Galicia), the head of the political department, Prince Janusz Radziwill, was certainly the most important man in this Cabinet. As a relative of the Prussian royal house and son of the leader of the Polish group in the German Reichstag, the prince seemed to be ideally suited to the role of mediator. His moral position was even strengthened to some extent by the German occupation policy in White Russia and the Ukraine. The White Russian People's Republic (BNR) set up in Minsk on 24–25 March 1918, which, like its model, the UNR, favoured agrarian revolution, was not recognized by the German commander, von Falkenhayn. The German command preferred to support the conservative and aristocratic Minsk governing committee headed by the Polish Count Roman Skirmunt, a Polesian squire and philosopher whose aim was a comprehensive Polish-White Russian union. In the Ukraine the Government of the UNR was overturned on 28–29 April 1918 with the assistance of the German occupation authorities and replaced by the landowners' Government of Hetman Pavlo Skoropadskyj, who maintained a benevolent attitude to the Polish landed aristocracy in the regions on the right bank of the Dnieper. Thus both in White Russia and the Ukraine a sort of alliance grew up between the German occupation authorities and the Polish aristocracy on the basis of a conservative agrarian policy. Both partners opposed the division of the big estates advocated by the Bolsheviks, the German officers of the occupation force partly from general conservatism but mainly to safeguard Germany's food supplies, the Poles because of their interests as landowners. Even in the Kingdom of Lithuania the social supremacy of the Polish landed nobility was not assailed, in spite of the pro-Lithuanian inclinations of the German occupying forces; the Berlin Government had even offered the throne of Lithuania to Prince Janusz, but he had declined it. It was above all fear of the tendency, unleashed since the October revolution, towards general agrarian revolution that drove Radziwill and the Steczkowski Government to collaborate with the Germans in spite of the Poles' many serious differences of opinion with them on questions of national sovereignty. Even in the Kingdom of Poland the socialist opposition – particularly the main body of the PPS, but also the PPS left wing and the SDKPiL, both of which were in sympathy with the Soviet Government – had grown sharper and more embittered.

These circumstances encouraged the readiness of the Warsaw Government for a Germano-Polish reconciliation to such an extent that as early as 17 April 1918 Prince Radziwill asked in Berlin for the negotiations to be hurried on. On 29 April 1918 the Steczkowski Cabinet sent the Vienna and Berlin Governments a note containing a number of very moderate demands. It suggested the definitive establishment of the Kingdom out of the territory of the two General Governments with extensions in the region of Chelm and in the Niemen area to the south of Vilna; access to the sea was to be secured by 'free navigation on the Vistula' down to Danzig. A Poland of this kind, bound to the Central Powers by a military alliance, would render superfluous the 'protective corridor' which Ludendorff wished to have ceded to Germany for strategic reasons, and would provide 'the best protection for central Europe against the east'. This note may be regarded as the high-water mark of Polish willingness to make concessions. An important factor in its conception was certainly the fact that the Central Powers' chances of victory had grown as a result of the great spring offensives in the west; but these very expectations of victory decided the German General Staff and with it the Berlin Government to make a somewhat reserved reply to the Polish offer. Thanks to the tireless efforts of Prince Janusz and Count Ronikier the links between Warsaw and Berlin did not break in the following months, but no further constitutional settlement was achieved.

Nevertheless, progress was made in the internal consolidation of the Polish State. On 22 June 1918 a national Sejm or Parliament met, in the form of a Council of State with 110 members, under Franciszek Pulaski, a historian who belonged to the Podolian landed nobility, for a six-week period of legislation. Of the 110 deputies only 55 had been elected by the local and town councils; 43 had been nominated by the Regency Council and 12 had been appointed as persons of importance. Thus the Council of State, in which 48 deputies belonged to the *bourgeois* Centre and 41 were members of the Inter-Party Club, by no means reflected the real political opinions of the people, especially as the Left had boycotted the elections. Its legislative achievements were slight. On the other hand, the organization of the Polish provincial administration was completed. Governor-General Beseler and the Regency Council even raised two regiments of a so-called 'Polish Defence Force' under a German inspector, the Saxon General Barth. This Defence Force included former officers of the Legion such as Marian Zegota-Januszajtis and Marian Kukiel; even the commander of the illegal POW, Colonel Edward Rydz-Smigly, applied for commissioned rank in it.

Summer 1918 saw one last possibility of a solution to the question of the Polish State. In the middle of August the two monarchs (i.e. the German and Austrian Emperors) negotiated with Ronikier, Radziwill and Hutten-Czapski about the candidature of Archduke Charles Stephen for the Polish crown. On the 22 August 1918 Emperor Charles of Austria offered Prince Janusz a 'great' Austro–Polish solution, which would have united the whole of Galicia with the Kingdom and thus created a Poland of some 80,000 square miles and a population of about 20 million, four-fifths of it Polish. Because of his high opinion of the Polish nation, which he described as 'rich in spiritual forces which only awaited development', Beseler supported an extension of the Kingdom to the east.

However, these plans foundered on the opposition between German and Austrian views, and above all on the obstinacy of Ludendorff, who was able to kill all genuinely political ideas by appealing to the supposedly military necessity of a 'protective corridor'. Yet by this time, after 14 August 1918, the 'black day' of the German armies in the west, the approaching collapse of the Central Powers was already becoming apparent. The military defect of the Central Powers in the west also decided the pro-Polish Charles Stephen to decline the throne offered to him by Prince Olgierd Czartoryski; for him, as for Prince Janusz, who had advised Kaiser Wilhelm not to support the candidature of the archduke, the Austro–German offers came 'too late'. Even the Polish aristocracy – the last group of Poles to persist in trying to reach an arrangement with Germany and Austria – no longer believed that the Central Powers would be victorious.

THE BREAK-THROUGH TO INDEPENDENCE

Since it seemed impossible to bring the question of Polish sovereignty to a satisfactory conclusion in co-operation with the Central Powers, the hopes of the Poles turned more and more in 1918 to the Polish policy of the Entente. Lloyd George and Wilson had finally spoken out – the former on 5 January, the latter on 8 January – in favour of an independent Poland, and the President of the USA had expressly emphasized the necessity of 'free and guaranteed access to the sea'. Yet Allied statesmen still preserved a noticeable reserve in their attitude to Polish questions, and this reserve was apparent once again in the joint statement issued on 3 June 1918 by the Prime Ministers of France, Great Britain and Italy. Dmowski and with him the Paris National Committee were hurt by the fact that they were unable to secure recognition from the Entente Cabinets as the Government in exile and to have the Warsaw Government rejected as illegal. It was not until the fortunes of war in France swung round in August 1918 that there was a change. The Polish army in France, which, under Colonel Haller, now numbered 20,000 men, was recognized by the Franco–Polish military convention of 28 September 1918 as an 'allied and belligerent army'. To it were also apportioned the scattered Polish units in Russia, such as the Kuban division under General Lucjan Zeligowski, the Polish Siberian division, the Murmansk brigade and numerous small cavalry units; all these troops were fighting against the Bolsheviks and regarded themselves as Entente troops. Basing himself on these Polish armies, supposedly amounting to 120,000 men, Dmowski laid before President Wilson on 8 October 1918 in the name of the National Committee a memorandum in which he proposed the formation of a strong, independent Polish Republic as a 'great, creative democracy in Eastern Europe' and a 'buttress against the German drive towards the east'. In the west Poland was to include – besides Congress Poland – Posen, West Prussia, Upper Silesia and parts of East Prussia; in the south, the whole of Galicia and Teschen; and in the east almost the whole of the Grand Duchy of Lithuania and parts of Volhynia and Podolia. In the next few years this memorandum was to become more or less the political creed of the National Democrats.

The impending military collapse of the Central Powers also decided the Regency Council to seek a way to Polish independence. Without consulting the two governor-generals the three Regents published on 7 October 1918, a 'Call to the Polish people', in which they invoked Wilson's solemn principle of self-determination and announced the formation of an all-party Government and elections for a constituent assembly. At the same time both Prince Radziwill, who was in close contact with the Regency Council, and the Galician socialist leader Ignacy Daszynski demanded the liberation of Pilsudski, since only a man of his authority seemed to be in a position to bridge the political opposition between Left and Right and to reduce the tension between the Poles and the occupation authorities. However, Berlin refused to set free Pilsudski. This alone made the situation of the Regency Council difficult, but in addition the POW, which was some 20,000 strong, was trying to procure arms, obviously to organize a rising. To frustrate this, on 12 October 1918 the Regency Council put the Polish Defence Force under its own authority and called for volunteers for this now purely Polish army. With the approval of the German General Staff, Beseler bowed to the inevitable and laid down his command of the Defence Force on 23 October 1918. The Austrian General Tadeusz Rozwadowski was appointed as the new commander of the little army. As it was becoming more and more difficult to steer a course between the right-wing and left-wing opposition, on 26 October 1918 the Regents installed in office the National Democratic Cabinet led by Jozef Swiezynski, in which Professor Stanislaw Glabinski, the leader of the Galician Endecja, took over the Ministry of Foreign Affairs and the War Ministry was given to Pilsudski, who was still interned in Magdeburg.

The disintegration of Austria now became complete. On 27 October 1918 a Polish Liquidation Commission was set up in Cracow under Ignacy Daszynski, Wincenty Witos and the National Democrat Count Aleksander Skarbek; it became the *de facto* provincial Government of western Galicia. It is true that in Lwow and eastern Galicia a 'Ukrainian National Council' took over power in the night of 30 October to 1 November with the help of Ukrainian rifle-clubs. Although a small Polish free corps under Captain Maczynski was able to hold out in Lwow, the authority of the Liquidation Commission was confined to the territory west of Przemysl. Nevertheless, the successes of the

Galician National Democrats under Skarbek made such an impression on the Swiezynski Government in Warsaw that it tried, for its part, to overthrow the Regency Council; however, it failed, and had to resign. But if the Regency Council had thus shown itself stronger than the Right, it could no longer control the open opposition of the Left. In Lublin, the seat of the disintegrating Austrian military government, the POW under Rydz-Smigly carried out a successful *coup d'état* in the night of 6–7 November 1918. A 'Provisional People's Government of the Polish Republic' was formed under Daszynski; Rydz-Smigly, as Pilsudski's representative, was appointed commander of all Polish troops; and the Regency was declared null and void. The Warsaw right-wing parties protested against this socialistic Lublin Government and therefore gave their tactical support to the Regency Council. Thus two Governments with no ground for agreement confronted each other; civil war amid the wreckage of the Austro–German occupation administration seemed inevitable.

In this almost insoluble situation two events occurred which assured the rectilinear development of the Polish State: these were the German republican revolution of 9 November 1918 and the release of Pilsudski from captivity in Magdeburg by the new German Government. Pilsudski arrived in Warsaw by a special German train on the morning of 10 November, just at the very moment when the military organization of the occupation authorities was finally collapsing as a result of events in Berlin and German soldiers' councils were being formed everywhere. The 'Commander' returned home with the firm belief that, now the last of the partitioning powers lay crushed and the hour of the rebirth of an independent Poland had arrived, there would be 'a rebirth of the Polish soul' as well. In Pilsudski's own words, 'the power of the Polish soul' would enable the Poles, 'a people of anarchy, disobedience and weakness', a people that had certainly gained 'sympathy' in its misfortunes but never 'respect', to conjure up again 'the great spirits of the erstwhile commonwealth'. And in fact the arrival of the national hero did cause party strife among the Poles to disappear as if by magic. The Regent, Prince

Lubomirski, welcomed him at the station, and the Warsaw commander of the POW – which was already taking over military command from the German soldiers' councils everywhere in Poland – announced that the People's Government in Lublin and the Cracow Liquidation Commission were ready to put themselves under his authority at once. By his mere presence, Pilsudski became the 'moral dictator' of the Poles. By virtue of this authority he was able to decree in his first order of the day, of 12 November 1918, that the Polish population should let the German forces withdraw in peace and order, 'as befits a nation certain of its great and glorious future'. In this way the removal of the occupation troops took place, in spite of their many severities, in an atmosphere of forbearance and on the whole without any fighting. Pilsudski's chivalry enabled Governor-General Beseler, who was seriously ill, to depart under a safe conduct for Thorn (Torun) on 12 November 1918 in a Vistula steamer. With the withdrawal of the occupying troops Pilsudski had created in Congress Poland and western Galicia a free space for Polish independence, a space which formed a sort of island in the realm of German power, for not only in the west and the north but also in Lithuania, the area round Brest-Litovsk and the Ukraine there were still German occupation troops, though it is true that they were in the process of disintegrating.

On the very day of his return, 10 November 1918, Pilsudski had travelled with Prince Lubomirski to the latter's residence in the Frascati Gardens. Here took place the historic conversation in which, even before the country's birth, the dethroned monarchy and the infant republic came to an agreement about the future shape of Poland. Pilsudski refrained from accepting power from the hands of his earlier socialist friends; he refused to play the part of a 'tribune of the people'. He was soon to say to the socialist leaders, Daszynski, Feliks Perl and Tomasz Arciszewski: 'We travelled a long way together in the socialist team; I got out at the stop called "independence".' Instead of letting himself be hoisted into the saddle by the Lublin socialist ministers, he conferred their offices on them. To gain this independent non-party position, he accepted his authority from the Regency Council, although the latter derived its power from the patent of the two emperors. Constitutional continuity from the Kingdom of 5 November 1916 to the Republic – for all authoritative circles seemed to be agreed on a republic – was thus assured. It is true that Prince Lubomirski made the condition that Pilsudski should only receive power provisionally, as the representative of a constituent assembly to be elected afresh. Pilsudski agreed to this, although he was by no means certain of the elections for the coming Sejm. Accordingly, the Regency Council's manifesto of 11 November 1918, by which Pilsudski was appointed generalissimo, contained this passage: 'Power and responsibility we put in your hands, Supreme Commander, to be handed over to the legislative Sejm.'[1] On 14 November 1918 the three regents renounced their civil authority too – unwillingly, but in obedience to the country's political requirements – and appointed Pilsudski Chief of State, a title already borne once before by Tadeusz Kosciuszko.

On the same day the new Chief of State entrusted Daszynski with the formation of independent Poland's first Government. He seemed to owe this to his old socialist comrade-in-arms. However, this cabinet provoked such a storm of indignation, especially from the National Democrats, that it had to be dismissed immediately. This obviously suited Pilsudski very well. He now commissioned the PPS politician Jedrzej Moraczewski, who was regarded as more moderate, to form a government, and on 17 November 1918 Moraczewski submitted to him a cabinet of the radical-idealistic intelligentsia, based on the PPS and the left wing of the Populist (Peasant) Party. The directives which Pilsudski gave Moraczewski, a former officer in the Legion, were positively military in their terseness: 'In your decrees you are not to tamper with social conditions, and in the course of a week you are to produce an electoral law, just as if you had a trench to dig.' Thus Populist intended to keep the promises which he had given to Prince

[1] Pilsudski was given the title of 'First Marshal of Poland' by the acclamation of his legionaries and POW officers in March 1920.

Lubomirski. Three days later, Moraczewski laid before him an electoral law which fulfilled all democratic requirements. The Chief of State's signature made it law on 28 November 1918.

However, during this period Pilsudski had to cope with the opposition of Dmowski and the Paris National Committee. If the Chief of State controlled the civil service, the administration and the army in Poland, the National Committee had the ear of the Entente Governments. Dmowski was influential enough to criticize Pilsudski to the Western Powers as 'pro-German' and even 'infected by Bolshevism'; he controlled a strong party in Poland and in the province of Posen, which still lay outside Pilsudski's sphere of influence. In the end the Chief of State realized that only Dmowski could secure the diplomatic recognition of Poland by the Entente and the assistance in the way of weapons and food which Poland so pressingly needed. Pilsudski was therefore ready to co-operate with Dmowski, as he said in his letter 'to my dear Roman'. But Dmowski was conscious of the strength of his position and refused.

Paderewski, who felt confident of the powerful protection of President Wilson, travelled to Poland in December 1918 as the representative of the National Committee. On 26 December 1918 he arrived in National Democratic Posen, where his presence caused unrest among both Germans and Poles. A few days later he reached Warsaw. It was regarded as due to his influence that on 4 January 1919 Prince Eustachy Sapieha and Colonel Marian Januszajtis, with the support of the National Democrats and some military units, attempted a rebellion which collapsed the very next day. However, it seems extremely probable that this *coup* was provoked by Pilsudski, who used the opportunity to put the National Democrats in the wrong and thus weaken their moral authority. The rebellion also made it possible for Pilsudski to sacrifice the Moraczewski Government despite the wishes of the Left. On 16 January 1919 Paderewski, who had some affinities with the marshal, since both of them came from the eastern border nobility, formed a compromise Cabinet based on the Centre parties. A Government of this sort could reckon on the right wing's

44

abandoning its previous opposition. It was thus in a position to carry through without friction on 26 January 1919 the elections for the constituent Sejm – Poland's first universal, equal, secret and direct election. The National Democrats gained 37 per cent of all votes, or 116 seats, and became relatively the stronger party; the whole Left succeeded in winning 38 per cent of the votes, or 123 seats, 52 of these going to the PPS and 58 to the Populist (Peasant) Party group, 'Liberation'. It was significant of the new political line-up that in Congress Poland – though not in Galicia – the Centre parties disappeared almost completely. With the attainment of independence the chief motive for the secession of the former middle-class Activists from the National Democrats had disappeared, and most of them now gave their support to the Endecja again. The strongest Centre party turned out to be the 'Piast', Peasant or Populist Party group, which won 44 seats, and in Galicia, thanks to its peasant voters, cornered 40 per cent of all the votes. On 14 January 1919, in accordance with the distribution of seats, the National Democrat candidate, Wojciech Trampczynski from Posen, hitherto a member of the German Reichstag, was elected Marshal or Speaker; the leader of the Piast, Wincenty Witos, was defeated by a small majority.

On 20 February 1919 Pilsudski put his dictatorial powers in the hands of the new Sejm, declaring that ever since he had taken power the 'basic aim' of his Government had been to allow unavoidable party conflicts 'to be decided only by democratic means'. The Sejm for its part handed back to him the offices of Chief of State and Supreme Commander; but in future Pilsudski and the Government he had appointed – Paderewski remained in office – was to be responsible to the constituent assembly. With this arrangement the first stage in the internal consolidation of the young republic had been attained.

The break-through to independence showed that, in spite of their strong opposition to each other, the two great political schools of thought, that of Pilsudski and the PPS on the one hand and that of the Endecja on the other, had fundamentally worked together and in practice complemented each other. Dmowski gained the sympathies and help of the Entente for Poland; in conjunction with Austria, Pilsudski created the symbol of the Legion. And again, both orientations would have been impossible but for the previous achievements of the Cracow school. It was their all-conquering Polish patriotism which enabled all these parties to sink their differences and work together. Yet all the Poles' efforts could scarcely have been successful had the Austro–German proclamation of the State not created the fundamental presuppositions for independence. The manifestos of 5 November 1916 not only founded an independent administration, which was there ready to be used when the Central Powers collapsed, but it also set the Polish question in motion on the diplomatic level both among the Entente Powers and in Russia. Pilsudski's historical achievement lay not so much in his faith in Poland's own strength as in his accurate prognosis of the course of the war, a prognosis which enabled him instinctively to choose the right policy. Dmowski on the other hand made a decisive contribution by founding the National Committee, with which he took over the idea of Polish independence at the very moment when its previous exponent, Pilsudski, voluntarily left the political scene. Thus, whatever claims may have been made, it was not thanks to any individual statesmen in the ranks of the Poles, the Central Powers, the Entente or Russia that the way was cleared for Polish independence. The work was accomplished by the complex and intricate interplay of a number of different political forces.

CHAPTER II

The Struggle for the Frontiers (1919-1923)

FIRST STEPS IN FOREIGN AFFAIRS AND THE SETTLEMENT OF THE FRONTIER WITH GERMANY

The future course of the Polish Republic's foreign policy was determined, even more than the home policy, by the objective and personal differences between Pilsudski and Dmowski. The chief aim of the National Committee and the National Democrats was territorial gains in the west, which they hoped to achieve by diplomatic negotiations with the Entente. Pilsudski, on the other hand, did not attach much value to such acquisitions, which he described contemptuously as 'a gift from the Allies'. All his efforts were directed towards enlarging Poland by conquests in the east, and he concentrated the whole military potential of the nation on this idea. While the National Democrats paid homage to the egalitarian and centralistic ideals of French democracy, Pilsudski and the PPS believed that a powerful Poland could only be built up by federation with the peoples on the western borders of Russia. Only a strong east European federal State seemed capable of standing up to the might of Russia. Because he thus regarded Russia as Poland's main enemy, Pilsudski was led to adopt a moderate attitude to Germany, which the Endecja, on the other hand, regarded as the essential adversary. Dmowski's conception was 'Piast', Pilsudski's was 'Jagellonian'. To Pilsudski, historical modes of thought were of great importance; in particular, he expected to be able to restore the old Lithuanian–Polish condominium of 1386–1772 in the form of a commonwealth of the peoples concerned. This conception formed the background to the motto he had used for forty years, namely that 'Romanticism in aims and realism in methods' would lead him to success. To Dmowski, a biologist and sociologist, who tended to think in terms of sociological abstractions, the question of nationalism was only relevant in so far as he condemned alien peoples in the future Polish State to swift assimilation and absorption. He too based his policy on a principle, and his principle was this: 'It is not the nation that creates the State, but the State that creates the nation.'

Confronted with such fundamentally differing ideas, Pilsudski tried in his foreign policy not only to follow his own conception but also to take into account the National Democrats. Hence his first important steps in foreign affairs were rather curious compromises. For example, in accordance with the aims of the Endecja, the electoral ordinance of 28 November 1918 embraced the German territories of Masuria, Ermland (Warmia), West Prussia, Posen and Upper Silesia, although they lay outside the domain of the Republic, while on the other hand in the east the division into electoral districts ended at Suwalki, Brest-Litovsk and Lwow, which marked the limits of the Government's actual authority. Yet the ordinance also made provision for the Poles in Lithuania and the Ukraine and thus forecast a future policy of federation. It was certainly in the spirit of National Democracy that on 15 December 1918 the Deputy Foreign Minister, Tytus Filipowicz, withdrew the credentials of the German *chargé d'affaires*, Count Harry Kessler – he had secured the release of Pilsudski from Magdeburg – without the Chief of State's foreknowledge; for this Pilsudski dismissed Filipowicz, and the Polish *chargé d'affaires*, Wilhelm Feldman, previously editor of the *Polnische Blätter*, stayed on unofficially in Berlin. The difference in views was made clear when a delegation of Pilsudski's led by the veteran PPS politician Kazimierz Dluski arrived in Paris in January 1919 and started discussions with the National Committee. The delegates from Warsaw had to put up with rather overbearing treatment from Dmowski. They had to listen to a hail of reproaches over the fact that Pilsudski was not supporting the demands for German territory and in addition was ready to give away 'Polish' land east of Lwow to the Ukrainians. Only after a series of stormy discussions did the two groups manage to unite into an official Polish delegation on 13 January 1919. As head of the delegation, Dmowski was given a free hand to push his frontier demands in the east and west, and the delegation's brief for the Paris Peace Conference was drawn up along the lines of his memorandum of 8 October 1918. In return, Pilsudski was to use the Polish army in whatever way seemed best to him. An important motive for Dmowski's partial surrender was the fact that since the abortive *coup* of 4–5 January 1919 the Chief of State was firmly in control of all power in Poland. Thus an internal compromise produced an expansionist – and extremely dangerous – foreign policy in both east and west.

In the interests of aggressive military action towards the east, Pilsudski directed all the country's energies, exhausted though they were by the war, towards the creation of a strong and efficient army. There were plenty of gifted military leaders available. The Austrian army had produced generals like Stanislaw Szeptycki, Tadeusz Rozwadowski, Wlodzimierz Zagorski, Jozef Haller and, indirectly, Wladyslaw Sikorski, while in the Russian army Waclaw Iwaszkiewicz, Jozef Dowbor-Musnicki, Lucjan Zeligowski and the young colonel Wladyslaw Anders – afterwards to lead the Polish army in the Second World War – had all distinguished themselves. In addition, there were the younger officers of the Legion and the POW, such as Slawek, Rydz-Smigly and Kazimierz Sosnkowski, and the officers of the Polish Defence Force. As a result of tensions, between the old Tsarist generals and the legionaries, for example, and between the Austrians and the POW, the internal structure of the young Polish army was far from being perfectly unified, although Pilsudski strove to be fair and gave his legionaries modest ranks. But an army was in fact formed; at first it was about 100,000 strong, but by April 1919 volunteers and conscripts had brought its numbers up to 200,000.

These efforts were in any case necessitated by the frontier conflicts which arose from the collapse of the Central Powers and which seemed to demand the military defence of Polish claims. In eastern Galicia a state of open war had existed between Poles and Ukrainians ever since, on 1 November 1918, the 'Ukrainian National Council' had seized power in Lwow, Stanislawow and

Tarnopol. On 30 November this National Council had proclaimed a 'West Ukrainian People's Republic' (ZUNR), to which, besides eastern Galicia, the Carpatho–Ukraine and the Ukrainian border strips of Bukovina were supposed to belong. The Government of the ZUNR was headed by former members of the Austrian Parliament such as Evgen Petrushevich and Kost Levitskyj, and was conceived very much in the spirit of the old Austrian tradition; the Ukrainians of Galicia had in fact been the only non-German group in the Hapsburg State which as late as October 1918 had still been demanding the perpetuation of the imperial monarchy. So here a *bourgeois* national state of an Austrian character had arisen, a state which was swiftly accepted by the Galician Ukrainians but rejected by the local Poles. On 20 November 1918 a Polish column under Colonel Michal Karaszewicz-Tokarzewski succeeded in advancing from Przemysl to Lwow and in relieving the Polish free corps fighting there under the leadership of Maczynski. By 22 November the town was firmly in Polish hands, and a stable Polish-Ukrainian front was now swiftly formed, running round Lwow from the north in a wide arc curving out to the east. The Polish commander, Iwaszkiewicz, was able to ward off the repeated offensives of the Galician–Ukrainian army in December 1918 and January 1919, and to hold on to Lwow. The authority of the ZUNR was confined to the region round Stanislawow and Tarnopol, especially as Bukovina fell into the hands of Roumania and the Carpatho–Ukraine into those of the newly-created Republic of Czechoslovakia.

The question of Posen turned out to be essentially different and in some respects more complicated than the Galician problem, especially as it was enlivened by internal political differences. On 3 December 1918 a 'sectional Sejm' met in the city of Posen and three days later elected a 'Supreme People's Council' with 82 members to represent all Poles in the German empire. A simultaneously created commission – in which the former deputies in the German Reichstag Wladyslaw Seyda, Wojciech Trampczynski, Wojciech Korfanty and the priest Stanislaw Adamski were the dominant figures – functioned as the unofficial governmental authority of the Poles in the province of Posen. It soon acquired an official character, since representatives of the republican Prussian Government entered into negotiations with it about autonomy for the Posen Poles. In accordance with the predominantly National Democratic views of the population as a whole, the Commission put itself under the orders of the Paris National Committee; out of hostility to Pilsudski and his Warsaw Government it even boycotted the electoral decree of 28 November 1918 and opted to remain in the German empire until the final peace treaty. Only the small but well-organized Posen POW group headed by the Prussian reserve officers Paluch and Hutewicz was on Pilsudski's side. When Paderewski visited Posen on 26 December 1918 with an Allied mission and the visit led to spontaneous clashes between soldiers of German and Polish nationality, the Posen POW made use of the unrest to unleash a general anti-German uprising; Pilsudski himself may have had a hand in this. At any rate, the Commission rightly recognized that if the revolt were successful it could only help Pilsudski and weaken the position of the National Committee, and accordingly tried to stop the fighting. But the anti-German slogans of the insurgents proved so popular that the revolt spread like wildfire; when Wojciech Korfanty attempted pacification he was even threatened with death by the leaders of the insurgents. By 8 January 1919 the rebel troops had brought almost the whole province of Posen under their control. However, on the frontiers of Silesia and Brandenburg and along the line of the River Netze they were halted by the German frontier guards. Pilsudski supported the insurgents by sending them arms and volunteers, and with a fine piece of psychological insight he put them under the command of two former Russian officers, General Jozef Dowbor-Musnicki and Colonel Wladyslaw Anders. The fighting was ended on 7 February 1919 by an armistice which Korfanty, Adamski and Anders concluded in Berlin with a German delegation led by Under-Secretary of State von Heinrichs. Through the rising, Pilsudski had acquired control of Posen and robbed the National Committee of the only territory in which it possessed the semblance of governmental authority. The *de facto* annexation of the province to the Polish Republic (an annexation by no means dictated by the principle of self-determination) was reflected in the fact that on 14 February 1919 Trampczynski assumed the position of Marshal of the Sejm.

The fighting in Posen took place in the shadow of the Peace Conference, which had met on 15 January 1919. On 15 February it set up a special 'Commission for Polish Affairs' under Jules Cambon. On 25 February the Polish delegation handed over to the Commission Dmowski's memorandum of 8 October 1918, on which Polish territorial claims were based. The territorial demands of the Poles were specified on 28 February; they embraced almost the whole of Upper Silesia, parts of Central Silesia, the provinces of Posen (Poznania) and West Prussia except for a few purely German border areas, the eastern tip of Pomerania, Danzig, Masuria, Ermland (Warmia) and the Memel flats – altogether an area of about 34,000 square miles. To support these demands, ethnic, linguistic, historical and economic arguments were advanced, together with technical ones touching transport and communications. In particular, the circumstance that Polish was the everyday language of the Masurians and Upper Silesians seemed to the Polish delegation an incontestable reason for giving these regions to Poland; it overlooked the facts that in these long-Germanized areas mother-tongue and nationality were not identical, and that most of the Masurians and a considerable portion of the Upper Silesians had become 'Polish-speaking Prussians'. Pilsudski rightly saw this and rejected Polish claims to Upper Silesia, although he was unable to prevent them from being put forward. Similarly, he said in his blunt way that 'only five or six fools' could possibly want East Prussia. In point of fact, East Prussia was a key factor in Dmowski's conception; at Versailles, he advocated that the province of East Prussia, so far as it was not apportioned to the Polish–Lithuanian State, should be separated from the German empire, in accordance with the principle of self-determination, and made into an independent republic. He sought in this way to assure Poland's access to the sea down the

Vistula and to avoid the creation of a 'corridor' through German territory. He had recognized the fundamental incompatibility of the notions of 'Prussia' and 'Poland', and hoped by this solution to be able to hinder future German attempts at frontier revision. When all was said and done, even Bismarck had declared that the creation of an independent Poland with access to the sea would cut through 'Prussia's best sinews'. The Polish delegation therefore used every means at its disposal to secure the adoption of its proposals without modification by the Peace Conference. It flooded the Entente Governments with memoranda, reports, plans and legal arguments. Although this Polish obstinacy aroused distaste in some quarters, it did achieve a measure of success, since the Western Governments felt that some consideration was due to a nation which had so long lacked a state of its own.

On 17 March 1919 the Commission for Polish Affairs agreed to support the Polish demands in general. However, at the instigation of Lloyd George, the Supreme Council of the Entente altered the proposals for settling the frontiers. Lloyd George, who had little faith in the Polish ability to build up a state – for this reason he had a poor reputation in Poland right up to his death and afterwards – had the proposals toned down in Germany's favour, even though this meant incurring the opposition of the French Premier, Clemenceau. Parts of West and East-Prussia, instead of being handed over unconditionally to Poland, were made subject to a referendum. Danzig, since it had a purely German population but was linked by economic ties to Poland, was to be made into a free city in accordance with historical tradition – for three hundred years it had been a German city-state allied to the Polish crown. This was the form in which the Allied draft treaty was handed over to the German delegation at Versailles on 7 May 1919. The German answer of 29 May rejected it as incompatible with 'ethnographical principles'. It offered the cession of Posen, which in any case was in practice already subject to the Warsaw Government, and sought to assure Poland's access to the sea not by the cession of West Prussia but by 'free ports at Danzig, Königsberg and Memel, Vistula navigation rights and

53

special railway agreements' under international guarantee. On the strength of these German counter-proposals, Lloyd George succeeded in obtaining a referendum in Upper Silesia. It is true that Posen and the central part of West Prussia – known as Pomorze by the Poles – were assigned to the Poles without a ballot. Since the bulk of East Prussia remained German, this meant the excision of a 'corridor' from German territory, the very solution which both the Polish and German delegations had wanted to avoid.

In accordance with the directions of the Supreme Council, the Treaty of Versailles, signed on 28 June 1919, gave Poland the whole province of Posen and border regions of central Silesia and Pomorze, with an access to the sea to the west of Danzig; altogether an area of about 17,000 square miles. In the Prussian census of these provinces in 1910, 1,714,000 persons had given Polish as their mother-tongue, 1,080,000 had given German, 105,000 Kashubian and 9,000 Masurian; 2,017,000 belonged to the Catholic Church and 904,000 to the Evangelical Church. Thus although the majority of the inhabitants regarded themselves as Poles, and although the German section of the population had been enlarged by the families of officers and civil servants and the German colonization policy of 1886–1916, Poland also received areas with exclusively German native populations and individual German colonies. That is why Stanislaw Grabski, a leading National Democrat politician, emphasized as early as October 1919 that the 'alien element' in Posen and Pomorze must be reduced from '14 or even 20 per cent to $1\frac{1}{2}$ per cent'. In fact, with the incorporation of the two provinces zone by zone, which began on 10 January 1920, the German population either migrated or was expelled, and finally only about 335,000 old-established Germans remained in these regions.

In addition, the Versailles Treaty prescribed the establishment of a Free City of Danzig, granting to the Polish Republic the right to conduct the city's foreign affairs, to include it in the Polish customs area, and to use freely its harbour, railways and waterways. The future status of Upper Silesia and the areas of Allenstein and Marienwerder were to be decided by referenda. No plebiscite was held in Upper Silesia for several years, but voting took place in the regions of Allenstein and Marienwerder on 11 July 1920. The result completely contradicted National Democratic views about the Polish character of the Masurians and Warmians, even if the participation of 152,000 voters who had already emigrated and the advance of the Red Army on Warsaw and Thorn (Torun) did influence the voting. At any rate, in East Prussia only 7,980 electors (2·2 per cent) voted for Poland and in the district of Marienwerder only 7,947 (7·6 per cent); all the rest opted for inclusion in Germany. Not only the vast majority of the Masurians but also two-thirds of the Catholic, Polish-speaking Warmians chose to be German. Thus on 12 and 15 August 1920 only eight East and West Prussian villages were assigned to Poland by the Allied Commissioners; the remainder of the territories where plebiscites had been ordered stayed German.

So far as Polish sovereignty was concerned, the Treaty of Versailles laid it down that Poland was only to be recognized as an independent state, as an 'allied and associated power', if she accepted the treaty as a whole. Moreover, the Entente Governments gave this state sovereignty only over the territories ceded by Germany and suspended sovereignty over the territories where plebiscites were to be held. The question of sovereignty over Congress Poland, Galicia and the eastern territories, and the question of frontiers other than those with Germany, remained open; the Supreme Council retained the right to decide these matters. The disappointment of the Poles at these decisions was general. According to the testimony of the well-known international lawyer Michal Bobrzynski, the Polish nation felt 'that it would still have to fight hard for its frontiers, without being sure of the result. Yet the result would decide whether Poland was to be a small state, existing by courtesy of two mighty neighbours, or an important element in the European balance of power.' The covering letter which the French Prime Minister, Clemenceau, attached to the Paris treaty was calculated to increase Polish dissatisfaction still further. This letter expressly described the restoration of Poland as a gift of the Entente Powers, and in return for the territories handed over to Poland it granted the national minorities rights which were guaranteed by international law and therefore could not be curtailed by the future Polish constitution. This guarantee was made explicit in the Polish Minorities Treaty of 28 June 1919, the primary object of which was the protection of the German and Jewish population. The non-Polish groups of eastern Poland, which for the most part were only incorporated in the Polish State after the drafting of the treaty, were not taken into consideration when it was first conceived, although it was extended to cover them later on. Although the provisions of the Minorities Treaty sprang from purely humanitarian principles, and although they were designed only to regulate, not to prevent, the absorption of the minorities by the majority, the Polish people nevertheless regarded them as insulting and degrading; they seemed to imply that the Poles stood on a lower cultural level than some other peoples. Because of these psychological effects, the Minorities Treaty was calculated to harm rather than help the minorities in Poland. The only reason why the Polish Parliament did not raise any objections to the Peace Treaty and the Minorities Treaty as a whole was that it did not wish to endanger the recognition of Poland as a State. Minister Stanislaw Glabinski observed that 'the Treaty was really "dictated" to "victorious" Poland in the same way as it was to defeated Germany, which was compelled to accept the peace terms'. Events seemed to have confirmed Pilsudski's view that acquisitions in the west could only lead to conflict with Germany and thus endanger expansion to the east.

CONQUESTS IN THE EAST

Pilsudski was not displeased by the general dissatisfaction with the Versailles peace negotiations and their disappointing result. With the collapse of the Central Powers and the retreat of their occupation troops from the western provinces of Russia, which were left temporarily without Governments and were drawn into the confusion of the Russian civil war, prospects for the reestablishment of the federal kingdom of the Jagellonians seemed to be growing; Pilsudski had no doubt that the Lithuanians,

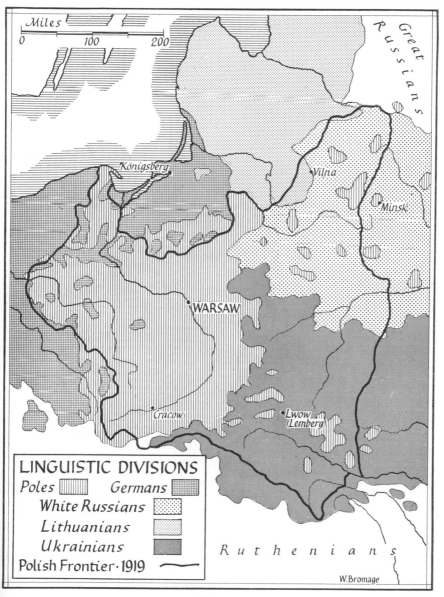

LINGUISTIC DIVISIONS
Poles ▨   Germans ▨
White Russians ▨
Lithuanians ▨
Ukrainians ▨
Polish Frontier · 1919 ——

W. Bromage

MAP 2

White Russians and Ukrainians would gather round Poland as their 'natural protector' against Muscovite power, whether 'Red' or 'White' in character. He thought he could achieve this aim on the one hand by military conquest of these 'historical eastern marches' and on the other by arranging plebiscites among the Lithuanians, White Russians and Ukrainians concerned before peace was concluded with the Moscow Government. This eastern European federal State was to be buttressed by alliances with the other border peoples of the Russian empire, namely the Finns, Estonians, Latvians, Crimean Tartars and Caucasian peoples. So far as extending the eastern frontiers of Poland was concerned, Pilsudski's old opponents, the National Democrats, were in agreement with him. Their former policy of renouncing the eastern parts of the old Polish realm in return for a fundamental Russo-Polish reconciliation had finally been invalidated by the October Revolution and the Russian civil war. Hence even the note of 3 March 1919, in which the Polish delegation in Paris expounded its eastern programme, advocated a considerable extension of Poland towards the east. This note demanded almost all the former Grand Duchy of Lithuania, except for a few border areas in the north and east inhabited solely by Latvians or White Russians, and also, to the south of the Pripet, substantial portions of the provinces of Volhynia and Podolia. However, the Polish peace delegation claimed these extensive regions not in the name of a new federal State but in the name of a Polish national state; thus even in the question of the eastern territories the unitary standpoint had triumphed over what Dmowski called the 'absurd federal ideas' of Pilsudski's followers.

The Polish nation's expansionist aims were centred primarily on the former Grand Duchy of Lithuania. The territory was inhabited in the west mainly by Lithuanians, and in the centre and east mostly by White Russians; Poles, as landlords, townspeople in Kovno, Vilna, Minsk and Dünaburg (Dvinsk), and as small landowners in the numerous 'aristocratic hamlets' of central Lithuania, formed the intellectually, socially and politically dominant class. The numerous Jews (about a tenth of the total population), who were for the most part craftsmen, merchants, workers or members of the intelligentsia, provided a kind of middle class. The ethnic patchwork was further enriched by Russian officials and landowners, Germans, Tartars, Karaites and, in the former Polish Livonia, Latvians. The religious situation was just as complicated and intricate as the ethnic and linguistic: in western Lithuania most of the non-Jewish inhabitants – that is, the Poles, Latvians and a considerable proportion of the White Russians – were Roman Catholics; the White Russians in the east belonged to the Orthodox Church; and central Lithuania formed a transitional zone. Lithuania was certainly not suited to attempts to create a national State; the Lithuanians, Poles and Latvians had a sense of nationality, but the White Russians had not yet developed one. Most of them regarded their language as a peasant language, in other words as the language of a class, not as a national language. In large parts of the country people were still in the 'pre-nationalistic' stage and felt that denominational and linguistic differences marked differences in social class rather than in race or nationality. Indeed, in central Lithuania (the Vilna region), the whole question of nationality seemed to be completely insoluble. Since the White Russian linguistic frontier was continually moving westward, the Vilna area was inhabited mainly by Catholics who had once spoken Lithuanian but had now been 'White Russianized'. Most of them favoured Poland.

Thus Polish claims to Lithuania were not based solely on historical arguments. In contrast to the predominantly 'physical' reasons which had been advanced by the Poles in connection with the western frontiers, namely language and racial character, those put forward to support the claim to Lithuania were mainly 'spiritual'. It was pointed out that Lithuania had been deeply affected by Polish culture and that in this case mother-tongue did not provide a reliable guide to nationality; many of the inhabitants who could not speak Polish nevertheless considered themselves members of the Polish nation. Many Poles regarded the bulk of the White Russians simply as 'ethnic raw material'. Thus, so far as Lithuania was concerned, the Poles employed the same sort of arguments as the Germans had adduced in favour of letting Masuria and Upper Silesia remain part of Germany.

The Polish claims to parts of Volhynia and Podolia, as recorded in the note of 3 March 1919, could hardly be supported with any very conclusive evidence. Apart from historical arguments, they rested mainly on the presence of a substantial Polish minority, whose members, as landowners and townspeople, tended to dominate the solid Orthodox Ukrainian peasant population. The situation in eastern Galicia, now subject to the West Ukrainian Government, was certainly different. Most of the Galician Ukrainian population, numbering at that time about 3·2 million, whose national consciousness had been developed both by membership of the Austrian empire and by their Greek Catholic or Uniate National Church, decisively rejected Polish dominion and supported their own national Government. For their intellectual leaders, the development of their own nationality had been absolutely synonymous with the struggle against Polish culture, language and administration. Nevertheless, eastern Galicia had a Polish Roman Catholic population of nearly two million, which was extremely influential politically, and from a social and cultural point of view held a leading position, especially in the towns. The same curious ethnic, linguistic and denominational mixture of the population to be observed in central Lithuania also gave central and eastern Galicia a character of its own. Just as in the Vilna area there were Catholic White Russians, whose religion gave them affinities with the Poles and whose language linked them to the White Russians, so in eastern Galicia there were strong groups of Roman Catholic Ukrainians and Greek Catholic Poles, who thus stood half-way between the two nationalities.

The actual distribution of power in these territories claimed by Poland by no means corresponded to Polish notions. The collapse of German military power in November–December 1918 had also involved the collapse of those conservative, monarchist régimes in Lithuania, White Russia and the Ukraine which had owed their existence to German World War policy. In Vilna, on 11 November 1918, the republican wing of the 'Taryba' appointed by the German military government had set up a Government of the Republic of Lithuania under Antanas Voldemaras. This *bourgeois*, pro-Entente Cabinet was able to take over the educational and administrative systems created by the German authorities in western and central Lithuania and thus quickly formed a solid civil power. The situation in eastern Lithuania was more confused. In Minsk, besides the older Cabinet of Skirmunt, which had had no influence since the departure of the German troops, there was still the Government of the 'White Russian People's Republic' (BNR) under J. Varonka and A. Lutzkievich; it fluctuated between *bourgeois* and agrarian-revolutionary programmes, but found little response among the White Russian peasants, who had little or no sense of nationality. The place where social revolutionary solutions were being tried most thoroughly was the Ukraine. On 14 November 1918 in the provincial town of Bila Cerkwa a 'Directory' of Ukrainian Nationalists had met; on 14 December, with the help of Galician Ukrainian riflemen under Colonel Konovalec, it succeeded in capturing Kiev and ending the rule of Hetman Pavlo Skoropadskyj. The Directory, in which the social revolutionary politician Symon Petljura soon acquired a dominating position, re-established the Ukrainian People's Republic (UNR) which had been suppressed on 29 April 1917. On 22 January 1919 this new state concluded with the West Ukrainian People's Republic a solemn 'Act of Union' which left both states full autonomy. Petljura was recognized as the common head of both states. Thus a Ukrainian national state had come into being, in which Austrian and Russian political traditions, *bourgeois* and agrarian-socialist ideas, parliamentary and revolutionary practices were rather curiously combined.

It is true that the territorial limits of the three republics of Lithuania, White Russia and the Ukraine were swiftly reduced. The retreating German occupation troops were followed up by the Soviet armies, which in December 1918 advanced to Minsk and Kiev. On 8 December 1918 the Government of the BNR had to leave Minsk, and on 31 December the Lithuanian Cabinet fled from Vilna, which the German soldiers' council handed over to

61

the local Polish defence force. The latter was only able to hold the city against the Red Army until 5 January 1919, though it continued to wage guerrilla warfare in the forests to the south of Vilna. The Lithuanian Government, which was joined by J. Varonka, the BNR minister, as representative of the White Russian minority, was able to hold out in Kovno (Kaunas) under the protection of the German free corps which was defending Courland and Samogitia against the Red Army. In this way the Lithuanian State could be consolidated behind the German defensive front, which at that time ran along the line Schaulen–Vilkomir–Kovno–Grodno, and at Suwalki was in contact with the Polish frontier guards. Further to the south Soviet troops were advancing towards Brest-Litovsk, but were turned back by Polish frontier guard units (this was the first clash between Polish and Soviet troops). The Red divisions were more successful in the Ukraine. On 4 February 1919 they succeeded in capturing Kiev, with the result that the territory of the Ukrainian People's Republic was now restricted to the western parts of Volhynia and Podolia. The Moscow Government was thus in a position to put into effect in the newly-won areas its policy of setting up national states. In the territory of the Grand Duchy of Lithuania arose the 'Socialist Soviet Republic of Lithuania and White Russia', the so-called 'Litbel', whose Government was set up in Vilna on 27 February 1919 under the leadership of J. Mitzkievich-Kapsukas. That the Central Government in Moscow preserved the historical unity of the country, although it normally advocated the strictest separation of nationalities, was probably to be ascribed to its insight into the intricate ethnic mixture of the population of Lithuania. Similarly, a Ukrainian Socialist Soviet Republic headed by Christian Rakovskyj was proclaimed in Kiev on 3 March 1919. Both republics were formally completely independent of the Russian Federal Republic; it was not until June 1919 that the Central Executive Committee in Moscow began to envisage a federation of all Soviet republics.

In these circumstances Poles intent on expansion to the east had to reckon with the fact that they would come up against two zones of differently conceived national States, a *bourgeois*-socialist one and a Soviet one. A military attack on the Lithuanian or Ukrainian Republic would have made future federation with these States more difficult and eased the position of the Bolsheviks, who were regarded as the chief opponents in so far as they were the territorial heirs of the Muscovite State. An attack on the Republic of Lithuania was also ruled out because German free corps still occupied the region of Suwalki and barred the way of Polish units. Only in the territory between Suwalki and Brest-Litovsk, that is, in the region of Bialystok-Grodno, did a direct advance against the Soviet power in the shape of the Soviet Republic of Litbel seem possible.

Pilsudski also had other reasons for wishing first of all to gain control of central Lithuania. The Vilna region was a piece of his homeland of which he was particularly fond. To him, a member of the Lithuanian princely house of Ginet, who in June 1893 had organized the first party congress of the PPS in the Ponary forest near Vilna, the union of Poland and Lithuania was an indispensable requirement. To him, Lithuania was not a national or political concept, but a half-historical, half-romantic one; in language, culture and national pride he felt himself a Pole, but in his political thinking he was a Lithuanian. At the beginning of April 1919, when thanks to the stabilization of the position in Posen and eastern Galicia and to numerous regroupings the Polish army was in a position to undertake an offensive, he began to make his preparations. On 8 April 1919 he wrote to his trusted friend Leon Wasilewski, a St Petersburg socialist who had acted since 1898 as his political adviser (Wasilewski was in Paris at this time), that he would shortly be able to make a start on his Lithuanian and White Russian policy, and this 'with a revolver in my hand'. He was very much inclined to gain some compensation for Danzig, which at that time, before the Versailles decisions, was still 'doubtful', by acquiring Libau and Riga. To provide diplomatic support for this planned advance, on 12 April 1919 the Prime Minister, Paderewski, laid before the Paris Commission for Polish Affairs his plans for the creation of the 'United States of Eastern

Europe'. The offensive itself brought the region of Vilna and Lida under Polish control on 19 April; the legionaries were burning to lay their idolized commander's home town at his feet 'as a gift'. On 22 April Pilsudski issued his famous proclamation, 'To the Inhabitants of the Former Grand Duchy of Lithuania', in which he promised that all the peoples of this country would be quite free to settle their own 'internal national and religious affairs without any pressure from Poland'. At the same time he set up under Jerzy Osmolowski a 'Civil Administration for the Eastern Territories', which was responsible directly to him and was thus safe from the interference of the Warsaw nationalists.

Pilsudski's federal programme, as expressed in this proclamation, gave his political opponents in the parties of the Right splendid opportunities for furious polemics. For example, the National Democratic leader, Professor Stanislaw Stronski, reproached the Chief of State with being ready to give away 'Polish land' in Lithuania to the Lithuanians and White Russians; Pilsudski, said Stronski, was an unpractical idealist, like the Polish generals of 1848–9, who had fought for the revolution all over Europe, but not for their own native land. This reproach was certainly unjustified. In Pilsudski's view, the strength of a State was measured in relation to the strength of its neighbour, and for this reason the guiding principle of his foreign policy was always to weaken Russia as much as possible by splitting up the western and southern provinces of the Russian empire into independent States. However, these newly created States could only be linked to Poland by a really attractive federal concept. Once incorporated in a federation, any States linked to Poland would be transformed by the superior nature of Polish civilization just as thoroughly as the peoples in Jagellon's union had been. Pilsudski was firmly convinced that in any agreement between a stronger and weaker nation the stronger had to give some kind of bounty or gratuity, since in the long run it would enjoy the advantage. That was why he wanted to curb the 'raging federalist' Paderewski, and also why he once admitted cynically: 'Now that the chatter about the brotherhood of men and peoples, and American doctrines, are beginning to triumph on the face of God's Earth, I am very glad to give my support to the Federalists.' The difference between the 'unitary' principle of the National Democrats and Pilsudski's 'federal' programme was simply that the former aimed at complete assimilation of alien peoples, so that they became Polish, while the Chief of State, in accordance with the old phrase *'gente Lituanus, natione Polonus'*, wished to leave the non-Polish peoples' ethnic character as it was, but to see a Polish-speaking upper class established over them to ensure the unity of the country. Only *vis-à-vis* the great Ukrainian nation did Pilsudski probably have a genuinely federal relationship in mind.

There was considerable underestimation of the national consciousness of the peoples envisaged for federation; even Pilsudski was guilty of it. This came to light in the negotiations for federation which were carried on in the first half of 1919 with the Republic of Lithuania, or, as the Poles called it, 'Kovno Lithuania'. These negotiations were more or less doomed to failure from the start, since the Kovno Government insisted on the principle of a completely sovereign Lithuanian national state and demanded Vilna for its capital. For this reason on 23 December 1918 it had even thrown away the chance of a joint Polish-Lithuanian defence of Vilna against the Bolsheviks. To Lithuanian nationalists, the awakening of the national consciousness and the creation of a national State were synonymous with the removal as far away as possible of Polish language and culture, whose superiority they feared more than they did Russian civilization. Even though the existence of a Lithuanian State had only been assured by the Polish capture of Vilna, which removed the continual Bolshevik threat to Kovno, the Lithuanian nationalists felt that they could not at any price renounce the unconditional possession of Vilna, which they regarded, just as much as the Poles or Jews, as the 'Lithuanian Jerusalem'. The Polish- or White Russian-speaking majority of the population were once again to be made into 'Lithuanian-speaking Lithuanians'. With the youthful impatience of a national consciousness that had only been awake for one generation, the Kovno Government transformed historical memories of the medieval Lithuanian empire into current political demands. How involved questions of nationality could be in the Vilna area of Lithuania was shown by the example of the Iwanowski brothers; one of them became a Polish minister, the second, as 'Iwanouskij', became a White Russian nationalist politician, and the third, as 'Ivanauskas', became a Lithuanian university professor. It was no less significant that the great Polish writer Adam Mickiewicz was claimed for their nation by both the Lithuanians and the White Russians. It was also a matter of common knowledge that the brother of the subsequent Polish President Narutowicz – the family belonged to the Samogitian landed nobility – had signed the Lithuanian Republic's declaration of independence under the name of 'Narutavicius', and that the temporary commander-in-chief of the Lithuanian army, Plechavicius, was in fact a Polish aristocrat, the former Russian general Plechowicz. The very fact that the cleavage according to nationality produced painful divisions in families caused Polish society in central Lithuania, where it played a leading role, to adopt just as nationalistic an attitude as the Lithuanians. Like the Baltic Germans, it was conscious of its position as a culturally and politically dominant minority and sought to defend this position with all the means at its disposal. Few of the landed gentry were prepared to agree to a union of 'Vilna Lithuania' with the Lithuanian Republic, either on the basis of a Polish–Lithuanian federation or without one. Most of the Poles in Vilna pleaded for unconditional union with Poland. As the most influential groups among both Poles and Lithuanians rejected the federal idea in favour of the concept of a national state in its most extreme form, there was little prospect of success for the negotiations which Leon Wasilewski conducted with the Lithuanian Cabinet headed by Slesevicius. Since the middle of 1919 a military demarcation zone had been formed between 'Kovno' and 'Vilna' Lithuania. It ran along to the west of the Grodno–Vilna–Dvinsk railway and was respected by the Polish army on the orders of Pilsudski; it left about as many Poles on the Lithuanian side as Lithuanians on the Polish side. In addition, demarcation lines, which corresponded more or less to the actual frontier zone, were fixed on 28 June 1919 by the Entente and on 27 July by Marshal Foch. Meanwhile, the POW in Lithuania – almost certainly in collusion with Pilsudski – was preparing to carry out a *coup d'état* in Kovno; however, it was discovered by the Lithuanian Government. The arrest of those concerned on 29 August 1919 and the completion of a first instalment of land reform aimed against the Polish landed aristocracy hardened the antagonism between the States of Poland and Lithuania.

The military conquest and consolidation of central Lithuania enabled Pilsudski to make preparations to settle the question of eastern Galicia. In April 1919 Haller's army, consisting of 60,000 well-equipped troops, had returned to Poland from France; it was deployed in the region of Zamosc–Kowel for an attack on the twin Ukrainian States. On 30 April 1919 Pilsudski issued his 'Plans for the offensive in Volhynia and Galicia'. Meanwhile negotiations under General Botha were still going on in Paris over a preliminary peace plan worked out by the 'Inter-Allied Commission for the Conclusion of an Armistice between Poland and the Ukraine'. It envisaged a demarcation line which gave Lwow and the oil region of Drohobycz to Poland, and was thus unfavourable to the Ukrainians. Yet the draft was accepted by the Ukrainian delegation on 13 May 1919 because it was conscious of the inferiority of the Galician–Ukrainian army; however, on the same day it was rejected by the Polish delegation under Dmowski and Paderewski. The offensive by Haller's army now began, on 14 May 1919; it swiftly led to the annihilation of the East Ukrainian troops deployed near Luck and thereby indirectly facilitated the Red Army's advance into Volhynia. Haller's army now swung southward and with the help of Iwaszkiewicz's army, which attacked from the west, had by 8 June 1919 conquered the whole of eastern Galicia up to the River Zbrucz, which formed the border. As the Red Army was advancing at the same time from the north-east against the eastern frontier of Galicia, the West and East Ukrainian troops were compressed into an area of only a few square miles round the little town of Husiatyn on the Zbrucz.

Petljura now asked the Polish army command for an armistice, which was granted on 15 June 1919, and gave the East Ukrainian State the protection of Poland in the rear against the Bolsheviks, but also left the western part of Volhynia under Polish control. Even if the East Ukrainians saw Soviet Russia and the Soviet Ukraine as their real opponents and were therefore forced to unite with Poland – negotiations for a peace treaty were begun – the Galician-Ukrainian State had to continue to regard Poland as enemy number one. Accordingly, the West Ukrainian army did not recognize Petljura's armistice, and in a desperate counter-offensive brilliantly led by General Grekov had by 27 June 1919 recaptured part of eastern Galicia. Meanwhile the Supreme Council, impressed by Haller's offensive, had decided on 18 June to allow the Polish army to occupy the whole of eastern Galicia, so that the 'lives and property of the peaceful population of eastern Galicia may be protected from the Bolshevist bands'. An important factor in this decision was the wish to see the oil region of eastern Galicia incorporated in Poland rather than in the Ukrainian State. The decision was communicated to the Polish delegation on 25 June 1919, but not to the Ukrainian delegation. The Polish army, under the personal command of Pilsudski, now started another offensive which by 15 July had finally brought the whole country under the control of Poland. The Galician–Ukrainian army withdrew across the Zbrucz; from now onwards it was to fight no longer against the Poles, but to join Petljura's East Ukrainians in the struggle against Soviet Ukrainian troops. The hard-won realization that in the last analysis Kiev was more important to the Ukraine as a whole than Lwow had reconciled the West Ukrainian leader Petrushevich and his politicians to the temporary yet painful renunciation of their native land.

Thus at the same time as Posen and Pomorze were assigned to Poland by the Versailles Treaty and Kovno Lithuania had to be given up as lost, the whole former Austrian crown land of Galicia was under the control of the Warsaw Government. It is true that it ruled here by force of arms not by right of sovereignty, although it was empowered by the Entente to set up a civil administration. The military occupation of the country necessarily involved the loss of any chance of making moral conquests among the West Ukrainians; all the same, Pilsudski could put it down to the credit of his policy that the concept of a pan-Ukrainian State was now aimed exclusively against the Bolsheviks.

After the military defence of Galicia the Chief of State concentrated the energies of the Polish army on the conquest of eastern, White Russian Lithuania. In summer 1919 the Polish troops began to advance eastward again; on 8 August they entered Minsk and in September they reached Borissov and Bobruisk. The Government of Litbel, already driven out of Vilna in April 1919, had to retreat to Smolensk. In autumn 1919 Pilsudski's armies formed a cordon, which ran along the Dvina from Dvinsk to Polotsk and from there, bending southward, along the Ulla, the Beresina and the Ptitsh; to the south of the Pripet, the rivers Ubort and Sluch formed the boundary between the Polish domain and that of Petljura. Poland had thus acquired for itself northern and eastern frontiers which corresponded fairly closely – except for the territory of the Republic of Lithuania – to Dmowski's demands of 3 March 1919. They also marked the extreme limit of scattered Polish settlement, for they enclosed the zone in which the Polish, Catholic population formed only about 5 per cent of the total population. The Poles who lived in the regions occupied, some two to three million, were almost exclusively townspeople or landowners, and provided the basis of the Polish civil administration.

Indeed, it was precisely the presence of a strong autochthonous Polish ruling class in the Grand Duchy of Lithuania that formed the biggest obstacle to Pilsudski's plans for federation. This was because of the social conflict between the Polish landowners and the land-hungry White Russian peasants. The Polish civil administration under Osmolowski strove at first to win the confidence of the native population by radical measures such as the nationalization of the factories. Pilsudski had a proclamation published in which he promised that White Russia should negotiate with Poland about a future constitutional link 'on absolutely equal terms, as one free man with another'. Anton Lutskievich, the erstwhile Prime Minister of the BNR, who had been summoned from Paris on Paderewski's orders, convened a 'Supreme White Russian Rada' (or Council) in Minsk, but found himself confronted with an agrarian-socialist majority hostile to the Polish land-owners. He was forced to form a moderate, conservative, minority Government which was supported by the Polish administration, especially in the cultural field. Meanwhile, the demand that the big estates should be broken up, a slogan which was disseminated by the exiled Government of Litbel in Smolensk and also by the secret White Russian Communist Organization in the country itself, steadily gained ground. Under pressure of the con-servative Polish population, the Polish administration therefore soon tried another tack; Polish was made the official language and Polish estates that had been broken up from 1917 to 1919 were restored. The example of White Russia showed quite clearly that the Polish concept of federation was no match for the Soviet one, especially the concept of federal union supported by Stalin, the commissar for minorities. Both Stalin and Pilsudski advocated the cultural emancipation of the 'alien' peoples in the Russian empire; but what made the programme of Lenin and Stalin more attractive was their power, which Pilsudski lacked, to distribute land to the peasant masses. Consequently, the Polish ascendancy in White Russia rested not on the whole-hearted support of the local population but fundamentally on the victory of Polish arms.

THE WAR BETWEEN POLAND AND SOVIET RUSSIA

The explanation of the weak resistance which the Soviet Government offered to the extension of Polish power to the Düna (Dvina) and Beresina was that in the summer of 1919 the Red troops had to fight the hardest defensive battles of the civil war against the White armies. At that time Yudenich was concentrat-ing his forces for the advance on Petrograd; it was true that Admiral Kolchak had to withdraw his troops, defeated by the Bolsheviks at Samara, right to the Urals, but he still controlled the whole of Siberia. In the south of Russia and the eastern Ukraine were Denikin's armies, which in June captured Tsarytsyn – later to be renamed Stalingrad – and in August Kharkov, Kiev and Odessa, though this involved them in a war with Petljura's East and West Ukrainian divisions. Nevertheless, Denikin was preparing to march on Moscow. In these circumstances the Moscow Government was prepared to abandon the whole of White Russia to the Poles so as to be able to throw all available troops against Denikin.

As a result, Poland, now the uncontested champion of the nationalist movements among the border peoples of the erstwhile Russian empire, acquired in summer 1919 a sort of arbitrator's role in the struggle between the Whites and the Reds. Pilsudski had at his disposal about 400,000 men, of whom over 230,000 were deployed along the eastern frontier of Poland; to the south of them, in Volhynia and Podolia, were about 100,000 men of Petljura's East and West Ukrainian units. Soviet Russia had only about 500,000 soldiers on all fronts put together, while Denikin commanded some 250,000, 150,000 of them Cossacks. It was an indication of the real balance of power that in the summer and autumn of 1919 Pilsudski was requested to take part in the Russian civil war not only by Lenin and Denikin but also by the Governments of the Entente Powers.

Pilsudski negotiated with all three sides simultaneously. As early as July 1919 he sent a military mission under General Aleksander Karnicki to Taganrog, Denikin's headquarters at the time, and a little later he sent Jerzy Iwanowski as his plenipotentiary. The commander of the White armies attached great value to Polish armed assistance, which would make his advance on Moscow in August and September 1919 considerably easier. In particular, he wanted a Polish offensive from the region of the lower Pripet against Gomel, as this could cut off the Bolshevik 12th Army, which was operating to the north of Kiev, from its supply base. He described the co-operation of all non-Bolshevist troops on Russian soil as a dictate of civilization, but was not prepared to make any concessions to Poland in territorial questions. He wanted to see the Polish State confined to the Congress Kingdom, or, as one of his officials remarked almost mockingly, 'the

Vistula basin'; the restoration of the 'Grand Duchy of Warsaw' seemed quite sufficient to him. For this reason he described the Polish claim to Lithuania as 'psychopathic megalomania'; and he regarded the conflict between Great Russia and the Ukraine as a 'purely internal Russian question', 'a fraternal quarrel between Moscow and Kiev'. In these circumstances Pilsudski saw no reason for meeting Denikin's wishes in any way. On the contrary, on 3 November 1919 he made contact with the Soviet mission which had been installed since the beginning of October in Mikaszewicze near Luck under the well-known Polish communist Julian Marchlewski, the friend of Rosa Luxemburg. Pilsudski's representative, Captain Ignacy Boerner, told Marchlewski – a special Polish emissary gave the same message direct to Lenin – that the Polish army was ready to remain on the line it held at present and not to advance in the direction of Gomel if the Red Army withdrew ten kilometres from the Polish line all along the front and refrained from disseminating communist propaganda among the Polish troops; in addition, Poland would support Latvian claims to Dvinsk and would expect the Red Army to refrain from making any attack on Petljura's troops. The need to make these demands was already urgent, since in October and November 1919 it was becoming evident that the Whites were going to lose the war. Denikin's troops, defeated before Moscow, were fleeing back through the Ukraine to the lower Don, while with the collapse of Kolchak's Ural front the conquest of Siberia by the Bolsheviks was beginning. A last call for help from Denikin to Pilsudski on 26 November 1919 drew no response. Pilsudski also resisted the diplomatic intervention of the Entente Governments, which tried to draw him on to the side of the Whites, and and for his part pointed out to the British ambassador, Sir Horace Rumbold, the importance of the proposed new belt of border states to England. The sacrifice of the Whites and the silent support of the Reds by Pilsudski formed, in the words of the Polish general Tadeusz Kutrzeba, 'an unpleasant, but necessary consequence' of Poland's eastern policy. The fact was that in the Polish view a *bourgeois* Russian Government which insisted on the principle of a 'one and indivisible Russia' and oppressed other peoples – Denikin's treatment of the Crimean Tartars was a good example of this – was a far greater danger than the Bolsheviks; in the last analysis, the latter were far more flexible in their dealings with non-Russian peoples and were even ready to accept the independence of Finland, Estonia and Latvia. This attitude of Pilsudski's was certainly an extremely important, if not decisive, factor in the military victory of the Bolsheviks in the Russian civil war.

This decision brought with it the final settlement of the differences between Poland and Petljura's Ukrainian People's Republic. On 20 July 1919 the East and West Ukrainian troops had begun an offensive against the Bolsheviks which led to the capture of Kiev on 31 August 1919. As Denikin's White divisions reached Kiev from the south-east on the same day, a military conflict flared up between Denikin and Petljura over the possession of the Ukraine to the west of the Dnieper. This conflict lasted until November 1919 and contributed to Denikin's downfall. On the other hand, this quarrel assisted the progress of the Polish-Ukrainian peace negotiations which were being conducted on Petljura's behalf by A. Livitskyj. Petrushevich, the head of the West Ukrainian State, energetically opposed the Polish demand for eastern Galicia, but after his Galician–Ukrainian troops fighting in Volhynia had been decimated by sickness he finally yielded to the arguments of Petljura, the head of the combined Ukrainian State, and on 15 November 1919 went into exile in Vienna. The Polish–Ukrainian peace treaty, which gave eastern Galicia and the western part of Volhynia to Poland, was signed on 2 December. Petljura had thus purchased Polish patronage and protection, as was shown by Pilsudski's message of 3 November to Lenin. However, in spite of their celebrated 'death march' to Poltava, his troops, weakened by disease, were unable to recapture Kiev, which on 22 December passed out of the hands of the Whites into those of the Bolsheviks. By that time Petljura's political programme was being outbid by that of the Bolsheviks, just as Pilsudski's was in White Russia, and the heroic struggles of the

Petljura divisions provoked little or no response in the Ukrainian people. A resolution of the Bolshevik Central Committee passed in December 1919 promised 'national self-determination' and 'independence' for the 'Ukrainian Soviet Republic', and the 'free development of Ukrainian culture'. This robbed Petljura – and consequently also Pilsudski – of his strongest propaganda weapon.

The problem of the territories disputed between Poland and Soviet Russia was at this time also occupying the Supreme Council of the Entente. In face of the unsettled political, ethnic and religious questions of these territories, it fixed on 8 December 1919 a provisional eastern administrative boundary of Poland proper. This line led from the East Prussian frontier at Goldlap round Suwalki to the Niemen; from the Niemen it ran east of Bialystok to the Bug at Mielnik, and then southward along the Bug to the Galician frontier. Quite independently of this, the Supreme Council was also discussing a frontier between Poland and the Ukraine in central Galicia, but it failed to reach a final decision. Factors which contributed to the failure were the questions of Polish sovereignty over eastern Galicia and of Ukrainian autonomy. In any case, the line of 8 December and its planned southern continuation in central Galicia ran on an average 300 kilometres to the west of the actual limit of Polish authority. Its creators meant it to be neither a definitive eastern frontier of Poland nor a western frontier of Soviet Russia – although in the Polish–Soviet conflict of the next few decades it was again and again falsely interpreted as such – but simply an administrative boundary of the territory already recognized as incontestably Polish. At any rate, although with this line the Supreme Council was meeting the wishes of the White Russians, it expressly reserved for a future decision 'any rights which Poland could establish to the territories east of the line described'.

In fact, the settlement of the Polish–Soviet frontier question hardly depended on the authority of the Supreme Council, but on the issue of the struggle between the two parties concerned. At the end of November 1919, after Lenin had replied evasively to his proposals, Pilsudski broke off negotiations with the Moscow

74

Government and reverted to military action again. In December 1919 a number of Polish divisions, in concert with Latvian troops, undertook a winter campaign against the Bolsheviks on both sides of the Dvina, and on 3 January 1920 captured the important fortress of Dvinsk. This action demonstrated to the Moscow Government that Pilsudski insisted on the principle of 'no change', and on 22 December 1919 Foreign Commissar G. V. Chicherin sent the Polish Government by wireless a peace offer which led to fresh negotiations. On 28 January 1920 Lenin, Trotsky and Chicherin addressed to 'the Chief of State, the Polish Government and the Polish people' a suggested frontier settlement which envisaged a demarcation line running from Drissa on the Düna (Dvina) via Polotsk, Borissov and Chudnov to Bar in Podolia, and thus corresponding fairly closely to the existing front line. Pilsudski answered these suggestions with some reserve and spun out the armistice negotiations over the winter months. He was obviously convinced that for all its apparent generosity the Soviet offer was not meant sincerely and was simply intended to gain time until the bulk of the Red Army could be thrown against Poland after the final annihilation of the Whites. And in fact the operations division of the Red Army General Staff under General Shaposhnikov was already working out in February 1920 plans for an offensive against Poland, which in its view would require twenty divisions and five cavalry brigades, a total of about 190,000 men. At that time the Polish troops were confronted by only five divisions and five calvalry brigades, but this small Russian western army gradually grew when withdrawals were made from other fronts until on 25 April 1920 it numbered twenty divisions and five cavalry brigades, the strength envisaged in Shaposhnikov's plan. The Polish staff was kept informed by its intelligence service of every detail of this regrouping. As a touchstone of Soviet sincerity, Pilsudski insisted on the demand that the peace negotiations should be concluded in Borissov, a small White Russian town situated in front-line territory on the western edge of the area where the Soviet troops were massing. The fact that the Moscow Government obstinately rejected Borissov as the site for the conference and preferred Reval, Petrograd, Moscow, Warsaw or even London seemed to him to confirm that they intended to launch an attack.

The assumption that the Red Army would attack Poland in the spring of 1920 decided Pilsudski to seek allies. Between 16 and 20 January 1920 he was negotiating with M. Chaikovsky and B. Savinkov, the leaders of the Russian Social Revolutionaires, who had been sent from Paris by the anti-Bolshevik Political Council. Through them – thanks partly to the discreet mediation of Winston Churchill – he came to an understanding with the Whites. However, this agreement had little military value, since in March Denikin's troops lost the lower Don and had to flee into the Crimea. The efforts of Leon Wasilewski at the Helsinki Conference (15–22 January 1920) to build up a united anti-Soviet front consisting of Poland, Latvia, Estonia and Finland were unsuccessful, mainly because of the impression created by Yudenich's catastrophic defeat in front of Petrograd. Estonia, which had started negotiations with Moscow on 3 January, made peace on 20 February, while Finland and Latvia, which felt safe since it had captured Dünaburg (Dvinsk) with Polish assistance, were preparing to hold similar discussions. The Poles now had to pay for standing by idly during the decisive defeats of the Whites a few months before. The only allies on which the Polish army could count were Petljura's weak Ukrainian divisions, the small White Russian free corps under General Balachowicz and the excellent Lithuanian Tartar cavalry under General Romanowicz. Pilsudski therefore exerted every effort and by the spring of 1920 had brought the Polish army up to 700,000 men, more than 300,000 of whom were deployed on the eastern frontier, where, however, they were strung out along a front line about 620 miles long. On 7 March, by a local advance towards Mosyr on the River Pripet, the Polish army cut the important railway line which ran behind the Soviet front and connected Orsha in the north with Zhitomir in the south.

Pilsudski made up his mind to attack the Red Army, although on 9 February 1920 the British Foreign Secretary, Lord Curzon, had informed him that in this case Poland could expect 'neither help nor support from Great Britain', and a corresponding warning from the Supreme Council had followed on 24 February. He made this decision in order to anticipate the complete defeat of the Whites and the Caucasian peoples by the power of the Soviet; considerable portions of the Bolshevik armies previously employed in fighting Denikin had already been sent to reinforce the Polish front in Volhynia. Although the bulk of the Soviet Russian offensive troops were stationed in the north, in the region of Vitebsk-Orsha, Pilsudski chose to mount his offensive in the Ukraine, on the right bank of the Dnieper. Such an operation may have had the value of a military diversion, but it was certainly intended primarily to restore the frontiers of 1772 in the south as well, and to complement control of White Russia with that of the 'right-bank' Ukraine. Strategically, an attack in the north on the Red troops engaged in massing for an offensive would have been of incomparably greater value.

On 21 April 1920 Pilsudski concluded with Petljura an offensive alliance which allotted the Ukraine to the right of the Dnieper to the UNR if the campaign was successful, but on condition that there should be a federal union with Poland. The Polish and Ukrainian divisions started their advance on 25 April 1920. On the tips of their lances the Polish Uhlans carried a proclamation drawn up by Pilsudski and dated 26 April 1920 which, like the Lithuanian proclamation of 22 April 1919, promised 'all inhabitants of the Ukraine, without distinction of class, race or religion', the protection of Polish arms; it expressed the hope that the Ukrainian people would drive out the 'foreign intruders' (this meant the Bolsheviks) and exert every effort 'to win freedom for itself with the help of the Polish Republic'. On 7 May 1920 Kiev fell into the hands of the Polish and Ukrainian divisions without a fight; the Government of the Ukrainian Soviet Republic under Christian Rakovsky had to abandon the Ukrainian capital for the fourth time since 1918. The capture of Kiev swiftly changed the mood of the National Democrats, who had maintained a reserved attitude to the 'Ukrainian adventure', in favour of Pilsudski.

Trampczynski, the speaker of the Sejm, declared emphatically that the writer Mickiewicz's vision of a free Poland with the frontiers of 1772 was now being realized; in a solemn resolution passed by the Sejm on 18 May 1920 he referred to Pilsudski as the general who 'walked in the footsteps of Boleslaw the Brave'. The marshal (for such he had become in March) was at the zenith of his fame. A *Te deum* was sung in all Polish churches.

The reaction followed swiftly. In the north the twenty-eight-year-old Russian general M. N. Tukhachevsky, a former guards officer, attacked on 14 May, although the Reds had not yet assembled all their troops. He did not achieve any direct strategic success, but made it necessary for Polish troops to be moved up from the Ukraine. This in turn facilitated the offensive of the 'Proletarian Cavalry Army' under Budienny, which had been hastily ordered from Caucasia to the Ukraine. Twelve thousand sabres strong, it broke through the Polish front to the south of Kiev on 6 June 1920 and on 8 June reached Zhitomir. With that the Polish southern front collapsed; on 11 June Kiev had to be evacuated, and the Polish army group retired swiftly to its starting points in western Volhynia and Podolia. In Warsaw there was a political crisis; in Moscow the Russian military successes were interpreted as the overture to a general European revolution. In a letter to Lenin on 20 June, Stalin outlined the vision of a future 'Soviet Germany, Soviet Poland, Soviet Hungary, Soviet Finland', in other words of Soviet States which would be compelled by 'the logic of events' to enter into a 'confederation', a federal union, with Soviet Russia.

On 20 July 1920 Tukhachevsky issued to the army group of twenty divisions under his command an order of the day which expressed the proud expectations of the Soviet Government: 'The fate of the world revolution is being decided in the west; the way leads over the corpse of Poland to a universal conflagration. . . . On to Vilna, Minsk and Warsaw!' The offensive which opened on 4 July seemed to justify these hopes. Minsk fell into Tukhachevsky's hands on 12 July, Vilna on 14 July and Grodno on 19 July. Meanwhile Budienny advanced towards eastern

Galicia. By the middle of August Tukhachevsky's armies were already fighting round Warsaw; at the same time Gay-Khan's cavalry corps, consisting mainly of Caucasians, was advancing between Masuria – which had only just voted on 11 July to remain part of Germany – and the middle Vistula towards Thorn (Torun) and Graudenz (Grudziadz). It looked as if the Polish army, compressed into central Poland, was going to be caught in a huge encircling movement. Tukhachevsky's troops, whose wing divisions had carried out an advance of some 600 miles, were thus carrying out the same manœuvre which had given victory to the Russian Field-Marshal Paskevich in the Russo-Polish war of 1831.

In this desperate situation the Polish Prime Minister, Wladyslaw Grabski, who had finally managed to form a Cabinet after a Government crisis lasting fifteen days, called on the Allies for help. He travelled to Spa, where the Supreme Council was sitting, but had to listen to bitter reproaches about Polish *hubris*, which seemed to have challenged the might of the Soviet. Consequently the conditions on which the Entente offered to use its good offices to arrange a peace were exceptionally hard. By the so-called Protocol of Spa, signed on 10 July 1920, the Polish Government had to undertake to accept the Supreme Council's decisions on the Polish–Czech and Polish–Lithuanian frontiers, to renounce its claim to Vilna in favour of the Republic of Lithuania, to recognize the Entente's future decisions about the fate of eastern Galicia and the arrangement between Danzig and Poland, and finally to withdraw its troops behind the line of 8 December 1919, and in eastern Galicia to the front line existing on the day of the armistice still to be arranged. After these conditions had been accepted, a French military mission under General Maxime Weygand and a diplomatic one headed by the British statesman Lord d'Abernon travelled to Warsaw. On 11 July the British foreign minister cabled his proposal for an armistice to the Moscow Government (his French colleague, Millerand, did not wish to be involved). The demarcation line suggested by Curzon, from which the Red Army was to withdraw fifty kilometres, was identical in its central section, from Grodno to the Galician frontier, with the line of 8 December 1919. To the north of Grodno the frontier between Soviet Russia and the Republic of Lithuania was to run more or less along the Grodno–Vilna–Dünaburg (Dvinsk) railway, while a southern continuation of the Line of 8 December 1919 was provided in the form of the so-called 'Line A' of 17 June 1919, which ran southward from the Galician border, west of Rawa Ruska and east of Przemysl, to the source of the River San. This line, subsequently christened the Curzon Line – the expression was coined by Soviet diplomacy – gave the Moscow Government, over and above its old demands for the territories of White Russia and the Ukraine which had formerly belonged to the Russian Empire, an apparently legitimate claim to Eastern Galicia, which had never been part of the Tsarist Empire. In addition, the Curzon Line, originally fixed in 1919 as a provisional minimum frontier between Poland and the non-Soviet territories of White Russia and the Ukraine, subsequently became a Polish–Soviet frontier approved by France and Great Britain. Henceforward, right up to the present, the Soviet Government has made this frontier the basis of its legal claims.

The enormous sacrifices which the Grabski Government had made – and which forced it to resign on 24 July 1920 – did little to improve the military or political situation of Poland. As early as the middle of July the Moscow Government, confident of military victory, had set up in Bialystok a 'Provisional Committee' under Julian Marchlewski and Feliks Dzierzynski which was to serve as the embryo of a Government for the future 'Soviet Poland'. At the Polish–Soviet peace negotiations, which began at Minsk on 17 August, Moscow declared itself content with the Curzon Line, including a few small alterations in favour of Poland, as the 'final frontier of Poland', but at the same time demanded the reduction of the Polish army to 50,000 men, the dismissal of the Allied missions and the complete dismantling of the Polish arms industry. During this period the promised Allied deliveries of war material were bringing no effective help. Germany and the Czechoslovak Republic prohibited their transit, and in the

Miles
0   100   200

L A T V I A

L I T H U A N I A

Kovno

Königsberg

EAST
PRUSSIA

Danzig

Grodno

GERMANY

Thorn

Minsk

R U S S I A

•WARSAW

Brest
•Litovsk

Pinsk

CURZON
LINE
1919

Breslau

RIGA
LINE

C Z E C H O

Cracow

Lwow
(Lemberg)

S L O V A K I A

CURZON
LINE · 1919
POLAND·1919
1914 Frontiers of Russia,
Germany & Austria-Hungary

W.Bromage

MAP 3

newly-created Free City of Danzig the dockers refused to unload Allied munition ships. The British Labour Party coined the slogan 'hands off Russia'; its secretary, Henderson, issued an emphatic warning on 6 August against giving any support to Poland; and on 10 August Ernest Bevin, the secretary of the Transport and General Workers' Union, protested against the sending of any munitions to Poland. For good measure, the Prague Government – which at that time was encouraging pro-Russian feeling among the Czechs and was toying with the idea of handing over the Carpatho-Ukraine to the Ukrainian Soviet Republic – refused to let through 30,000 cavalry which the Hungarian Government wished to send to the help of Poland.

Nevertheless, by the middle of August 1920 the worst point in the Polish crisis had been reached. The 'Government of National Defence' formed on 24 July under Witos and Daszynski, in which all parties except the communists took part, mobilized a volunteer army of 80,000 men, including farmers' battalions armed in the old Polish style with straightened scythes. The War Ministry produced another 172,000 men, and the strength of the army thus rose to 900,000. The unconditional, enthusiastic devotion and self-sacrifice of all Poles assumed grandiose proportions. General Lucjan Zeligowski's army, which defended the eastern approaches to Warsaw, stood firm at Radzymin. On 17 August General Sikorski's army even mounted a counter-attack northward from Modlin.

The whole change in the military situation was due to Pilsudski, who boldly made use of a temporary gap between the two attacking Soviet army groups. After advancing into eastern Galicia the Soviet south-western army group had not carried out the swing to the north which would have threatened Warsaw from the south and enclosed the Polish army in three-quarters of a circle. Instead, on Stalin's advice, it pushed on westward towards Lwow (Lemberg); its link with Tukhachevsky's army group was thereby stretched too far and the Deblin–Lublin region became a subsidiary front. In this space, in the middle of August, Pilsudski collected a striking force of his best divisions, in order to attack northwards and encircle Tukhachevsky's army group, which was fighting east, north and north-west of Warsaw, from behind. As Tukhachevsky had adopted Paskevich's strategy of 1831, Pilsudski's plan of operations recalled the ideas of Ignacy Pradzynski, the 'Polish Clausewitz', who in 1831 had not been in a position to carry out his plan against Paskevich. Pilsudski's historic decision to attack, taken on 6 August 1920, was influenced neither by General Weygand's methodical defensive plan nor the operational intentions of Rozwadowski, the Chief of the Polish General Staff, who wanted to attack from the Wkra north of Modlin; not only the responsibility but also the plan for the subsequently famous offensive were Pilsudski's alone. The attack was launched on 16 August from Wieprz in the Deblin–Kock sector, and gained ground to the north so quickly that on 22 August the striking group reached the Narew on a broad front between Ostroleka and Bialystok. Tukhachevsky did all he could to save his army group by a hasty retreat to the east, but could not prevent his whole 4th Army from being cut off north of Lomza and forced to enter East Prussian territory. Defeated a second time in the battle on the Niemen in the neighbourhood of Grodno-Wolkowysk (20–28 August 1920), the harassed troops of the erstwhile Soviet western army group just managed to reach eastern White Russia, pursued by the Poles, who in September 1920 once again occupied Minsk and Slutsk. At the same time the Polish southern armies threw the south-western army group back into central Volhynia and Podolia. The Polish victory was complete.

The war weariness and exhaustion of both sides hastened the drafting of a preliminary peace treaty, which was signed in Riga on 12 October 1920 and in practice ended the war. When the ceasefire came into effect on 19 October, the Polish troops held a line which ran from Dzisna on the Düna (Dvina) southward just to the west of Minsk, followed the Sluch south of the Pripet, and at Bar in Podolia reached the Roumanian frontier on the Dniester; this front line formed the basis of the subsequent frontier settlement. The importance of the military victories of August 1920 could hardly be over-estimated. The concentration of Soviet military power on Poland put the Cabinets of the Baltic States in a favourable position in the peace negotiations which they were conducting with the Moscow Government in summer and autumn 1920. Thus Lithuania concluded a favourable treaty on 12 July, and Latvia and Finland were able to do the same on 11 August and 14 October respectively. Over and above this, the battle on the Vistula was of historical significance, because it had prevented the Red Army from advancing into Germany and hence removed the possibility of revolution in central Europe, a possibility which seemed quite conceivable in view of the communist revolts in the Ruhr in March to May 1920. The whole episode provided further proof of the rightness of the decision which on 9 November 1918 had dispatched Pilsudski from Magdeburg to Warsaw and through him turned Poland's attention away from Germany and towards Soviet Russia. Even the authors of the decision can hardly have been fully aware just how right it was. The contribution of the battle of the Vistula to the defeat of Trotsky's theories of world revolution and to the development of Stalin's thesis of 'socialism in one country' was probably considerable. So the judgement of Lord d'Abernon, who described Pilsudski's victory as 'the eighteenth decisive battle of the world', equal in importance to the battles of Salamis and Plataea, can be allowed to stand, although nineteen years later Hitler destroyed Pilsudski's work by once again letting Soviet Russia into central Europe.

For internal political reasons, the Polish National Democrats tried to diminish the marshal's fame. Led by Professor Stanislaw Stronski, their Press declared that, in so far as any strategic talent was involved at all, the 'miracle of the Vistula' was to be ascribed rather to General Weygand. This view was certainly not shared by real experts such as Weygand himself or the young Charles de Gaulle, who had been serving since 1919 as a staff officer with the Polish army. De Gaulle thought just as highly of Pilsudski's genius as, for example, Hans von Seeckt, who praised in Pilsudski the rare combination of general and statesman and compared him to Frederick the Great. Because of his profound contempt for the Press, the marshal himself did little to combat the National Demo-

The Struggle for the Frontiers (1919–1923)

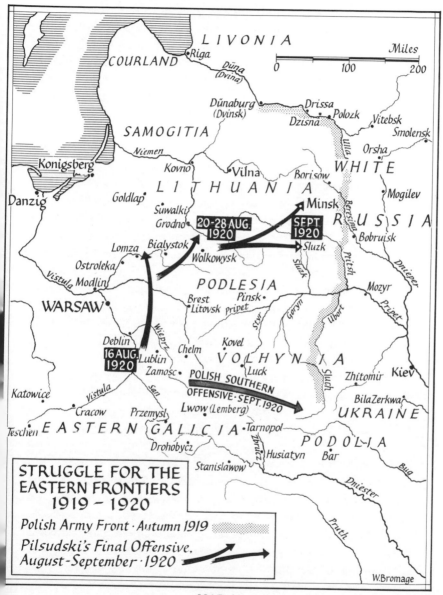

MAP 4

85

cratic myth, which was adopted enthusiastically by German and French publicists and proved remarkably long-lived. In his order of the day to the army when the war ended on 18 October 1920, he did not emphasize his own achievement, but that of his soldiers. To him, the 'thousands of mounds and funeral crosses, which cover the old Republic from the distant Dnieper to our native Vistula' were proof that Poland had left behind it the age of weakness and anarchy.

THE UNSETTLED FRONTIER QUESTIONS

The most important postulates for the final clarification of those legal and territorial questions which were still unsettled were those laid down in the Protocol of Spa of July 1920, which Wladyslaw Grabski had been compelled to sign in the hour of Poland's greatest distress. Both Government and nation saw in the hard conditions of Spa the unjust exploitation of Polish difficulties. These decisions therefore affected the confidence – it had never in any case been very great – which Poles felt in the knowledge and policy of the Entente Cabinets; the Polish Government felt legally but not morally bound by the 'dictates' of Spa. It reserved the right to make claims for revision in the future. This was particularly true of the frontier problems in the west, which were subject to the *de facto* decisions of the Supreme Council. These problems were the fixing of the Polish frontier in Teschen and Upper Silesia, and the ordering of the relations between Poland and the Free City of Danzig.

The erstwhile Austrian Duchy of Teschen had already been the subject of strife between Poland and Czechoslovakia for some time. Czech troops had occupied the western half of the disputed territory on 23 January 1919 and thus created a *fait accompli*, which could not be set aside even by an agreement made between Benes and Dmowski on 1 February, though this agreement envisaged a referendum. The Supreme Council's decree of 27 September 1919 dealing with the proposed plebiscite was equally ineffective, since the Inter-Allied Commission under Count Manneville appointed in February 1920 recognized that a referendum was impracticable, and direct Polish-Czech negotiations ended in failure. On 28 July 1920 the Inter-Allied Commission, in accordance with the directives of Spa, made an award which gave Poland only the districts to the east of the little river Olsa, with about 142,000 German and Polish inhabitants. The larger and more valuable portion of Teschen, with its mines and foundries and the town of Teschen itself, was assigned to Czechoslovakia. In the Beskids mountains twenty-seven border villages with about 30,000 inhabitants were ceded to Poland. The territorial claims which Poland continued to make delayed the final fixing of the frontier until 16 September 1924 and were to cast a shadow over Polish–Czech relations in the future. The reason why a just division of the disputed Teschen area of Silesia was so difficult was that the centre of the region was inhabited by 'Slonzaks', people who spoke a Polish dialect but were distinguished from the Poles of Galicia by their Evangelical religion and Germano–Austrian culture. Slonzaks formed the majority of the 140,000 Polish speakers who were left on the Czech side of the new frontier.

In Upper Silesia, hitherto German, where the Treaty of Versailles stipulated that a plebiscite should take place, the ethnic and linguistic situation was still more complicated than in the Duchy of Teschen. The centuries-long superimposition of German civilization, intensified by the development of the mining area, had led to a steady and continual Germanization of the native Polish population. The towns, the intelligentsia, the landowners and the inhabitants of the western and northern districts, including many people who were bilingual or used only Polish, regarded themselves as German; only in the south and east of the territory had the purely Polish character of the population been preserved. The process of Germanization had only come to a halt since about 1900 with the awakening of Polish national consciousness, which was due mainly to the tireless agitation of the native miner's son Wojciech Korfanty. Thus Poland's claims to Upper Silesia were based on grounds which were just the opposite of those which had inspired the claim to Central Lithuania; the Germans in Upper

Silesia fulfilled the same social function as the Poles in the Vilna region, and Germany did not fail to point out the inconsistency of the Polish arguments.

In view of the comparative weakness of the Polish position in Upper Silesia, the POW, on the 16–17 August 1919, unleashed a 'First Silesian Uprising', which sought to influence the territorial decision, but was in fact quickly suppressed. On 20 January 1920 Allied troops moved in, and on 11 February an Inter-Allied Commission under the French General Le Rond took over the administration of the plebiscite territory. When Poland's electoral defeat of 11 July 1920 in Masuria and Ermland (Warmia) became known, and when rumours began to spread that the Polish Government was ready to hand over Upper Silesia to Germany in return for military aid against the Red Army, which at that time was threatening Warsaw, the leaders of the POW decided on a second uprising. It broke out in August 1920 right on the Polish–Silesian border to the east of Katowice and gained control of several districts; however, thanks to German concessions and the action of the Control Commission, it was ended on 2 September by the so-called 'Beuthen Agreement', concluded by the plebiscite commissioner Wojciech Korfanty with his German colleague Urbanek. The plebiscite which had been so long in preparation finally took place on 20 March 1921, but Poland won only 478,820 votes or 40·3 per cent of the total, while Germany gained 707,554 or 59·6 per cent. There were 597 communes with a Polish majority as against 664 communes with a German majority. In view of the result of the ballot the Supreme Council rejected the German argument that the territory was indivisible and decided to divide it. Korfanty, who knew what was intended, now began to organize, together with the POW, a third uprising, although hitherto he had considered revolts not only useless but even harmful. No doubt the – to him – surprising failure of the plebiscite was one of the factors which induced him to take this decision. Numerous Polish volunteers from outside Silesia also took part in this serious and bloody insurrection. Between 3 and 6 May 1921 the insurgents gained control of the whole region which they claimed for Poland. Nevertheless, German free corps under General Karl Hoefer prevented the extension of Polish power, in particular by storming the Annaberg (22–24 May 1921). The revolt collapsed on 18–19 June, mainly through the intervention of the Supreme Council.

On 20 October 1921 the Council of the League of Nations arranged the division of Upper Silesia in such a way that Poland received about 1,300 square miles containing roughly a million inhabitants and most of the mining and industrial area. In this henceforth Polish region 284,052 voters (55·8 per cent) had opted for Poland and 225,431 (44·2 per cent) for Germany. The new 'voivodship of Silesia', to which the Polish portion of Teschen was assigned, enjoyed the benefit of the 'Organic Statute', which the National Assembly in Warsaw had already passed on 15 July 1920 and which guaranteed the voivodship autonomy, with its own provincial Sejm in Katowice. Finally, the Geneva Convention of 15 May 1922, which was valid for the whole plebiscite area, tempered the harshness involved in the division of a region which had been economically and culturally united for hundreds of years.

Of all the questions governed by the Protocol of Spa, the relations between Poland and the Free City of Danzig were certainly the most delicate. In Polish eyes the Free City constituted on 10 January 1920 had been compromised ever since on 20 August 1920, in the crisis of the war between Poland and Soviet Russia, its Assembly had passed a declaration of neutrality and its dockers had operated an anti-Polish strike. Mutual mistrust also hung over the negotiations between Danzig and Poland about the Paris Convention which the Ambassadors' Conference had drawn up to settle all disputed questions in accordance with the decisions of Spa. In principle, the Convention granted Danzig political independence, which the League of Nations also guaranteed on 17 November 1920, but it put the administration of the port under the control of a mixed committee. It was finally signed on 9 November by Heinrich Sahm on behalf of Danzig, and on 18 November by Paderewski on behalf of Poland. A complementary

Warsaw Convention of 24 October 1921 settled further details. Although the relationship between Danzig and Poland was now formally defined and there was a League of Nations high commissioner in Danzig to act as arbitrator from 26 November 1920 onwards, Poland's actual rights in Danzig were in many ways not entirely clear. The regulations governing the curious international status of the Free City, which was certainly a sovereign State but was to be represented in foreign affairs and defended by the Polish Government, could be interpreted in differing and even contradictory ways. Thus the obstinacy with which each of the two partners sought to defend legal positions which they had once adopted led to continual tension. In May 1923, under the pressure of this miniature juridical war, the Polish Government began to develop the port of Gdynia, so as to have an assured outlet to the sea. It must be admitted that it thereby destroyed the assumptions on which Poland had been granted rights in the port of Danzig.

The decisions about Poland's eastern regions and about the question of Polish sovereignty in these territories which had after all formed the kernel of the Protocol of Spa were fundamentally altered in their basic assumptions by the Polish–Soviet War. This was particularly true of eastern Galicia. On 25 June 1920, after his break with Petljura, Petrushevich had formed a Government-in-exile of the West Ukrainian People's Republic. This Government was recognized as legal by the majority of the Galician–Ukrainian population, which regarded the temporary occupation of the country by the Red Army and also – unlike the local Poles – the renewed Polish occupation as only a passing episode. Neither in the Treaty of St Germain – signed on 10 September 1919 and in force from 16 July 1920 – nor in the complementary Treaty of Sèvres (10 August 1920) did the Entente Governments stipulate to whom the sovereignty over Galicia belonged, although these treaties formally put an end in international law to the existence of the Austrian empire. On 3 December 1920 the Polish Government included the area in the general division of Poland into provinces, whereupon the Council of the League of Nations once again made it quite clear that in Galicia as a whole Poland possessed only occupation rights.

The fate of the Vilna region was even more subject to change. On 12 July 1920 the Moscow Government had concluded with the Republic of Lithuania a peace treaty which gave it the city of Vilna and the surrounding territory. Two days later Tukhachevsky's troops had captured it in the fighting with Poland, but had at first kept it under a military government; Vilna was only handed over to the Lithuanian authorities on 25 August 1920, during the course of the Soviet retreat. The new Polish advance once more threw the question of the Polish–Lithuanian frontiers into the melting-pot. A control commission under the French Colonel Chardigny was quickly dispatched by the Council of the League and on 7 October 1920 secured the Polish–Lithuanian 'Arrangement of Suwalki', which established a demarcation line and left the city of Vilna to Lithuania. This agreement had no political significance; it was a purely military pact. Nevertheless, the Polish Government could not simply disregard Lithuania's legal claim to Vilna, which rested *vis-à-vis* the Western Powers on the Protocol of Spa, and *vis-à-vis* Soviet Russia on the Peace of Moscow. In this situation Pilsudski had a real stroke of genius. He gave General Zeligowski, the defender of Radzymin, the secret commission to occupy the Vilna region with his division on the pretext of starting a rising against the Polish Government. Such a 'rising' looked all the more credible in so far as both Zeligowski and his soldiers were in fact natives of central Lithuania. Zeligowski occupied the region on 9 October 1920, forced out the troops of the Lithuanian Republic and set up a supposedly sovereign State called Central Lithuania, with Vilna as its capital.

Since the Warsaw Government declined to accept responsibility for Zeligowski's 'disobedience' and the Kovno Cabinet championed its claims more persistently than ever, the Council of the League sought to escape from the insoluble legal dilemma by suggesting a plebiscite in the disputed territory. It also succeeded in arranging a protocol, signed in Kovno on 29 November, which ended the fighting between the Kovno and Vilna forces and established a neutral zone between them. However, the carrying out of the plebiscite was hindered by Zeligowski's refusal to evacuate central Lithuania and by the Moscow Government's protest against the dispatch of an international police force to supervise the voting. The Kovno Government adopted to a certain extent the same attitude as Moscow – probably from fear that the result of the plebiscite would be unfavourable to itself – and this naturally did not improve its position at the League of Nations. In these circumstances the Council of the League, in its resolution of 3 March 1921, gave up the idea of a plebiscite and recommended both parties to undertake direct negotiations in Brussels under the chairmanship of the Belgian minister Paul Hymans.

The central Lithuanian and eastern Galician questions were at the same time the subject of the Polish–Soviet peace negotiations, which after the preliminary peace of 12 October 1920 went on in Riga all through the winter of 1920–21. There were serious differences inside the Polish delegation, which was led by Jan Dabski of the Populist (or Peasant) Party, between the 'Federalists' and the 'Centralists'; the latter demanded less territory than the former, but wanted to annex it directly to Poland, not to assign it to future federal states. The victory of the Centralists was clearly reflected in the Polish renunciation of Minsk. The Peace of Riga, signed on 18 March 1921, thus represented the definitive defeat of the federal idea and the victory of the concept of a purely national state. By accepting a frontier line which corresponded more or less to that of the preliminary peace, the Polish delegation included only as much White Russian and Ukrainian territory in the Polish State as the Polish people seemed capable of assimilating. The Soviet delegation under Adolf Joffe offered little resistance to the generally moderate Polish demands, since the armistice in the west gave the Moscow Government an opportunity to destroy the remains of the White army in the Crimea and to end the independence of the Republic of Georgia. It renounced all rights and claims west of the new frontier, while Poland renounced its claims to the people's republics of White Russia and the Ukraine.

The Struggle for the Frontiers (1919–1923)

The sacrifice of Petljura by the Warsaw Government was thus matched by the Soviet Government's sacrifice of eastern Galicia. Moscow was prevented from interfering in the Vilna question, in so far as the Peace of Riga made the problem of central Lithuania exclusively a matter to be decided between Poland and Lithuania. As the defeat of the federalists showed, Pilsudski had little influence on the course of the negotiations; this fact reflected the overpowering war-weariness and longing for peace of the Polish nation.

By virtue of the Peace of Riga, the Vilna question became solely a matter for the Polish–Lithuanian negotiations being conducted in Brussels under the aegis of the League of Nations. Pilsudski's political colleague, Prince Eustachy Sapieha, suggested a plan which Hymans put forward on 20 May 1921. This project envisaged a union between Poland and Lithuania, in which Lithuania would be divided into a Kovno and a Vilna canton, each with its own parliament. The second Hymans plan of 3 September 1921 even sanctioned the incorporation of the Vilna region in Lithuania as an autonomous canton; otherwise its conditions were the same as those of the original proposal. The Hymans plan certainly provided the only possibility of solving the Vilna question without doing violence to the populations concerned, and it was therefore all the more regrettable that the Kovno Government – indubitably out of nationalistic narrow-mindedness, which, however, had only been provoked by Zeligowski's *coup* – rejected both proposals. The Council of the League now gave up its attempt at mediation (13 January 1922).

The Warsaw Government had certainly anticipated the collapse of the negotiations by passing a resolution, on 26 November 1921, about the holding of a general election in central Lithuania. The Zeligowski Government issued the writs on 30 November 1921 and the election itself took place on 8 January 1922. 64·4 per cent of the electorate voted, although the Lithuanians and some sections of the White Russians and Jews abstained. In the new provincial Sejm of Vilna the Centralists, who favoured the unconditional incorporation of the region in the Polish State, had a majority of 69 seats out of a total of 101. Accordingly, on 20 February 1922, the Sejm resolved on annexation to Poland, which was put into effect on 24 March in a solemn Act of Unification. Poland thereby gained an area of about 15,000 square miles with a population of roughly a million. All attempts to give central Lithuania autonomy within the Polish Republic were blocked by the Warsaw and Vilna nationalists, although the majority of the central Lithuanian population did not speak Polish. Pilsudski, who as a native of the area was bound to know its needs best, regarded this rigidly unyielding attitude as a real misfortune. In fact he came into such sharp conflict with the leaders of the right-wing parties in Warsaw on this question that he threatened to leave Warsaw and to create out of Kovno and Vilna Lithuania, with the help of the central Lithuanian troops, a Lithuanian State independent of Poland. However, in the end he had to yield to the all-powerful National Democrats as he had in the questions of the incorporation of Upper Silesia and the Riga Peace.

The inelastic, 'Polonization' programme of the National Democrats was also adopted in the treatment of the Galician Ukrainian problem. Confronted with fairly far-reaching proposals by the Left, the Warsaw Sejm refused to sanction territorial autonomy for the Ukrainians of eastern Galicia; it only agreed to grant (on 26 September 1922) a certain degree of self-government within the three eastern Galician voivodships of Lwow, Stanislawow and Tarnopol. This 'provincial autonomy' was to be introduced within two years, and it was to be complemented by the foundation of a Ukrainian university. This law was never put into effect; but it was an important factor in the final transfer of sovereignty over eastern Galicia to Poland.

After the Polish Government had thus consolidated its authority over the eastern territories partly by *de facto* control and partly through the Peace of Riga, the Entente Governments delayed their recognition no longer. The decision of the Ambassadors' Conference of 15 March 1923 approved the existing Polish–Soviet and Polish–Lithuanian frontiers – the latter had come into being

Miles
0   100   200

LATVIA

LITHUANIA

Riga

Dünaburg
(Dvinsk)

Niemen

POLISH
CORRIDOR

Königsberg •Kovno

Gdynia

EAST

Danzig

PRUSSIA

Minsk

•Allenstein

Netze

Thorn

•Bialystok

G E R M A N Y

Vistula

Posen

P O L A N D

Warta

WARSAW

Brest
Litovsk   Pripet

Oder

Lublin

Breslau

Cracow   Vistula

Teschen

G A L I   C I   A

Lwow
(Lemberg)

C Z E C H O S L O V A K I A

POLAND
AFTER THE
PEACE TREATIES

Territory & Free
City of Danzig

W. Bromage

MAP 5

through the division of the neutral zone in February 1923 – in the name of the Allied Powers. It recognized Polish sovereignty over all the regions involved, including central Lithuania and eastern Galicia. In the reasons for the decision it was emphasized that by the law of 26 September 1922 the Polish Government had recognized the necessity for Galician Ukrainian autonomy – a formula which had no legally binding force.

The decision of the Ambassadors' Conference meant that the Warsaw Government was finally able to conclude the process of shaping Poland, a process which had taken four years of conflict. The Republic now possessed an area of over 155,000 square miles and a population of about twenty-seven million, of whom only a bare nineteen million were Polish by nationality. Some four million Ukrainians, more than two million Jews, about a million Germans and a million White Russians, together with smaller groups of Lithuanians, Russians, Czechs and Tartars, lent the Polish Republic the character of a conglomeration of minorities. This linguistic and ethnic variety was the result of a compromise between the concept of a national unitary state and a supranational federal state. In the west, by taking over bilingual and purely German districts, Poland had incurred the hostility of Germany; in the east, on the other hand, it had not succeeded in winning over as a body the Lithuanians, Ukrainians or White Russians. The Peace of Riga was certainly the first international agreement in which the Poles gave up their legal claim to the eastern territories, the very territories which from 1815 to 1914 had wrecked all attempts at Russo–Polish reconciliation. The Riga frontier ran more or less midway between the original Polish claims and the Curzon line. It included too few White Russian and Ukrainian communities to make a real federation any longer possible, but on the other hand too many for the purposes of the National Democrats, who wished to transform the alien peoples gradually into Poles. The frontier drawn at Riga was thus really an indication that Poland was destined to become a multi-national state with a uni-nationalist ideology. The Poland created by the treaties of Versailles and Riga not only represented a political defeat for

Pilsudski and a victory for the doctrines of Dmowski; it also implied the renunciation of the old Jagellonian 'Commonwealth of Nations', which had lived on so long in the writings of Adam Mickiewicz and Henryk Sienkiewicz. Instead of the traditional idea of a combination of peoples with equal rights living under the shield of a common Polish culture, it was the new conception of 'Poles' and 'minorities' which triumphed. With the gradual realization that the ethnically non-Polish countries east of the Riga frontier had to be banished from Polish political thinking came the impatient demand that the minorities west of this frontier should be turned into Poles. This mode of thought and the political behaviour dictated by it involved serious dangers. In the west and north Poland was threatened by the territorial claims of Germany and Lithuania, in the east by those of the Soviet Union, set up in 1922, which encouraged the development of the national cultures of the Soviet republics of White Russia and the Ukraine; and finally in the south Poland was at loggerheads with Czechoslovakia over the question of Teschen. On no frontier – apart from the small strips facing Latvia and Roumania – did Poland enjoy real security. Thus the Poland of 1921–23 was a sort of provisional entity, which either had to expand again into the realm of the Jagellonians or else – as Chicherin, the Soviet Commissar for Foreign Affairs, remarked – 'be reduced to its narrowest ethnographical limits'.

CHAPTER III

Poland as a Parliamentary Republic
(1919-1926)

THE 'GREAT CONSTITUTION' AND THE QUESTION OF THE ELECTION OF THE PRESIDENT

In the early months of 1919, when through the formation of Paderewski's Cabinet and the ratification of the 'Little Constitution' the young Polish Republic had achieved a certain degree of consolidation, the political parties formed the strongest bond holding the former partition zones together. Most of the middle class and some of the nobility and farmers, in other words most of the former National Democrats, belonged to the National Populist Party, created on 5 February 1919, which with 116 seats out of about 300 possessed a relative majority in the Constituent Sejm. The men who emerged as its main leaders, in addition to the 'grand old man' Dmowski, were Professors Wladyslaw Grabski, Stanislaw Glabinski and Stanislaw Stronski and the Posen politicians Wojciech Trampczynski and Marian Seyda. Right from their first congress (11–12 May 1919), the National Populists – still often called National Democrats – supported a programme corresponding to the interests of the property-owning classes. This programme included the creation of a strong central government, state encouragement of private enterprise, industrialization and the greatest possible moderation in agrarian reform. The nationalist aspect of the party was reflected in the demands for the energetic Polonization of the minorities and a foreign policy friendly to the Entente. The most decided opponent of the National Populists or Endecja was the Polish Socialist Party, the PPS, which at its sixteenth conference (23–27 April 1919) amalgamated with its sister parties in Galicia and Prussian

Poland, and represented the great mass of the workers and also strong groups of the left-wing intelligentsia. Its aim was the 'realization of an independent, united socialist republic' by means of the 'revolutionary class struggle'. As its only important political demand, independence for Poland, had meanwhile become a reality, it lost many middle-class voters; nevertheless, under the leadership of such experienced Galician parliamentarians as Ignacy Daszynski, Herman Lieberman and Zygmunt Marek, of Tomasz Arciszewski from Congress Poland and of Mieczyslaw Niedzialkowski from Vilna, it was able to win 65 seats. The Communist Party of Poland remained insignificant; it had been formed on 16 December 1918 under the aegis of Rosa Luxemburg out of the SDKPiL and sections of the PPS left wing, and in accordance with its internationalist and pro-Soviet attitude rejected the *'bourgeois'* Polish Republic. Most of the peasants, who still had little political experience, were adherents of the Polish Populist or Peasant Party. The Peasant Party was divided by differences in policy; the 'Piast' branch, under Witos and Maciej Rataj, which had originated in Galicia and had a Catholic, tenant-farmer bias, was content with a programme of moderate land reform, while the 'Liberation' group from Congress Poland and the left wing of the Galician party demanded a radical redistribution of the land. So in spite of a temporary amalgamation in January 1920 the Peasant Party broke up again into 'Piast' and 'Liberation' wings; like the many small middle-class Centre groups, it did not possess a rigid party organization. Indeed, apart from the PPS and the Endecja, all the political parties of this period tended to resemble loose groups which collected round the person of a politician; their continually changing coalitions were not unlike the Confederations of the old Poland.

It is true that behind the political parties there were very often influential secret societies, which had arisen in the period of Partition and preserved their conspiratorial character even after the foundation of a State. Thus the National League still formed the secret core of the Endecja. The 'Convention' of the Polish Military Organization, founded in the middle of 1917, also continued in existence; it formed the secret centre of Pilsudski's supporters. But the most powerful secret organization was the 'Union of Polish Youth', or 'Zet' for short, which from about 1890 to 1908 had functioned as the youth organization of the National League, but subsequently formed an independent organization. In some regions the Zet supported the National Democrats, in others the Pilsudski camp. From 1919 onwards, under the leadership of its 'centralizer', Kazimierz Wyszynski, it formed a number of legal organizations such as the Frontier Watch and the Western Marches Association. The enormous importance of the Zet for Polish political thinking is reflected in the fact that four-fifths of all the leading politicians of the new republic came from its ranks. Besides these big, old-established organizations a number of smaller, ephemeral secret societies after the style of the French *Cagoulards* came into being, such as the 'Knights of the White Eagle' and the 'Action Squad of Polish Patriots'.

The great theme of all the political forces in the country was the debate about the constitution, which was intended to weld together the three very different zones into which Poland had formerly been divided. All parties – except for a few conservatives and the communists – were agreed that the constitution must be a democratic parliamentary one. There were sharp disputes about the status of minorities, a point which was of particular importance in view of the continual extension of Polish control over territories with non-Polish majorities. It turned out to be particularly unfortunate that the minorities were hardly represented at all in the constituent Sejm and that the decision about their status consequently fell to the Poles. Of the draft plans put forward in May 1919, the socialist one, sponsored in particular by Niedzialkowski, favoured the granting of territorial autonomy to the non-Polish peoples, while the character of the National Democrats' proposals was unitarian and in favour of the assimilation of minorities into the new State. In December 1919 the Government took a middle path with a draft providing for self-governing bodies without territorial links. In general – and this was of the greatest importance for future policy towards the minorities –

the view of the Endecja won the day, simply because of their dominating position in the Sejm.

After consultations lasting two years the constitution was finally adopted on 17 March 1921, that is, more or less at the same time as the signing of the Treaty of Riga and the plebiscite in Upper Silesia. Although it contained many echoes of the Polish Reformed Constitution of 3 May 1791, it was on the whole modelled on the French constitution and reflected the *bourgeois* liberal ideas of the nineteenth century. Notwithstanding a some-what complicated division of functions, the real power resided in the National Assembly, which was divided into two chambers – Sejm and Senate – and elected by universal, equal, secret, direct and proportional suffrage. The Government, including the War Minister, who was responsible for the appointment of the com-manders-in-chief in time of war, was fully accountable to Par-liament. The supreme authority was formally embodied in the President, who was chosen by the National Assembly for seven years and was to appoint the government; however, his compe-tence was confined to purely representational duties and did not even include the right to dissolve Parliament. The National Democrats had weakened the office of President in this way in case Pilsudski became a candidate for it. The parliamentary omni-potence thus achieved contained certain dangers for the continuity of political authority, since the bulk of the voters were not yet accustomed to the somewhat complicated franchise, and political power thus devolved on a group of parliamentarians who, as in France, arranged among themselves the distribution of posts in the Government and Opposition. The prevailing multi-party system produced by proportional representation, the impossibility of building a reliable majority and the complete dependence of every Government on fluctuating parliamentary coalitions opened the way to abuses and corrupt practices in the State and even in the army.

Immediately after the ratification of the constitution there was a sort of interregnum, since the powers of the Chief of State still rested on the Little Constitution, while Parliament sought to

A History of Modern Poland

exploit its newly-won prerogatives. The formula in the old constitution which stated that the Chief of State was to appoint the Government 'in agreement' with the Sejm left the legal question open. After the victory on the Vistula, the 'Government of National Defence' under Witos had lost the character of a coalition Cabinet owing to the resignation of the ministers belonging to the Left and Right, and on 13 September 1921 it was overthrown. There followed a period of swiftly changing Cabinets; Korfanty, who by virtue of the 'wedding gift' of Upper Silesia, presented on 15 June 1922, felt strong enough, with the help of a parliamentary majority, to call on the Chief of State to resign, even provoked a serious governmental crisis. It was only with the formation of a compromise Cabinet under the Cracow university professor Julian Nowak, a trusted friend of Pilsudski's, that the tension eased on 31 July 1922. The holding of orderly elections in accordance with the new constitution was now guaranteed.

The elections for the first Legislative National Assembly took place on 5 and 12 November 1922. Once again the united Nationalist parties were the strongest political group, with 163 seats out of 410 in the Sejm; the 'Piast' gained 70 seats, the Liberation group 49 and the socialists only 41. In contrast to the almost complete disappearance of the old Centre parties, the 87 representatives of the minorities represented a new parliamentary element, and one which, as a result of the dissensions among the Polish parties, was often able to tip the scales one way or the other. The parties in which Pilsudski was interested – the Democratic Union and the 'State Associations in the Eastern Marches' did not win a single seat. The composition of the Senate was similar to that of the Sejm, but there were rather more Nationalist members (11 out of 48), obviously because of the higher minimum voting age for the Senate. In general, the political intelligentsia of the Centre and Left, which had contributed so much to the winning of independence and idealistically handed over all power to the people, suffered a decisive loss of influence in these elections. The result of the voting made it clear that the questions of independence and the struggle for the frontiers, now solved, had given way in the minds of the electorate to the new problems of home affairs and the economic situation.

In the question of the election of a President, Pilsudski was opposed by the Right and consequently championed by the Left. However, on 4 December 1922, in view of the powerlessness of the office of President, the Chief of State decided not to let his name be put forward; he declined to let himself be enclosed in a 'gilded cage'. This left the best chance of victory to the candidate of the Right, Count Maurycy Zamoyski, who at the first ballot obtained 222 votes of the 555 in the National Assembly and thus had a relative majority over his competitors, Professors Jan Ignacy Baudouin de Courtenay and Gabriel Narutowicz, Ignacy Daszynski, the leader of the socialists, and Stanislaw Wojciechowski, the organizer of the co-operative movement in Poland. However, Zamoyski, with about 500,000 acres, was the biggest land-owner in the country, and this induced both branches of the Peasant Party to vote against him. The scale was actually turned by the representatives of the minorities, who rejected him because of the nationalistic programme of the Endecja and finally helped Professor Gabriel Narutowicz to triumph at the fifth ballot on 9 December 1922. Pilsudski, the Chief of State, handed over power to Narutowicz in a solemn ceremony on 14 December. However, only two days later, on 16 December, Narutowicz was shot dead in the Warsaw Gallery of Fine Arts by the painter and National Democrat Eligiusz Niewiadomski. The reason for the assassination was that Narutowicz's presidency was regarded as a 'symbol of shame', because the election had been decided by the votes of the non-Polish Members of Parliament. Most National Democrats at first condemned the murder, in accordance with the Polish national mentality which always abhorred acts of violence. However, during the course of Niewiadomski's trial the attitude of the public changed so completely that the assassin was celebrated as a hero and a fighter for the ideal of Polish nationalism; the fact that at his execution he ostentatiously held a rose in his hand and directed his last words against the alleged moral dictatorship of Pilsudski won the hearts of all 'Patriots'. Thus the assassination of the first legitimately elected President of the Republic deepened the gulf between the Right and the Left in a disastrous way.

However, Rataj, the Speaker of the Sejm and as a member of the Piast Party a man of the Centre who favoured peaceful compromises, was able to bridge over the conflict by effecting the appointment of a non-party Government under General Wladyslaw Sikorski. On 20 December Stanislaw Wojciechowski – whom Pilsudski had supported at the time of the first ballot – was elected president by the votes of the Left and Centre, who joined forces against the Right. The assumption of the presidency by this deserving politician, who enjoyed the respect of the workers and peasants, at any rate made possible a return to orderly political life, even if it could not eliminate political and social antagonisms.

Since resigning the office of Chief of State, Pilsudski had devoted himself to purely military tasks. The formation of Witos's second Cabinet on 28 May 1923 also caused him to lay down the posts of Chief of the General Staff and President of the Supreme War Council. He withdrew to his modest estate at Sulejowek and after renouncing any form of pension from the State henceforth lived on his small income as a writer. The reason which probably dictated this resignation was his recognition of the hidden dangers to the State and the army inherent in the predominance of the Sejm; he was also sensitive to his defeats over the question of an eastern federation and in the parliamentary elections. So he 'played the game' in the hope that his departure would serve to increase his stature. In fact, the experiment of a 'Poland without Pilsudski' was to give him in the future far greater power than he could ever have attained through the presidency.

THE AGRARIAN QUESTION

By far the most important, indeed the decisive task of any Polish home policy was land reform. When the Republic was founded two-thirds of Poland's population made its living out of farming. But in all the provinces of Poland, especially in Congress Poland and Galicia, there were millions of peasants with little or no land of their own; the old Polish custom of dividing up estates, combined with the Tsarist agrarian reform of 1864, had led to the fragmentation of the land into small, even tiny, farms. Half the farmers in Congress Poland and four-fifths of those in Galicia possessed farms of less than twelve acres, which were hardly viable and could not even fully absorb the labour of the members of the family. Comprehensive industrialization, which would have drawn away the surplus labour from the land and thus abolished the concealed unemployment, seemed to be out of the question in view of Poland's poverty and the absence of foreign financial assistance. The only solution left therefore was to split up the big estates, which in central and southern Poland accounted for a fifth of the total area of cultivated land and in the western and eastern provinces for over a third, and to satisfy the demands of the small farmers with the land thus acquired. This was the exclusive aim of the Peasant Party which held 119 seats in the Sejm and represented roughly a quarter of all Polish voters; its two wings, Piast and Liberation, differed only in the degree of radicalism involved in their demands.

As early as 10 July 1919 the Constituent Sejm had passed a basic resolution on land reform. At that time the moderate views of the Piast had triumphed, and in accordance with these views the creation of middle-sized farms of thirty-five to fifty acres – like those established in Posen by Prussian agrarian policy – had been made the core of the reform. On 15 July 1920, during the Polish–Soviet War (and not without the intention of gaining the support of the peasants in the defence of the existing Polish State), a first agrarian law had been ratified by the Constituent Sejm. It enacted that land over and above an average freeholding of 450 acres could be divided up in return for compensation. This put land reform in motion through the parcelling out of plots, consolidation of strips and release from feudal service, especially in the east. A start was also made on the improvement of land.

With the constitution of the first legislative Sejm in November 1922 the formation of a parliamentary coalition became necessary for the representatives of the peasants as well. The strongest party in the Sejm, the National Democrats, could not form a stable Government without the support of the 70 Piast deputies; on the other hand, they could not afford to lose the support of those of their own members who represented the landed aristocracy, which was naturally hostile to reform. However, Count Adolf Bninski, the leader of the Posen nobility, who favoured moderate reform, arranged a settlement between the Endecja and the Piast which was reflected in the so-called agreement of Lanckorona of 15 May 1923. Witos met the wishes of the National Democrats with a very cautious agrarian programme, and in return was enabled to form a predominantly National Democratic Cabinet on 28 May. In this Government the Ministry of Foreign Affairs was taken over for a time by Dmowski himself; it was the only time that he took part in the formation of a Government. The coalition of the National Democrats with the Piast, which hitherto had usually supported the Left, was a turn of events which had important consequences in home affairs. It finally put the Endecja in power for three years, caused the resignation of Pilsudski and drove not only the PPS but also the Liberation section of the Peasant Party into strict opposition. In addition, Witos was forced to see the radical wing of his own party split off and create another Peasant Party, under Jan Dabski, with close affinities to the Liberation group. This split forced Witos to resign on 14 December 1923; his plans for a further measure of land reform – the very reason for which he had formed a Cabinet – were temporarily shelved. It was not until two years later, on 28 December 1925, that the Sejm ratified a second reform law, which remained in force – with some amendments – up to the Second World War. It retained the norm of 450 acres, but made some concessions to landowners: henceforth forests up to 75 acres and lakes up to 125 acres were not reckoned in the figure. The part of an estate to be left intact was no longer to be chosen by the Government land offices but by the owner of the estate to be divided up. In addition, the yearly quota of land to be distributed was fixed at 500,000 acres.

Yet even when this last agrarian law was drawn up it could be foreseen that it would not go far enough. Between 1919 and 1938 over six and a half million acres of land were distributed, that is, a tenth of the cultivable area of the whole of Poland; in addition, another million and a quarter acres were improved. But the 153,000 new farms thus created could hardly be sufficient, seeing that in 1901 there had been at least 200,000 landless peasant families in Congress Poland alone; and the distribution of land to 153,000 peasant families remained far short of what was required. The most successful part of the operation was the consolidation of farm strips, which with more than twelve and a half million acres embraced a fifth of the area under cultivation. In spite of all efforts to solve the agrarian question, the reserve of land at Poland's disposal was too small to satisfy its peasants' hunger for land. A real reduction of the agricultural over-population could only have been achieved by the creation of numerous industrial projects, and Poland's poverty made this solution impossible. Thus Polish Governments were simply not in a position to combat effectively the progressive pauperization of the peasants. This impoverishment was encouraged by the steady increase of the population, and with the arrival of the world economic crisis of 1930–37 was to lead to political extremism in both the peasants and the Peasant Party.

INFLATION AND CURRENCY REFORM

Owing to the way in which it had come into being, the Republic of Poland was burdened with economic mortgages which it was far beyond the economic and financial strength of the country to pay off. The war of 1914–20 had used both capital and savings in the country; in addition, almost 1,900,000 houses had been destroyed and about half the roads, railways and public buildings. The enormous amount of armaments required at the time of the struggle for the frontiers also consumed the supplies of gold and currency put at the Government's disposal by Polish emigrants, a sum amounting to more than a thousand million gold francs. In the year 1919–20 the taxes covered just a tenth of public expenditure, and in 1920 a loan floated among Poles in the United States brought in insufficient assistance. In these circumstances

Governments could do nothing but print more bank notes: the circulation of paper money, which at the end of 1918 had amounted to about one thousand million Polish marks, climbed to 229 thousand millions by the end of 1921. Poland was thus on the road to inflation. The short-lived Governments of 1921–23 were usually overthrown because they were unable to halt the fall in the value of money.

As early as November 1920 Wladyslaw Grabski, the Finance Minister in the 'Government of National Defence', had drawn up a comprehensive plan to put the country's finances on a sound footing, but on 27 November had been forced to resign. By 1923 the nation's inflationary losses had risen to 550 million dollars or about three thousand million gold francs, and not a single budget could be properly ratified by Parliament. On 15 January 1923, at the urgent wish of President Wojciechowski, Grabski took over the Ministry of Finance again, and finally, on 18 December, the Presidency of an extra-parliamentary Government. The defeat of inflation in Germany by Schacht's measures of 15 November 1923 seemed a favourable omen for the plans of the new cabinet of experts. On 5 January 1924 Grabski received special powers from Parliament – a concession necessitated by the swift rotation of previous Governments – and by the spring he had in fact succeeded in partly balancing the State's books and thus winning back the public's shattered confidence. The real stabilization was effected on 14 April 1924 by a currency reform, which replaced the mark with the gold guilder – in Polish, zloty – in the proportion 1:1,800,000, and by the foundation on 15 April of the Bank of Poland. The first favourable results were a hesitant influx of foreign capital, a drop in unemployment and a temporary period of peace in home affairs.

However, in the same autumn (1924) a fresh crisis arose. It was caused mainly by the failure of the property tax, but also partly by the failure of the loan from the USA arranged in December 1924, which brought in only 23·5 million dollars instead of the expected 50 million. The Grabski Cabinet had to endanger the currency again, for to buttress the national economy it was compelled to draw upon the currency reserves and to increase the issue of notes. A fresh blow was dealt to the currency by the trade war which the German Government opened on 15 June 1925 by raising the duty on Polish coal. The zloty sank to half the value which it had held in world markets in the middle of 1924.

This critical situation considerably increased the political and social tensions between the Right and the Left. Even before Grabski formed his Government there had been a general strike, which had led to disturbances and bloodshed in Cracow, Tarnow and Boryslaw between 6 and 8 November. When, in the middle of 1924, prices began rising, the number of unemployed rose again and there were financial scandals in which Wladyslaw Kuckarski, the National Democratic Minister for Trade, was involved. A fresh wave of strikes broke out in the summer and autumn in Upper Silesia and the region of Dabrowa, though it is true that the simultaneous activity of the Communist Party of Poland was stigmatized by the PPS as 'Communist criminality'. In view of these internal dissensions, Grabski's Government now also met growing hostility from the Right, which had previously supported its policy. On 13 November 1925, after holding office for nearly two years, he had to resign. How far fundamental criticism of the internal structure of the State had already gone, was shown by the words of the hitherto loyal Witos: 'Our constitution is too liberal.'

The formation of Aleksander Skrzynki's coalition Cabinet on 20 November 1925 was the last attempt to overcome the economic crisis by parliamentary means. Besides the Right and Centre parties previously in the government, the PPS also shared in the Government for the first time, 'to save the State and the working class from catastrophe'. The situation was certainly a threatening one, for towards the end of 1925 the number of unemployed rose to over 300,000 – a third of the total labour force. On the advice of the American expert Edwin Kemmerer, the Finance Minister, Jerzy Zdziechowski, tried to settle the economic crisis by a deflationary policy of Draconian severity, and did in fact achieve certain initial successes. Nevertheless, on 20 April 1926 the PPS went into opposition and withdrew its two ministers, because it thought that the curative measures were laying a burden on the workers and small farmers. Skrzynski's Cabinet, which no longer had a parliamentary majority, resigned on 5 May 1926. Riots among the unemployed in Kalisz, Stryj and Lublin formed a sinister accompaniment to this swan-song of the parliamentary republic.

PILSUDSKI'S COUP D'ÉTAT

The continual state of emergency in the period of pure parliamentary government from 1923 to 1926 gradually convinced Pilsudski that the Republic once again needed the guidance of a strong hand. One of the considerations which led him to this conclusion was certainly the conviction that parliamentarianism had not only failed to master the political and economic crises, but had also opened the door to general corruption. However, the fundamental reason for his rejection of the prevailing system of government was his view, expressed frequently and impatiently, that the army, as the only really reliable guarantee of Polish independence, must be kept free under all circumstances from the influence of the parliamentary machine. Since his retirement most of the high military posts had been filled by former Austrian generals, who regarded the existing provision for parliamentary supervision of the army as quite legitimate. The intellectual leader of this so-called 'Viennese War Academy' was General Wladyslaw Sikorski, who since the wars of 1914–20 had been the marshal's great opponent; from 1914–15 onwards relations between Poland's two most eminent army commanders had grown more and more strained, for both objective and personal reasons. The question of the organization of a supreme command caused a sharp dispute between the two. On 29 February 1924 Pilsudski wrote to Sikorski, at that time Minister for War, with a bitterness that was certainly not entirely justified: 'You move in an atmosphere in which discourtesy to me is considered good form.' The marshal's anger was certainly due partly to the fact that Stanislaw Haller, the Chief of the General Staff, was apparently having him watched by the military secret service. Such enmities led to the formation of factions within the army; officers who had served in the Legions and some of the erstwhile Russian general officers hoped that Pilsudski would seize power again.

To the Left and the parties representing the minorities, Pilsudski was a man of integrity whose reputation was not tarnished by National Democratic policies. He could therefore be sure at least of their secret support, though it was true that even before the foundation of the State the marshal had severed his connections with Marxist socialism and its economic theories. 'There is no God but Marx,' he had remarked mockingly, 'and the PPS is his prophet on earth.' That is why, at the Nineteenth Party Congress of the PPS at the beginning of 1924, Feliks Perl, the theorist and historian of the PPS, spoke against the 'sudden love' of many socialists for Pilsudski, 'We should like to see him in an important and responsible post,' declared Perl on behalf of the party leadership, 'but we must make it clear that Pilsudski is not our man. He cannot be made into a left-wing Mussolini.' In these circumstances Pilsudski had to rely rather on his direct followers, who were to be found in every party – even the Endecja – and were recruited predominantly from the upper classes of the eastern border regions and the Poles from Russia proper. Men like Slawek, Prystor, Holowko, Bartel, Jedrzejewicz, Koc and Moraczewski represented a more broad-minded and imaginative mode of political thought, but also a harder and less scrupulous one, than the ruling parliamentary class, which came mainly from central or western Poland.

On 13 November 1925, when Grabski resigned, Pilsudski intervened and gave President Wojciechowski his views on the need for some control of Parliament and the protection of the army against political interference. The two men had been close to each other ever since, a generation earlier, they had shared the leadership of the PPS in its struggle against the Tsarist authorities, and the President did not close his ears to the marshal's friendly arguments. Nevertheless, he felt obliged to observe the principle of constitutional legitimacy, that is, a principle which did not allow him to interfere. There was real tragedy in this decision, which not only broke up an old friendship but also strengthened

Pilsudski's resolve to carry out a *coup d'état*. At a rally of Legion officers in Sulejowek two days later the marshal expressed his bitter disappointment that the rebirth as a State 'of a powerless people which had continually degenerated in slavery' had not brought with it the hoped-for rebirth of the Polish soul. He implied that in future he would use more than words against those who, in his view, 'were making the State powerless and holding back the punitive hand of justice'.

Pilsudski was able to secure the appointment of a man devoted to him, General Lucjan Zeligowski, as Minister of War in Skrzynski's Government. By gradually collecting those regiments which were attached to Pilsudski, Zeligowski created the military conditions for a putsch. A last conference between Wojciechowski, Grabski and Pilsudski on 9 May 1926 – after Skrzynski's resignation – failed to solve the Cabinet crisis, and on 12 May Pilsudski occupied Praga at the head of fifteen regiments. By 14 May, after hard fighting against Government forces, his troops had captured Warsaw. Several attempts at mediation had been made, but they all failed. Pilsudski's victory was ensured by the PPS, which on 14 May called for a general strike and with the help of the railway workers' union hindered the transport of Government troops to the capital. The President and the Government resigned during the night of 14–15 May. The marshal now had in his hands the power to remodel the State in accordance with his own ideas.

That in carrying out his *coup d'état* Pilsudski was inspired by thoroughly noble and unselfish aims was shown by his well-known order of the day of 22 May, which ended the fighting. Nearly a thousand men had been killed, and the Government's bravest defenders had been the cadets, Poland's future officers. In spite of his long and intimate friendship with Pilsudski, Kazimierz Sosnkowski, the commanding general in Posen, had felt unable to break his oath and rise against the Government; the attempt at suicide by which he tried to escape the irreconcilable conflict between loyalty to the State and loyalty to a friend left him hovering between life and death for months. Shattered by this fratricidal strife, which he himself had caused, Pilsudski refrained from taunting or humiliating his beaten opponents. In chivalrous homage to the defeated he recognized that the dead of both sides had fallen for Poland, for a land 'which is as dear to one man as another and equally loved by both sides'; he hoped that the blood which had been shed 'would produce a new crop of brotherliness and proclaim a truth common to all brothers'. The strongest chords were struck by the evocation of death, the 'common brother' of all Polish soldiers, and by the confession which Pilsudski often made of his own guilt: 'May God in His mercy forgive us and turn aside His avenging hand from us.' These words, perhaps the finest and softest which ever came from Pilsudski's pen, seemed to confirm the hopes of many Poles that the marshal would make the changeover from parliamentary to authoritative government in a spirit of forbearance and reconciliation. After all, he had ended his order of the day with this proclamation: 'As for us, we want to begin the work which shall lend our country strength and renew it.'

CHAPTER IV

The Pilsudski Era (1926-1935)

THE YEARS OF 'MORAL DICTATORSHIP'

It was a tragedy for Poland as well as for Pilsudski that the *coup d'état* took place at a time when the marshal was physically worn out. The enthusiastic revolutionary, the gifted general, had long ago turned into a sickly, moody, mistrustful statesman, who had certainly retained his proved foresight in foreign and military affairs, but had little time for home or economic questions. Bitter disappointment at the moral bankruptcy of Polish parliamentarians, which even caused him on one occasion to call the Parliament a 'Prostitute Sejm', had contributed as much to the hardening of his character as disgust at the corruption to which even officials and high-ranking officers had yielded. Only this spiritual loneliness could explain his action in forcing the resignation of a number of generals – first and foremost Sikorski – who had incurred his displeasure and in having others, such as Wlodzimierz Zagorski, secretly murdered. Even the Prime Ministers whom he appointed himself had to put up with being watched by his agents. Yet even so, both he and his old comrades-in-arms, Walery Slawek and Aleksander Prystor, retained so much decency and integrity in their period of power that they preferred to live in personal poverty. Pilsudski's praiseworthy intention was to restore Poland to 'moral health' – this phrase became the watchword of his régime – but he had no clearly defined programme. He was satisfied with the explanation with which he had prefaced his *coup d'état*: 'There must not be too much injustice in a State if it is not to perish.' During the *coup*, Ignacy Daszynski, his colleague and adviser from the days of partition, had put the classic question to him: 'Where are you going to, Jozef?' All that Pilsudski had been able to say in reply was, 'I do not know.'

The Pilsudski Era (1926–1935)

After taking over power, Pilsudski refrained, with his usual restraint, from setting up an unrestricted dictatorship. He attached value to the formal continuation of political life, and Rataj, the Speaker of the Sejm, to whom President Wojciechowski had handed over supreme authority when he resigned on 14 May 1926, was thus able, on 15 May, to entrust Pilsudski's nominee, Professor Kazimierz Bartel, with the formation of a Cabinet. Bartel had emerged in 1925 as the leader of the 'Labour Party', a small group in the Sejm which supported Pilsudski. In the new Government, which consisted mainly of experts, Pilsudski took over the post of Minister of War, a position which was to remain the basis of his 'moral dictatorship' until his death. When the National Assembly met to choose a new President on 31 May 1926, Pilsudski was elected by a two-thirds majority, but he declined the post for the same reasons as he had declined it in 1922, and preferred to have a trusted supporter as President. He considered choosing Prince Lubomirski, the former Regent, or Marian Idziechowski, the well-known Vilna historian, both of whom he admired as honest and unselfish politicians; however, he had to refrain from putting either of these two forward out of consideration for his left-wing followers, for both men were conservatives. His choice fell eventually on his old acquaintance Professor Ignacy Moscicki, a democrat who had played a secondary role in the PPS round about 1890. Moscicki was elected on 1 June 1926 by the votes of the Left and Centre. His unsuccessful opponent was Count Adolf Bninski, the National Democrat candidate. An amendment to the constitution passed on 2 August 1926 – this time by the votes of the Right – gave the President the right to dissolve Parliament and to issue decrees with the force of law in the intervals between sessions. Such decrees were subject to ratification later by the National Assembly. In addition, the Government could now spend money on the scale of the previous year's budget if Parliament had not ratified the current budget in time. Thanks to these powers, a measure of continuity and stability in the government of the country was obviously now possible. Pilsudski regarded this legal bridging of an interregnum as a unique historical achievement, since it seemed to him that he had succeeded in carrying out a successful revolution, but had managed to avoid the harmful consequences of one.

Clear confirmation of a fundamental political law seemed to be provided by the fact that Pilsudski sought to rule with the support of the Right although he had been helped into power by the Left. Like Millerand, Laval and Mussolini, he thought he could see that it was easier to win power through the dynamic Left, but desirable to stabilize the State through the support of the conservative Right. Already on 26 May 1926 he had openly declared that Poland 'would have to remain for a long time' in a state of 'social equilibrium'; on the one hand the 'experiment of (Poland's) eastern neighbours was by no means attractive', and on the other Poland was 'a very poor country' and lacked the 'moral strength' for social reform. These words formed an open rejection of the PPS and at the same time an offer to the conservative camp. What the marshal wanted to do was to separate the 'older Right', the landowning aristocracy, from the 'younger Right', the National Democrats, and thus weaken the latter. Moreover, he himself displayed many of the typical characteristics of a hot-tempered old landowner and felt personally drawn to the nobility, especially that of the border regions. He was also busying himself at this time with plans for a Polish monarchy, and these too may have been a factor in his political thinking. At any rate, on 2 October 1926 he formed a largely conservative Cabinet, the leadership of which he assumed himself. On 25 October 1926 he paid a visit to the Radziwill castle, a visit which sealed his alliance with the eastern landed aristocracy in the persons of Albrecht Radziwill, Artur Potocki, Eustachy Sapieha, Aleksander Meysztowicz and others. The leadership of this new group was assumed by Prince Janusz Radziwill, who thanks to his enormous wealth and his connection with heavy industry enjoyed considerable influence. As a result, on 10 November 1926 the Supreme Council of the PPS decided to oppose, not Pilsudski himself, but the 'monarchist and reactionary elements' in his Cabinet. The chief organ of the PPS, the *Worker* – Pilsudski himself had founded the paper in

1894 and published it illegally until 1900 – depicted the transformation of Pilsudski's political views by means of two caricatures, in one of which the marshal appeared as a socialist with cap over one ear and torn trousers, and in the other as an old Polish magnate wearing greatcoat and sword. However, the opposition of the PPS was still not very serious, especially as Pilsudski remained in secret contact with Daszynski through Jerzy Stempowski, the head of the Cabinet secretariat.

For the time being Pilsudski favoured a policy of veering between the Right and the Left. In view of his lack of a firm parliamentary basis, in January 1927 he gave Colonel Walery Slawek the task of building up a Government Party. On the basis of their personal relations with Pilsudski, politicians of all parties now united in the non-party bloc of co-operation with the Government (BBWR). The Centre of the BBWR was formed by Pilsudski's direct adherents under Walery Slawek; others who supported the marshal were a group from the Zet called the 'Improvers of the Republic', Janusz Radziwill and the conservatives, a group representing the big capitalists, splinters of the Piast and Liberation Parties, a breakaway group from the PPS under Jedrzej Moraczewski and even a few 'Government Catholics'. Apart from the almost mystical idea of serving Poland, this heterogeneous bloc had no unified programme; it was held together solely by the authority of Pilsudski. Its *élite* was formed by the members of the eastern border nobility, and thus the foundation of the BBWR led to a fresh period of 'Lithuanian' supremacy in Poland.

Meanwhile the right-wing opposition had regrouped. On 4 December 1926, under the tested leadership of Dmowski, the 'Camp of Great Poland' (OWP) was formed, as a focal point for all nationalist forces – National Democrats, Christian Democrats and the Piast. The main efforts of the BBWR propaganda were directed against this coalition. And in fact the elections, which took place on 4 and 11 March after the elapse of the normal period, gave the bloc 122 seats in the Sejm and 46 in the Senate, that is, about a quarter of all the votes cast and a relative majority. In the Populist or Peasant Party, the Liberation wing won a good many votes

from the Piast wing; this was a result of the inadequacy of the
land reform. The whole Left, headed by the PPS, stiffened its
opposition. It succeeded in securing the election of Daszynski as
Speaker of the Sejm against Pilsudski's candidate, Bartel. On 27
June 1928, as he could now reckon on reliable support in the
Sejm, the marshal handed back the premiership to the conciliatory
Kazimierz Bartel. It is true that the Right too now strengthened
its resistance; on 7 October 1928 the National Democrats, who
had hitherto been organized in the 'National People's Union',
transformed themselves into the 'National Party' (SN) and also
retained the leading position in the 'Camp of Great Poland'.

An open conflict then flared up between Government and
Parliament on the question of budgetary rights, which had been
left obscure since the amendment of 2 August 1926. On the personal instructions of Pilsudski, the Finance Minister, Gabriel
Czechowicz, had spent public money without parliamentary
authority, and he had almost certainly spent it on the Government's election propaganda. As a result, on 20 March 1929, at the
instigation of a PPS member called Herman Lieberman, who had
the backing of the party, he was arraigned before the State Tribunal. Pilsudski gave his full protection to Czechowicz, who had
in fact done some service in the organization of the State finances;
on 7 April 1929, in the belief that here too he was faced with
'moral insanity', he spoke publicly in a most insulting way of the
Sejm and the State Tribunal. On 12 April 1929 he formed his
first fighting Government, the Switalski Cabinet, half of which
consisted of generals and colonels devoted to him. This 'indemnity conflict' finally ended the secret collusion between
Pilsudski and the PPS. On 24 June 1929, in a personal conversation
with Daszynski, Pilsudski rejected his last attempts at mediation
in very strong terms. On 29 June 1929 the intimidated State
Tribunal – Pilsudski had described the proceedings against
Czechowicz as 'ritual murder' – declared the Finance Minister
formally innocent, though it recognized Parliament's right to
control expenditure. Daszynski and the PPS now took up the
struggle for parliamentary legitimacy in earnest. Mieczyslaw

The Pilsudski Era (1926-1935)

Niedzialkowski wrote in the *Worker*: 'The Pilsudski of 1905, of 1914, of 1918 or of 1920 belongs to history; the Pilsudski of 1926-9 is the leader of the disappearing world of Old Poland, the Poland of the aristocratic societies, of the "Leviathans" [this was what the industrial concerns were called], of bureaucracy and the "moral cleansing".' In imitation of his admired model, Napoleon I, the marshal now thought of carrying through an '18 Brumaire'. On the 31 October 1929 he appeared in person to open the Sejm, which had been forcibly adjourned for six months. He was accompanied by a hundred armed officers. However, Daszynski, the Speaker, refused to open the session; fearlessly he called out to Pilsudski, 'I am not going to open the legislative chamber under the threat of bayonets, guns and sabres!' Once again Pilsudski shrank from openly breaking the constitution; he left the house with his officers and ordered a fresh adjournment.

On 31 October 1929 a new opposition bloc of the Left and Centre was called into being. On 1 November, under Daszynski's leadership, six parties – the PPS, the Piast, the Liberation group, Jan Dabski's Peasant Party, the National Workers' Party and the Christian Democrats – combined to form the 'Centre Left' (Centrolew), which controlled over two-fifths of all the seats. When the Sejm finally opened on 5 December, the Centrolew was able to overthrow the Kazimierz Switalski Cabinet by parliamentary means. Confronted with the choice between Dmowski's camp and that of Daszynski, Pilsudski once again chose the latter. On 29 December he appointed a moderate Cabinet under Bartel, which sought a political truce with the Centrolew. However, the Centre Left refused to drop its opposition; on 1-2 February 1930 the Supreme Council of the PPS voted for the 'Liquidation of the prevailing system in favour of parliamentary democracy'. On 15 March the PPS and the Centrolew caused the fall of this fifth Bartel Government and thus made open conflict unavoidable. The era of 'Bartelism', as the policy of governing with an intimidated Sejm was popularly described, was at an end.

At this period the world economic crisis made itself felt in Polish political life. Thanks partly to the good financial administration under Pilsudski, but above all to the general state of the world, the years 1926–9 had brought a certain prosperity and were among the most successful, from an economic point of view, of the whole inter-war period. Unemployment had almost disappeared, and even a certain amount of investment had been made possible. With the winter of 1929–30 poverty, rising prices and unemployment began to spread again, and these circumstances lent the Centrolew opposition tremendous social significance. The Government practised the strictest economy; but from a political point of view the general tendency to radicalism began to have its effect as it did in Germany under Brüning. Like the German Chancellor, Pilsudski decided in favour of an authoritarian policy. On 29 March 1930 he appointed the first Slawek Government, which as a pure fighting Cabinet consisted only of devoted adherents of the marshal and tried to do without the independent politicians previously involved. Slawek governed for months simply by repeatedly adjourning the Sejm. The Centre Left, on the other hand, tried to defend the sovereignty of Parliament. On 29 June its leaders held a congress in the Old Theatre at Cracow. This congress showed how the economic, social and political emergency had united the most heterogeneous parties; there were quite a few priests sitting beside the socialists and Peasant leaders, and the Christian Democrats' pictures of the Virgin contrasted curiously with the red banners of the PPS and the green flags of the peasants. Prime Minister Slawek accused the Congress of intending to organize a *coup d'état* or at any rate the violent overthrow of the Pilsudski régime. On the basis of the Austrian criminal code valid in Galicia he had about twenty politicians arrested on a charge of high treason; later the number rose to about seventy. Among those arrested were Wincenty Witos and Wladyslaw Kiernik, the leaders of the Piast, Kazimierz Baginski of the Liberation party – once a distinguished POW officer – Herman Lieberman, Norbert Barlicki, Adam Ciolkosz, Zygmunt Mastek and Adam Pragier of the PPS, and finally Wojciech Korfanty, the leader of the Christian Democrats. These arrests were indubitably aimed principally against the Left, even though Pilsudski sought to conceal this purpose by ordering the arrest of Aleksander Debski, the chief organizer of the OWP – he had in any case once been a socialist – and even of one of the BBWR deputies.

On 25 August 1930 Pilsudski himself once again took over the post of Prime Minister. In a series of policy speeches he made his sharpest attacks so far on the 'anarchic methods' and 'disgusting mess' of the Sejm and on its members as a whole. He bluntly described the politicians of the Centre Left as 'scoundrels'. On 30 August he dissolved both chambers of the National Assembly and later announced that fresh elections would take place on 17 and 23 November. The election campaign was slanted in favour of the Government under strong pressure from the administration. At the same time it became known that Pilsudski had removed the arrested politicians from the jurisdiction of the civil authorities and sent them illegally to the fortress of Brest–Litovsk, where they were exposed to ill-treatment and humiliation by the commandant, Waclaw Kostek-Biernacki. The elections took place on 17 and 23 November, during the period of two months in which the opposition politicians were incarcerated at Brest; they gave the Government camp the desired absolute majority of 247 seats in the Sejm. The Left and Centre parties formed only small splinters; even the PPS obtained only 24 seats (5·5 per cent). On the other hand, the National Party improved its position from 37 to 62 seats (14 per cent), which was certainly not displeasing to Pilsudski; the struggle against the Left demanded the support of the Right, and thanks to the Government's conservative policy the opposition of the National Party had long changed from social and political opposition to a purely parliamentary one. Pilsudski had thus won the struggle with Parliament for power in the State, and on 4 December he handed the post of Prime Minister back to Slawek.

The price paid for this victory was unfortunately too high. The Brest-Litovsk affair aroused the nation's sense of justice, and the brutal suppression of the Left even provoked the opposition of many politicians in the Government camp, such as Prince

Radziwill and the leader of the BBWR, Tadeusz Holowko. Prince Lubomirski expressed his anger quite openly. Compared with Stalin, Hitler or Mussolini, Pilsudski had certainly been able to overthrow the opposition with incomparably milder measures; but then, unlike the Bolsheviks or National Socialists, he had not questioned the independence and sanctity of justice. So by his behaviour he demoralized the administration of justice, alienated the bulk of the nation and henceforth had to rely on the officers who supported him. The result was all the more horrifying because the honesty and purity of Pilsudski's aims could not be doubted. The poet Maria Dabrowska, widow of a man who had fought for independence and herself at one time an admirer of Pilsudski's genius, was forced to this bitter conclusion: 'The moral links between the Government and the majority of the population were shattered. From now on, all attempts to restore them, however well intentioned, turned out to be vain.'

THE RÉGIME OF THE COLONELS

The last few years of Pilsudski's régime were overshadowed by the world economic crisis, which affected Poland from 1930 to 1935 and besides impoverishing the workers and peasants caused passionate political extremism. Since the Brest–Litovsk affair the Centre Left had been crushed; but the opposition of the left-wing workers and peasants lost none of its sharpness. The peasant parties – Piast, Liberation and Dabski's Peasant Party – united again in March 1931 into a unified Peasant Party (SL), which held only 48 seats in the Sejm but represented half the nation. Its leader, Wincenty Witos, once so moderate, had now adopted such radical views that he came out against 'out-dated capitalism' and demanded the complete redistribution of all big estates. After its Twenty-Second Congress in May 1931, at which it demanded 'the coalition of all democratic forces in the country', the PPS formed an alliance with the Peasant Party. The two parties were soon to move towards such extreme solutions as a 'government of workers and peasants' or 'immediate nationalization of big estates without compensation'.

The Pilsudski Era (1926–1935)

In these circumstances the Government camp tried to come to some kind of understanding with the National Party. Pilsudski obviously approved of this courtship; Dmowski's ideas had not only long penetrated the BBWR; they had also gained the adherence of most of the younger intelligentsia. Up to the elections of November 1930 the older 'democratic' tendency represented by Stronski had been the dominant one in the National Party; now the young men under Tadeusz Bielecki took over the leadership. They championed purely nationalistic and national-radical aims, and favoured – with the support of the old man Dmowski – a hierarchically organized, half-fascist state. This produced the curious situation that in spite of their traditional political antagonism the Government camp and the National Party (i.e. the former National Democrats) drew nearer and nearer to each other in their ideology.

From 1930 onwards the marshal gradually withdrew from home affairs; he left them to his 'colonels', who ran the Government in accordance with his general instructions. To the rhythm of regular 'changes of the guard', like those customary in Fascist Italy, Walery Slawek, Aleksander Prystor, Adam Koc, Janusz Jedrzejewicz, Leon Kozlowski, and Jozef Beck passed the important offices of State round among themselves. They ruled with the aid of a caste of officials and functionaries who were mainly recruited from the impoverished minor nobility. The world economic crisis had dealt the death blow to the smaller landowners, who had in any case been struggling against difficulties for decades. This new class of officials tried to live like the landowners of days gone by without being able to practise their generosity or to recreate their patriarchal relations with the people. The apparatus of authority, which even in 1928 had comprised over 600,000 officials, led in addition, as in other States, to a depersonalization of public order. In Poland this necessary consequence of the modern State seemed like a swindle in comparison with people's dreams of romantic messianism and the aristocratic freedom of that old Poland which those who had fought for independence believed they could restore. The rigidity of organization which was particularly necessary in this period of economic difficulty came as a painful disappointment to the enthusiasts and idealists of days gone by. Moreover, the dominant town society displayed a curiously divided, inorganic character. It was neither aristocratic nor middle-class in the Western sense, but it was above the 'grey mass of men'. It also fell into closer and closer economic dependence on the State and industry. In face of this, the art of government was reduced to the mere exercise of power, and the colonels, or at any rate the younger ones, did not fail to exploit for their own benefit the worship of power long prepared in theory by Dmowski. Thus in the ruling classes, as Pilsudski himself noted with bitterness, the number of self-seekers, careerists and soldiers of fortune rose considerably. This was not the least of the reasons why the gulf between governors and governed grew wider and deeper.

The colonels' Governments sought to deal with the general crisis by authoritarian means. Aleksander Prystor, Prime Minister since 27 May 1931, was able to end the indemnity conflict with the help of the now compliant Sejm; he ruled with Draconian economy measures and emergency decrees. Since in February 1932 the PPS organized mass strikes in the region of Dabrowa, Upper Silesia, Gdynia, Cracow and Lodz, he restricted the freedom of assembly and judicial independence. Legislation dealing with work and social conditions was intensified. The gradual shift to purely dictatorial forms of government was reflected in the 'Enabling Act' of 23 March 1933, which allowed the President to issue decrees with the force of law, and in the smooth re-election of Moscicki on 7 May 1933.

Prystor's successor, Janusz Jedrzejewicz, who came into office on 10 May 1933, carried out a temporary *rapprochement* with the Left for tactical reasons. Already on 15 November 1932 Bronislaw Pieracki, the Minister for Internal Affairs, had dissolved Dmowski's 'Camp of Great Poland'. By favouring the 'Youth Legion', which made use of socialistic and militaristic slogans, Jedrzejewicz tried to draw young blood to the BBWR; however, the attempt failed, especially as Jedrzejewicz irritated the lower middle-class intelligentsia with his unfortunate school and university policy and his salary reductions. The most active sections of Polish youth combined in the 'National Radical Camp' (ONR), which split off from the National Party on 17 March 1934 and – perhaps under the influence of German National Socialism – represented extreme Nationalistic and anti-Semitic ideas. When Pieracki was murdered on 15 June 1934, the Government blamed the ONR for the crime, forbade the organization and sent its leaders to the concentration camp of Bereza Kartuska, which had been set up in June 1934 on the advice of Goebbels. This very persecution lent the ONR, which continued to exist illegally, tremendous moral authority. But the younger men were gaining ground in the PPS and SL too. The peasant youth organization 'Wici' and the Young Socialist groups wanted solutions involving extreme socialism or agrarian revolution. The younger intelligentsia was particularly loyal to the prisoners of Brest – Witos, Lieberman and Korfanty – who had emigrated after their legal conviction on 5 October 1933. Witos in particular was honoured like a saint in many peasant circles. This kind of attitude not only showed how unpopular the colonels' régime and the 'moral recovery' had become; it also showed the breach between the generation which had founded the State and its successors, who already took independence for granted and had received their political education amid the new problems of the world economic crisis.

THE ROAD TO AN INDEPENDENT FOREIGN POLICY

Before he seized power Pilsudski had often observed that, besides military affairs, the real domain of the man in charge of a State must be foreign policy. For this reason, although he interfered little in home affairs, he retained the control of foreign policy in his own hands. In accordance with his fundamental attitude, which had always caused him to regard Russia as Poland's main adversary, he seemed called to make a break with the principles of Poland's previous foreign policy, which since 1923 had aimed mainly, in loyal alliance with France, at keeping Germany in check. And in fact Pilsudski's arrival in power saw a fresh flare-up in Polish–Soviet relations. In 1926–7 this flare-up assumed the character of an acute crisis, with the Lithuanian Republic taking the Soviet side because of the question of Vilna. To meet this threat, in December 1927 Pilsudski tried to conclude a Germano–Polish agreement in Geneva with Gustav Stresemann, so as to be able to concentrate all Poland's forces in the east. However, Stresemann rejected the proposal, as he obviously wanted to keep a free hand for an active German foreign policy in the questions of the revision of the Germano–Polish frontiers and of the German minority in Poland – a conception which also corresponded to the internal political scene in Germany at that time. Thus Pilsudski's first attempt at a re-orientation of Polish foreign policy came to nothing.

This failure showed that the effect of the frontier arrangements of 1919 to 1921 was much stronger than that of Pilsudski's initiative. Since the peace treaties of Versailles and Riga, both Germany and Soviet Russia had shown the desire to revise their frontiers with Poland to their own advantage, although for the time being they were of course far too weak to advance such claims seriously. Nevertheless, rightly recognizing future dangers, Pilsudski, when he was still Chief of State, had concluded on 19 February 1921 the alliance with France which was to form the basis of Polish foreign policy. The pact was complemented on 21 February by a secret military convention and provided for French military assistance if Poland was the victim of an unprovoked attack by either Germany or Soviet Russia. On the other hand, with the Rapallo Treaty of 17 April 1922 the Berlin and Moscow Governments introduced a period of political and military co-operation which was aimed primarily against Poland. A further worsening of Poland's situation was effected by the Locarno Treaties of 26 October 1925, in which the Germano–Polish frontiers, unlike the Franco–German ones, were not guaranteed, and hence in Polish eyes were demoted to 'second-class frontiers'. Thanks to the skilful diplomacy of Stresemann, the Locarno Treaties thus left the German Government free to pursue a policy of frontier revision *vis-à-vis* Poland. The Franco–Polish Guarantee Pact of 15 October 1925 was not sufficient to counterbalance German territorial claims on Poland, especially as it was very vaguely formulated. Moreover, it no longer provided for French armed assistance in the case of a Soviet attack. Finally, the Germano–Soviet neutrality pact of 24 April 1926, the so-called Berlin Treaty, put Poland still more firmly in the pincers, since at the time when it was conceived the possibility of concerted frontier claims against Poland by both Germany and Russia was expressly discussed by Stresemann and the Soviet Foreign Minister, Chicherin. It was at this period, too, that the secret military collaboration between the Reichswehr and the Red Army began. Thus when Pilsudski assumed power he was confronted with a *fait accompli* in foreign affairs: the Polish–French grouping was faced by a Germano–Soviet one, and in addition Poland could not be too sure of French support, as was shown by Locarno and deficiencies in French deliveries of arms. This situation caused Pilsudski, as early as May 1926, to make the prognosis that in foreign affairs Poland's position would scarcely change at all in the next five years. From this point of view, Pilsudski's initiatives of 1926–7 may be regarded not so much as real attempts at a new orientation, but rather as evolutions to soften up hardened positions. No doubt the marshal had recognized that the existing situation left Poland little room for manœuvre.

In these circumstances, from 1926 to 1931 Polish foreign policy operated within the framework of the French system of alliances. The conduct of all external affairs – such as meetings of the League of Nations – which could be regarded as more or less routine was left by Pilsudski to his Foreign Minister, August Zaleski, a moderate democrat who had done good service in London during the First World War promoting the idea of independence. More essential problems, especially the question of Poland's eastern policy, were dealt with by the marshal himself with the aid of his collaborators Tadeusz Holowko and Leon Wasilewski. With the signing of the Litvinov Protocols in February 1929 a very tolerable relationship with the Soviet Union was achieved. Relations with Germany, on the other hand, grew worse and worse, since after Stresemann's death the trade war which had begun in June 1925, the German revisionist policy, and Germano–Soviet co-operation were all continued and intensified by Curtius and Treviranus in 1929–30. From 1930 onwards, therefore, Pilsudski used his favourite trick of countering political pressure with military measures, and carried out military manœuvres on the German frontiers as a form of deterrent. He even toyed with plans for military preventive action. Measures of this sort in turn increased the Brüning Government's fear of a Polish attack – a fear which was a real nightmare to the German High Command – and caused it to build up the secret 'Eastern Frontier Guard'. Pilsudski for his part was kept informed by an excellent intelligence service of all the details of Germany's illegal activities in re-arming contrary to the Treaty of Versailles, and this hardened his attitude, especially as since the First World War he had had an exceptionally high opinion of German military efficiency.

Autumn 1931 saw the beginning of a period of greater political freedom of movement for Poland. The Soviet Union was tied down by the Japanese invasion of Manchuria, a situation which relieved Poland of any threat to her eastern frontiers for some years. In concert with Finland, Estonia, Latvia and Roumania, Poland started negotiations with the USSR for a non-aggression pact, thus resuscitating to some extent the tradition of the 'border state front' of 1920. Polish diplomacy could now concentrate on Germany and also move over to an active foreign policy in the north and south. Warsaw Governments had always regarded the Baltic and the Danube basin as their particular fields of action, even if they had felt tied down so far as Germany and Russia were concerned. In view of these new prospects, at Christmas 1931 the marshal gave Colonel Jozef Beck, his Secretary of State at the Foreign Office, general instructions to attach particular importance to the solution of the Teschen, Danzig, Lithuanian and minority questions. In addition, he designated Beck as the future Minister for Foreign Affairs. He regarded Beck – an energetic and flexible diplomat, who since 1929–30 had made himself indispensable to Pilsudski as his assistant in home affairs – as a better man to direct the new foreign policy than the conservative Zaleski.

The overture to the 'Beck era' was provided by the successful conclusion of the Polish–Soviet non-aggression pact on 25 July 1932. Poland was now in a position to adopt a firmer attitude to German demands for frontier revision and re-armament, which had become particularly active under the Brüning Government. Pilsudski feared nothing so much as German re-armament, since in his view it would lead to an internal unification of the German people, enable Germany to exploit the strategic advantages of her eastern frontiers and thus lend every demand for frontier revision – the emphasis of power. For this reason the marshal intensified his policy of intimidation, which assumed such dimensions, with troop concentrations round East Prussia in March 1932 and the appearance of the destroyer *Wicher* at Danzig on 15 June, that it contributed to the fall of Brüning and also, later on, to that of Papen. At the news of German–Soviet military conversations, Pilsudski dismissed Zaleski on 2 November 1932 and finally handed over the Foreign Ministry to Beck. Beck's most important assignment was to paralyse the German demand for military 'parity' and to maintain the existing superiority of the Polish army to the German army.

Hitler's seizure of power on 30 January 1933 was at first regarded not unfavourably by Pilsudski, since he expected less interest in revision of the eastern frontier from this 'Austrian' than from the previous 'Prussian' Weimar Governments. However, when Hitler ordered the secret re-arming to be continued and took up the demand for revision again, if only for internal reasons, Pilsudski resumed his tactics of intimidation again. Between 5 and 16 March 1933 he provided the Polish arms dump at the Westerplatte in the port of Danzig with a military guard whose strength exceeded Polish rights in Danzig, and made preparations for a 'preventive war' against Germany. This description, which is of later date, concealed a plan which Pilsudski had frequently considered since 1930 to carry out a 'police action' in conjunction with the French Government under the aegis of the League of Nations. In this action Poland was to occupy Danzig, East Prussia and German Upper Silesia, after the model of the occupation of the Ruhr, as 'territorial pledges' in order to force Germany to observe the provisions of the Treaty of Versailles governing re-armament and frontiers. When these aims had been attained – in March 1933 Pilsudski also had in mind Hitler's resignation – the occupied territories, with the exception of Danzig, were to be evacuated again. However, as the French Government would have nothing to do with such suggestions, which were made in the middle of March and again in the middle of April 1933, the marshal turned directly on Hitler. On 2 May he sent him an inquiry, couched in the terms of an ultimatum, about German intentions in the matter of revision. Hitler had meanwhile been informed of Polish plans for a 'preventive war' and gave an assurance that he meant to respect the existing Germano–Polish frontiers. The result of this exchange led to a complete transformation in Germano–Polish relations, hitherto so critical.

The impetus for this change came from Hitler. Since the middle of 1933 he had been feeling more and more inclined gradually to reduce German collaboration with the USSR. The first sign of this decision was the ending of the co-operation between the Reichswehr and the Red Army in June 1933. However, renunciation of the Soviet Union necessitated the restoration of good relations with Poland. Unlike Wilhelm II, Hitler recognized that any German Polish policy must be a function of German policy towards Russia, and that consequently it was essential to cultivate friendly relations with Poland in the case of a break with Russia – just as, vice versa, the good Russo–German relationship of the nineteenth century had largely determined German hostility to Poland. For this reason Hitler sought to reach an understanding with Pilsudski, whose personality in any case fascinated him at that time – he regarded him quite wrongly as a dictator of his own stamp. At the back of his mind there was also the still secret intention of winning, later on, the desired living space in the east; this, he hoped, would come about when Germany was strong, with the help of the Polish alliance. His first go-between was Rauschning, who was elected President of the Danzig Senate on 28 May 1933. It was he who put an end to the dispute between Danzig and Poland that had lasted since 1920. This very circumstance made Pilsudski – who regarded Danzig as the touchstone of Germano–Polish relations – more inclined to a settlement with Hitler. But the decisive factor for Pilsudski was the failure – clearly evident by October 1933 – of his preventive plan. He could see no further possibility of thwarting German rearmament, and therefore had to come to an agreement with Germany while Poland was militarily stronger and could obtain favourable conditions. Consequently on 26 January 1934 a Germano–Polish non-aggression pact was signed. This ended the political antagonism and eventually also the trade war; in addition, Hitler gave up his revisionist policy and stopped supporting the German minority in Poland. Yet Hitler was the real gainer in this agreement, since the Franco–Polish alliance was loosened and the path smoothed for German rearmament.

The signing of this agreement also showed that Pilsudski had come to the conclusion that the old foundations of Polish security – the peace treaties, the League of Nations and the alliance with France – had lost some of their strength since 1931. This development, which Poland had been powerless to influence, confirmed his prognosis of 1926. Polish statesmanship now had to concentrate on preserving the strictest independence *vis-à-vis* both Germany and the Soviet Union and on keeping the country's relations with both powers equally balanced. Neither the Moscow nor the Berlin Government must be given grounds for assuming that Poland was allied with one of her neighbours against the other. For this reason in February 1934 the marshal directed Beck to make the Polish–Soviet agreement exactly parallel to the Polish–German one. The Soviet Government approved this new version of the pact of 1932 on 5 May 1934. With that, the principle of a 'policy of equilibrium' had been formally implemented, even if in fact the policy represented an unstable balance resting on the antagonism between Germany and Russia which had become evident in the middle of 1934. Nevertheless, Pilsudski honestly intended to maintain this impartiality. He certainly still regarded the ussr as enemy no 1, as his last General Staff memoranda of 1934 showed, but he resisted all attempts by Hitler to persuade him to join in a campaign against the Soviet Union. He regarded such suggestions (those, for example, which Göring submitted to him in January 1935) as invitations to '*travailler pour le roi de Prusse*', and that in a double sense. In his view, in the case of defeat, Poland would have been exposed to the vengeance of the ussr, while in the case of victory she would have fallen into hopeless dependence on Germany by virtue of Germany's presence on the Baltic and in the Ukraine.

At any rate Pilsudski had been able to ensure Poland's external independence in the spring of 1934, that is, at a time when the rearmament of Germany and the Soviet Union had begun in earnest. It was assumed that in a few years' time both neighbouring powers would be stronger than Poland; then the question of frontier revision could be brought up again from both east and west. It was not in the marshal's power to prevent this development. He had taken all the precautions which lay within Poland's power. In internal affairs he may have followed too rigidly conservative or even reactionary tendencies, but his elasticity and clear-sightedness in foreign affairs compelled admiration. In this domain the legacy of the Jagellonians, which at home had often had unfortunate results, took on the appearance of a gift which no other Polish statesman enjoyed in this period.

BASIC CHARACTERISTICS OF THE POLICY TOWARDS MINORITIES

The revolution of May 1926 awoke great hopes in the minority parties and in the Left that there would now be a comprehensive revision of the minority policy, which between 1923 and 1926 had been conducted in a purely National Democratic spirit. It was true that the non-Polish peoples enjoyed international protection by virtue of the Minorities Treaty, and the constitution of 1921 certainly guaranteed a minimum of national rights; but these arrangements were not sufficient to prevent a systematic policy of 'Polonization'. Such a policy had been enforced in particular by the National Democratic politician Grabski, a man who had been among the founders of the PPS in 1892-3, but had soon changed into a zealous nationalist. By the law of 31 July 1924 and by his activities as Minister of Education in 1925-6 Grabski had largely replaced the flourishing minority schools with bilingual institutions of a decidedly Polish character. Land policy as well as educational policy was also made to serve nationalistic ends. The so-called 'Liquidation Law' was aimed particularly against the German minority, as was also the administration of the land-reform laws in German-speaking regions. Against the eastern minorities – Lithuanians, White Russians and Ukrainians – the method of military settlement was employed. The Jewish community had a relatively well-developed system of religious and cultural self-government, but in the whole of western and central Poland it was subjected to an economic boycott by the Endecja. It was thus simply the law of political self-preservation which made the non-Polish Members of Parliament in the 'minority Block' usually vote with the liberal Left against the nationalist Right and, until 1926, support Pilsudski, from whom they hoped for an improvement in the political situation of the minorities, if not the federalization of the Republic and the creation of territorially autonomous regions for the non-Polish groups.

These high hopes were not fulfilled in any way. The Treaty of Riga had knocked away the foundations of the old federal programme of Pilsudski and the PPS. Moreover, Pilsudski was pinned down by the minority laws of 1923-6, which he found he had to leave in operation even after he had seized power unless he was going to attack the whole legal basis of the State. In addition, 'Polonization' practices had become so much the habit, indeed a sort of self-evident right, of the lower levels of the administration that it seemed senseless to try to combat them with official regulations. Finally, a secret estimate made at the marshal's request immediately after his seizure of power pointed to the conclusion – a conclusion that differed from the one based on the official census figures – that over 35 per cent of the total population of Poland was non-Polish. This alone made it seem likely that any attempt at federalization would endanger the unity of the State.

But the decisive factor was connected with external rather than internal affairs. In the Berlin Government the German minority possessed a powerful advocate; Stresemann in particular liked to appear at the League of Nations as the 'spokesman of the minorities'. In face of the anti-Polish tendency of the Weimar Cabinets, not only the National Democrats but even men like Pilsudski were convinced that Germany was exploiting the provisions for the protection of minorities to support her foreign policy, and in particular to secure a revision of the frontier. For this reason alone it was considered essential to demonstrate the purely Polish character of the western provinces by an intensified policy of 'Polonization'. The Jews, too, thanks to the international backing which they enjoyed, were regarded with a certain amount of distrust. The eastern minorities – White Russians and Ukrainians – had not only the Minorities Treaty and the League of Nations to call upon for support, but also the neighbouring White Russian and Ukrainian Soviet Republics. Since 1922 there had been a lively national life which had been tolerated and even encouraged by the central Government in Moscow, and this unquestionably possessed a certain attraction for the White Russians and Ukrainians in Poland, where the Government was trying to turn them into Poles. In the case of the White Russians and Ukrainians, socialist or revolutionary demands were combined with the nationalist ones, and for this very reason their political aspirations seemed particularly dangerous to the Warsaw Government. The Lithuanians and some of the White Russians were backed by the Republic of Lithuania, with which Poland had been at loggerheads since 1920. All these considerations no doubt decided Pilsudski to let the previous 'Polonizing' minority policy continue in broad principle. Of the old federal conception only a few vestiges remained. These were nurtured at, among other places, the 'Warsaw Institute for Minority Questions', under the aegis of Leon Wasilewski, Tadeusz Holowko and Stanislaw Paprocki. In Volhynia the voivode or provincial governor, Henryk Jozewski, with the help of former UNR politicians, was able to guide the newly awakening national consciousness of the Ukrainians into pro-Polish and anti-Soviet channels. The Lithuanian Tartars and the Karaites in the Vilna region enjoyed autonomy in religious and cultural affairs for historical and romantic reasons. But such phenomena were by no means characteristic of the Government's general policy. As against the few examples of generous treatment of minorities there was, for example, the attitude of Michal Grazynski, appointed voivode of Upper Silesia by Pilsudski in 1926, who even regarded the methods of his National Democrat predecessors as too liberal. Grazynski, a former POW officer who had come to the fore in the Silesian revolts of 1920 and 1921, carried through in the thirteen years of his governorship a consistent 'Polonization' of Silesians with German sympathies by applying economic pressure, although this sometimes brought him into conflict with the Geneva Convention. In general, the minority policy of the Pilsudski era was highly influenced by the nationalistic wing of the Zet, in which both Paprocki and Grazynski held leading positions.

In this way the tension between the State and the minorities, especially the big, solid blocs in the east, grew steadily from about 1926 onwards. In their Uniate National Church -- it was led by Sheptytskyj, the Metropolitan of Lwow, a brother of the Polish general Szeptycki – the Galician Ukrainians possessed a powerful custodian of the Ukrainian national spirit. The partly Catholic, partly Orthodox White Russians lacked such ecclesiastical help, since the Orthodox Metropolitan of Warsaw was dependent on the Government and, the Catholic Archbishop of Vilna, in accordance with the provisions of the Concordat of 1925, impeded the introduction of the White Russian language for sermons. It was in fact among the White Russians that the conflict with the

Government first flared up, as their strongest party, the 'Hramada', founded in 1924, favoured both nationalism and agrarian revolution, and was supported by the Soviet Government in Minsk. The leaders of the Hramada, including among others the aged scholar Bronislaw Taraszkiewicz, were convicted after a lengthy trial which lasted from 23 February to 22 May 1928, and their organization was smashed. The Galician Ukrainian counterpart of the Hramada, the 'Sel Rob', founded on 10 October 1926, was much weaker; it disappeared after a few years under gentle pressure from the Polish authorities. In view of the *bourgeois* attitude of most Galician Ukrainians, the 'Ukrainian National Democratic Organization' (UNDO), founded on 11 July 1925, wielded the decisive influence in eastern Galicia; it was led by parliamentarians of the Austrian school such as Stepan Baran, Dmytro Lewitzkyj and Wasyl Mudryj. The radical fighters for independence belonged to the illegal 'Ukrainian Military Organization' (UVO), founded in 1920 under Colonel Evgen Konovalec. UNDO and UVO stood in the same relationship to each other as their Polish prototypes, Endecja and POW, did in the period from 1905 to 1918. At a congress held in Vienna in 1929 (27 January–3 February), the UVO united with other independence groups to form the 'Organization of Ukrainian Nationalists' (OUN), which in contrast to the UNDO favoured nationalistic, revolutionary tactics. With the attack on Bobrka on 29 July 1930, the OUN opened a proper guerrilla war, like the one waged by the Irish Sinn Fein, against the Government and the Polish landowners. Pilsudski regarded the situation as a revolt, especially as the OUN's terrorist activities coincided with the activities of the Centrolew after the Cracow Congress. On 15 September 1930 he started a series of 'pacifications', comparable with the dragonnades of Louis XIV, in which Polish cavalry were guilty of severely mishandling the populations of whole villages. The OUN's miniature war was suppressed by the end of November by means of this counter-terror. The leaders of the OUN remained irreconcilable; in 1931 their agents succeeded in murdering the Government leader Holowko, and in 1934 they assassinated Pieracki, the Minister for Internal Affairs. On the other hand, by the severity of his 'pacifications' in eastern Galicia, Pilsudski lost the sympathies of many people, abroad as well as at home, although on 30 January 1932 the League of Nations declared that the suppression of the OUN was fundamentally justified. Nevertheless, how far Pilsudski had travelled from his earlier mode of thought under the pressure of apparent reasons of state was shown by the circumstance that he rejected the plea for mercy for Holowko's assassins put forward by the PPS politician Arciszewski. It was in vain that Arciszewski pointed out that the OUN men had done no more than fight for the idea of national independence in just the same way as he and Pilsudski himself had in the ranks of the PPS of 1905. The other minorities never clashed so sharply with the Polish authorities as the Ukrainians did. However, the year 1930 was a sort of climacteric for all the minorities in their struggle to improve their position, for as a result of the manipulation of the November elections they lost most of their parliamentary representatives. The minority bloc was now no longer able to tip the balance between the various political parties.

Moreover, after 1930 the Polish Government was able to count on a steady worsening of the external and international situation of the minorities. The persecution of nationalist forces in the Soviet republics of White Russia and the Ukraine round 1930 and the collectivization carried out in 1932–3 turned the hopes of the White Russians and Ukrainians in Poland away from the Soviet Union. Germany's departure from the League of Nations in October 1933 robbed the German minority of the international tribunal before which their petitions had hitherto been heard, and with the Germano–Polish agreement of January 1934 Hitler in fact gave up any effective support of German interests in Poland. Finally, on 13 September 1934, the Warsaw Government unilaterally renounced the Minorities Treaty, which it had long regarded as humiliating, and thus withdrew the minority question from the jurisdiction of the League of Nations. This action effected the complete isolation of the minorities from outside influences. All that their representatives could do now was to conclude a kind of political truce with the State. However, this tactical agreement was incapable of bridging the profound differences between the minorities and the Poles. Under the powerful influence of the idea of a 'people', particularly cultivated in the Third Reich, the Germans really started to grow into a solid national bloc from 1933 onwards. The Jews gradually drew apart from the Poles as a result of the anti-Semitism which started to increase again from 1934 onwards and of the prospect of emigration to Palestine. So far as the Lithuanians, White Russians and Ukrainians were concerned, the undiminished 'Polonizing' tendency of Government policy was continually creating new grounds for conflict. It was true that the prevailing public order, the good treatment of members of the minorities in the army and the abundant social contacts between Poles and non-Poles resulted in the overwhelming majority of the minority population remaining loyal to the state; individual groups, such as the bulk of the Catholic White Russians, were to preserve this loyalty even after the collapse of the Republic. Nevertheless, the Polish State alienated the leaders of the non-Polish groups, and this showed once again to what a marked degree the nationalist attitude of the Endecja had taken hold of the Polish people.

THE NEW CONSTITUTION OF 1935

From the end of 1928 and the beginning of 1929 onwards, a period which was distinguished by the outbreak of a fundamental conflict between Government and Parliament, one of Pilsudski's main aims was a reform of the constitution. The amendment of 2 August 1926 seemed all the less satisfactory because it left Parliament with the power to overthrow Governments which it did not like and – at any rate according to the letter of the law – to form new Cabinets. In Pilsudski's view it was not the business of the Sejm to rule; it should simply act as a check on the Government. Impressed by these considerations, the Sejm club of the BBWR introduced as early as 6 February 1929 a draft reform worked out by Jan Pilsudski – the marshal's brother – which was quite moderate and still preserved the forms of parliamentary government. But in 1929 the BBWR was still too weak to force through this project against the opposition of all the other parties. Up to the elections of November 1930 the Government resorted to tricks of interpretation; acting on the advice of the lawyer Stanislaw Car, it interpreted the existing provisions of the constitution in a way that verged on distortion of the law. The Conservatives in the BBWR objected to this practice, for they were afraid of its demoralizing effects. In these circumstances they would have preferred the straightforward dictation of a new constitution, which would then have had to be accepted as binding. However, they did not succeed in forcing the adoption of their point of view.

When the elections of November 1930 gave the Government a parliamentary majority, Pilsudski possessed the means to have the constitution altered in a legitimate, or at any rate legal, way. In conjunction with his brother, the marshal had devoted a great deal of work to testing all the recognized kinds of constitution. On 26 November 1930 he made it known that the future State would be based on 'three main factors': the Presidency, the Government and the Parliament. The constitution would comprise 'a sort of agreement or treaty between these main motive forces'. In an interview which he gave on 13 December Pilsudski left no doubt, it is true, that he wanted to give the position of President, which had once been deliberately weakened with a view to his own candidature, particularly strong powers, and then to take it over himself by means of a nation-wide election. On the other hand, he did not want to govern as Prime Minister at the same time, like the American President. Stanislaw Car and the Vilna judge Bohdan Podoski worked out a draft based on Pilsudski's ideas. Work on the constitution was directed by Slawek, who resigned his second premiership on 26 May 1931 for this purpose. After two years' work Slawek was able to lay his proposals before the Sejm on 26 May 1931. Apart from modern anti-liberal theories and American models, the most decisive influence on the new draft constitution was Car's 'Six Power Doctrine', which instead of adopting Montesquieu's classic tripartite division aimed at splitting authority between the President, the Government, the military high command, the Sejm, the Senate and the judicature. The principle of the Government's responsibility to Parliament was preserved, but Leopold Jaworski conceived the idea that in all the more important matters of state the President should be released from the obligation of having his decrees counter-signed by the Prime Minister. The legislative powers of the Sejm were restricted by the creation of a strong Senate. However, Slawek's sentimental suggestion that the Senate should consist of the holders of high decorations did not meet with Pilsudski's approval. Two-thirds of the Senate were to be elected and the remaining third appointed, but the whole of the Sejm was to be elected; the method of election was to be subject to special legal arrangements. The final draft was adopted by the Sejm on 26 January 1935. The new constitution was given the force of law by the President's signature on 23 April 1935.

The ratification of this constitution illuminated Pilsudski's last political aims. He was not concerned, as Hitler was, to establish an unrestricted autocracy, but to educate his people, to form a new *élite* to guide the democracy. It was not for nothing that he had warned Hitler on 11 December 1933 of the dangers of 'overdoing dictatorial measures' and repeatedly quoted Goethe's reminder that it is self-discipline that makes the master. Thus the opposition's argument that this constitution would turn Poland into an 'Asiatic satrapy' and its President into an 'uncrowned king' missed the point of Pilsudski's aims. The marshal had never aimed at consolidating personal absolutism; he simply wanted to transform the parliamentary form of government into a constitutional one. That is what he meant when he used the story of Alexander and Bucephalus to illustrate that only a master could control the people, a rider with a soft hand, as it were. Unfortunately in the years in which his hand had to hold the reins in Poland it had become too stiff; too many trials of strength had worn his nerves out, and the fascinating talker, who had once been able to cast a spell on his political opponents, had turned into a lonely, embittered man, who amazed those close to him with his terse and often cynical aphorisms. But even now the wealth of his ideas, his capacity for observing moderation and the nobility of his intentions could not be doubted. With the new constitution he sought to ensure the permanence of his life's work, and he unquestionably succeeded in this aim to a certain extent. His constitution managed at any rate to preserve the continuity and international existence of the Polish Republic through the Second World War. The constitution of 1921 would not have been capable of doing this. A final proof of the vitality of the Pilsudski constitution was the fact that in many respects it provided the model for the constitution which General de Gaulle succeeded in inducing France to adopt in 1958.

If the constitution of 23 April nevertheless rendered poor service to the Polish nation in the years from 1935 to 1939, that was because Pilsudski was already mortally ill when it was ratified, and the office of President, meant for him, fell into the hands of an untalented man. If the weakness of the 1921 constitution was its distortion to thwart Pilsudski, the Achilles heel of the new one was the fact that it was tailored to suit the person of the marshal. On top of this came the later, unhappy conception of an electoral class, which freed the Government from any control by society and gave the constitutional structure a similarity to totalitarian constitutions which was quite alien to the spirit and the letter of the Pilsudski constitution.

Pilsudski died on 12 May 1935, a few weeks after the ratification of his constitution and nine years to the day after his *coup d'état*. He may well have been haunted by premonitions of death at the time of his seizure of power; the words of his Order of the Day of 22 May 1926 seemed to hint at this. His death seemed a catastrophe, a forewarning of dark days to come, like the storm which burst over the army's funeral parade in Mokotow field. The whole Polish nation mourned its marshal as his coffin made its way on a gun-carriage from the Belvedere Castle in Warsaw to the royal tombs on the Wawel at Cracow. Grief made Poles forget the era of the 'moral dictatorship' and remember instead the achievements of the revolutionary, the fighter for freedom, the creator of the State. There was anxiety about the insufficiently assured future of the State, and Poles of all parties became aware that in Pilsudski they had lost, as it were, the last great ruler of the epoch of the Jagellonians.

CHAPTER V

Poland as an Authoritarian State
(1935-1939)

PILSUDSKI'S SUCCESSORS

In 1935 the world economic crisis was still affecting Poland, although in the rest of Europe it had long passed its most critical point. On the one hand it caused the general impoverishment of the peasants, since the prices of farm produce had fallen even lower than those of industrial products, and on the other it drove unemployment to its highest point. There were about a million and a half unemployed – a sixth of the working population. At the same time the over-population resulting from the structure of the country made itself felt, for in spite of the intensive efforts of previous Governments it had not been possible to do more than slightly reduce this problem and in 1935 it embraced between five and nine million people, that is, between a fifth and a quarter of the total population. These tensions in the structure of society produced a tendency to political extremism which was reflected in a hardening of the opposition movements. Hitherto the opposition had at any rate felt some compunction for Pilsudski as a personality, but they had no reason to spare his successors. Thus the death of the 'direction-setter' of the Left left those who stepped into his shoes with a series of very difficult if not impossible tasks.

The first question posed by Pilsudski's death was that of a stable succession. Among the ruling colonels, Walery Slawek was indubitably the most powerful political personality, for he held not only the post of Prime Minister but also the leadership of the Government party, the BBWR; moreover, it had been the marshal's wish that Slawek should take over the presidency and thus succeed to his political position. However, in the week after Pilsudski's death it was agreed among those in power that for the time being Moscicki should remain President; on the other hand, Slawek was formally confirmed as Prime Minister on 20 May 1935. Supreme command of the army was assumed by General Edward Rydz-Smigly as 'Inspector General of the Armed Forces' (GISZ). Some colonels would have preferred to see General Sosnkowski, who was undoubtedly far more capable, in this post; but it turned out that Rydz-Smigly had purposely been kept away from political questions by Pilsudski and thus apparently marked out for the supreme command, while Sosnkowski was *persona non grata* because of his attitude in the *coup d'état* of 1926. In connection with the reshuffle of the Government, Moscicki dissolved the National Assembly, so that it could be reconstituted in accordance with the constitution of 23 April 1935.

For the new elections Slawek introduced on 6 June 1935 a set of electoral regulations drafted by himself and his predecessor, Kozlowski; they received the force of law on 8 July. The method of electing the members of the Sejm, now 208 in number, remained the same ('free, equal, direct, secret and proportional'), but Kozlowski had managed to ensure that the district electoral assemblies played a decisive role in the designation of candidates. These assemblies[1] were dominated by the representatives of the authorities, of the territorial or communal autonomous institutions and of the professional organizations. Previously, 50 independent citizens had been able to put forward a candidate; now this number was raised to 500. Provisions of this sort were aimed against the political parties, and Slawek approved them because, like Pilsudski, he wanted to limit the freedom, often abused, to make party political decisions and alliances; on the other hand, with these electoral laws he opened the gates to the pursuance of a policy of pure self-interest by the propertied classes, and also gave the Government the opportunity to manipulate the elections

---

[1] There was one for each of the 104 zones or constituencies into which Poland was now divided. Each constituency sent two members to the Sejm. (Trans.)

through their district electoral commissioners. The electorate which chose the 64 elected senators – another 32 were to be appointed by the President – consisted of a political *élite* embracing the holders of high decorations, high-ranking officers, academics, teachers – including non-academic ones – and officials of the autonomous institutions and professional bodies. These electors were to constitute voivodeship (i.e. provincial) colleges, from whose members the senators were to be chosen. The electoral campaign began on 14 August 1935, but it was a purely fictitious one, since it was boycotted by all parties from the National Democrats to the Communists. As a result, in the actual elections, which took place on 8 and 15 September, only 46·5 per cent of the electorate voted in the country as a whole, and in Warsaw only 30·1 per cent. The Government won a complete victory, but it was only a formal one. One hundred and fifty-three out of the 208 members of the Sejm, and 45 out of the 64 elected senators, belonged to the Government camp. The number of Government supporters was still further increased by the nomination of another 32 senators; among them were three former Prime Ministers – Prystor, Jedrzejewicz, and Kozlowski – Foreign Minister Beck, and Prince Radziwill, who had opposed the electoral laws right to the end. How disadvantageous the boundaries of the constituencies were to the minorities was shown by the fact that over ten million citizens belonging to minorities – in other words, about a third of the total population – were able to capture only an eighth of the elected seats; yet in the eastern provinces 56 to 67 per cent of the electorate had voted, and in Upper Silesia as high a proportion as 77 per cent. The White Russians, Lithuanians and Czechs were left without any representation at all, while the German minority, which was over a million strong, was represented by two senators of German nationality appointed by Moscicki.

The apparent consolidation of the régime by these elections provoked struggles for power inside the ruling circle. Slawek did not wish to force Moscicki to resign the presidency – a step which Slawek certainly possessed the power to take – in case he incurred the charge of selfishness. In addition, on 12–13 October 1935 he handed over the premiership to Marian Zundram-Koscial-kowski, once a member of the Liberation party. The new Cabinet included two experts co-opted at Moscicki's wish, Eugeniusz Kwiatkowski as Finance Minister and Juliusz Poniatowski as Minister of Agriculture. A college of high officials came into existence, a sort of inner Cabinet which was the real ruling body of the State; it comprised Moscicki as the holder of the highest civil power, Rydz as the supreme commander of the armed forces, the Prime Minister as head of the Government, Colonel Beck as the director of foreign policy and sometimes also Kwiatkowski, the 'economic dictator'. With the dissolution, on 30 October 1935, of the bbwr, which until then he had been able to control as rigidly as if it had been a cavalry regiment, Slawek committed political suicide. It was a testimony to his idealism, which was as unpractical as it was attractive, that from his premierships and his almost uninterrupted leadership of the bbwr from 1927 to 1935 he gained nothing but a small box of personal effects and a collected edition of the works of Pilsudski.

As a result of the dissolution of the bbwr, the Government camp broke up into individual 'lobbies', which included a Rydz party, a Moscicki party, a group springing from the Zet, known as the 'Improvers of the Republic', and many other small factions. The most important man in Parliament was still Slawek, whom most of the members supported because of his blameless character; Prystor, the Speaker of the Senate, and Car, the Speaker of the Sejm, were also on his side. Moscicki, who until Pilsudski's death had confined himself to somewhat extravagant representational functions, was able, thanks to his political cunning, to preserve and develop the power given to him by the constitution. In opposition to him, many of the older colonels supported the soft and indolent Rydz. This situation led gradually to the formation of a Rydz–Moscicki duumvirate, which received a sort of institutional confirmation by the nomination of Rydz on 12 May 1936 as commander-in-chief – a post which really existed only in wartime – and the appointment on 15 May of Felicjan Slawoj-Skladkowski, hitherto Deputy War Minister, as Premier. After that, and right up to the catastrophe of September 1939, the Cabinet was divided into the Rydz faction, which centred round Skladkowski and Tadeusz Kasprzycki, the War Minister, and the Moscicki faction, which included Kwiatkowski and Poniatowski. In Parliament, Colonels Koc and Boguslaw Miedzynski transferred their support from Slawek to Rydz. Prime Minister Skladkowski, a brave and dauntless if somewhat limited soldier, carried out his duties 'at the command of the Inspector General', as he admitted himself in his policy speech of 16 May 1936; on 13 July 1936 he circulated a decree in which he made it the duty of all officials – he did not exclude himself – to show 'respect and obedience' to Rydz. This instruction seemed to show a contemptuous disregard for the constitution of 23 April 1935. With his elevation to the rank of marshal on 10 November 1936, Rydz was finally thrust into the role of a military successor to Pilsudski. Yet the 'Supreme Leader' brought no other gift to the myth woven round him than personal bravery. Without any real political or strategic talent, he had to rely on his charm, his good seat on a horse and the elegance of his speeches in order to make an impression.

The most pressing political tasks of the régime were to overcome the economic misery and quickly reduce the agrarian overpopulation. The Government tried to measure up to these tasks partly by adopting the views of the Endecja and partly by taking over ideas from contemporary movements like National Socialism and Bolshevism. The 'Four Year Plan' which Kwiatkowski launched on 10 June 1936 sought to remove the social reasons for the internal crises by gradually reducing unemployment; on 5 February 1937 it was modified to serve the economic needs of defence by a new Four Year Plan which aimed particularly at the creation of a 'Central Industrial Region' (COP). However, this programme too could be only partly carried out owing to the lack of investment capital and the inadequacy of the assistance provided by France. The only possibility left was the compulsory distribution of land, and Poniatowski carried this out as a last resort, although he was perfectly conscious of its inadequacy. The mockery which 'Poniatowski's villages' provoked was really quite undeserved.

In these circumstances, the organization of a new Government bloc – a task which Rydz commissioned Colonel Koc to carry out in June 1936 – was only accomplished with considerable difficulty. The opposition parties stood aside on principle, and after nine months of negotiation even Slawek and his group, Moraczewski and the Government trade unions and the conservatives all refused to co-operate. Koc's 'policy declaration' of 21 February 1937 was therefore predominantly based, in spite of its ideological eclecticism, on the National Democrat programme. The 'Camp of National Union' (OZN) was finally set up on 1 March 1937; although it sought to imitate the genuine mass movements of contemporary Europe, it actually consisted mainly of officers, officials, functionaries and small organizations loyal to the Government or dependent on it. It only formed an institutional substitute for the old BBWR, whose breadth it did not attain.

Opposition to the régime and the OZN was centred in the left-wing workers' and peasants' parties. Since April 1936 the PPS had unleashed a series of powerful large-scale strikes. Alongside the PPS, the Communist Party of Poland (KPP) was gaining a certain importance for the first time; in May 1936 it took the initiative in proposing a Popular Front which, like those in France and Spain, was to embrace all parties of the Left and Centre. In people like Adolf Warski, Wera Kostrzewa (a pupil of Rosa Luxemburg's) and Julian Lenski (a friend of Lenin's) the KPP possessed a number of gifted leaders who were nearer to Trotsky than to Stalin in their thinking and whose sense of patriotism led them to try to find their own middle way between Stalinist Soviet nationalism and proletarian internationalism. In fact, their mode of thinking won over some of the younger workers and peasants, but the bulk of the PPS and the Peasant Party (SL) rejected the idea of a Popular Front. Socially and numerically, the SL was the most important party in the left-wing opposition. The degree of despair already reached by the peasants was shown by the action of Adam

Doboszynski, who in June 1936 occupied the little provincial town of Myslenice with a band of peasant partisans and deposed the Government authorities. At its congress on 17 January 1937 the SL chose leaders with radical views headed by the Posen co-operative secretary Stanislaw Mikolajczyk; this was a sign how much ground the Conservative–Catholic wing under Rataj had gradually had to yield. The social revolutionary attitude of the SL was reflected in a country-wide strike of agricultural workers (15–25 August 1937), which in some places was suppressed with bloodshed, and the steady demand for a peasant Government under the exiled Witos. The right-wing opposition also reorganized itself. At the instigation of Paderewski and Sikorski, some of the older Catholic politicians such as Jozef Haller, Stanislaw Wojciechowski, Stanislaw Grabski and Wojciech Korfanty founded on 10 October 1937 the 'Labour Party' (SP), which was based on the union of the Christian Democrats with the National Workers' Party. The Labour Party, which resembled the German Centre Party in its ideology, tried through its influential Press to lead public opinion in a Francophil and anti-Pilsudski direction. In the National Party (SN),[1] the influence of the 'young men' made itself felt even more decisively; the older group centred round Stronski drew closer to the SP. Finally, on 12 December 1937, the conservatives also united to form their own party under Adolf Bninski; Janusz Radziwill lost much of his influence. However, in comparison with the four big parties – SN, SL, SP and PPS – which from now to the end of the Second World War were to govern the formation of Polish political opinion, the conservatives were hardly more than the representatives of a stratum of society.

Compelled to choose between right- and left-wing oppositions, Koc steered the OZN in the direction of the right wing of the National Party. He sought to win over the National Radicals, especially the young intelligentsia which they controlled, and therefore started negotiations with the semi-legal, conspiratorial successors of the ONR such as the 'ABC' group and the 'Falanga' of Boleslaw Piasecki. Piasecki seconded his adjutant, Rutkowski,

[1] i.e., the old National Democrats.

to the 'Union of Polish Youth' (ZMP) founded by Koc on 22 June 1937, so that Rutkowski could organize it on lines suggested by Koc as a sort of State youth organization; but owing to the antagonism of the opposition parties the ZMP remained a small group, and Piasecki recalled Rutkowski. However, the decisive factor was that Koc – and with him Rydz – came up against the resistance of the Slawek group and the 'Improvers of the Republic', who regarded the totalitarian and functional rigidity of both the OZN and the ZMP as harmful, and demanded a certain liberalization of parliamentary life. They were supported by Moscicki, who in the Cabinet meeting of 7 October 1937 decided in favour of a swing to the left and on 13 November received a delegation of the PPS – the first such delegation to be received since June 1929. Even though the leaders of the PPS, headed by Arciszewski and Niedzialkowski, declined to co-operate in any way with the Government, the OZN's totalitarian claims could no longer be sustained. On 1 December 1937, by forming a 'parliamentary club', the OZN turned itself into one party among others; Koc had to be dropped by Rydz. With the appointment of Stanislaw Skwarczynski, a general on the active list, as head of the OZN – a step which Rydz took on 10 January 1938 – the organization lost most of its political character. The OZN, whose only motive according to Skwarczynski was to be the 'gathering together of all true Poles', became an organization auxiliary to the army for minor officials and opportunists. The 'Improvers' group alone gave its 'Supreme Council', set up in April 1938, a certain political colouring.

Slawek and his friends in Parliament worked against the OZN both directly and by infiltration; after Koc's dismissal numerous OZN politicians, especially those of the older, democratic persuasion, went over to Slawek. The strength of Slawek's parliamentary position was shown when Car died on 18 June 1938 and left the office of Speaker vacant. At the proposal of old General Zeligowski, on 22 June 1938 Slawek was chosen as Car's successor, by 114 votes to 62. Of the 62 votes against him, 30 were cast by the 'Improvers' and 32 by the Government bloc. Since Slawek's group was in contact with the left-wing opposition and in certain respects took over its legal parliamentary representation, it seemed exceptionally dangerous to the Government. On 22 September 1938 President Moscicki therefore dissolved both chambers. It was possible to manipulate the elections in such a way that when voting took place on 6 and 13 November 1938 (67·4 per cent of the electorate actually voted) the OZN was able to win almost all the elected seats in the Senate and 161 out of 208 seats in the Sejm. Slawek himself was not re-elected, and was thus silenced. The minorities were just as inadequately represented as in the previous National Assembly. Thus the last Parliament of the period between the wars provided a field of action for one-party rule, at last achieved, and President Moscicki did not fail to consolidate the governmental system by issuing on 21–22 November 1938 decrees dealing with the protection of the State and the Press. That these elections had by no means reflected the true state of opinion in Poland – at any rate so far as the non-peasant population was concerned – was shown by the municipal elections of 18 December, which were conducted in the traditional democratic way. In the municipal councils of Warsaw, Lodz, Cracow and Posen, the OZN received only between 13 per cent and 39 per cent of the votes cast; the PPS and the Jewish–Socialist 'Bund' together won 43 per cent of the votes in Warsaw, 35 per cent – a relative majority – in Cracow, and 55 per cent – an absolute majority – in Lodz. The National Party, which in Congress Poland lost vast numbers of votes to the OZN, remained dominant in Posen with 74 per cent. The Labour Party could only attain regional significance because it was a party of 'old men' and received its impetus from Poles in exile. Thus, on the whole, political opinion in the towns of Poland was divided into socialist and *bourgeois* currents – the latter being more or less equally represented by the OZN and the SN – while in the country the SL was the dominant party.

The coming Germano–Polish conflict, which was evident by March 1939, produced a superficial agreement between Government and Opposition in internal affairs. The prime importance of foreign affairs and national defence robbed internal differences of any practical significance even if it did not resolve them. In March and April 1939 the President received the representatives of the Opposition parties and listened to their declarations of loyalty; the politicians who had gone into exile after being imprisoned at Brest were allowed to return home and after a short period of 'symbolical arrest' to resume their political activities. Thus Polish political thinking was once more transferred to the four great Opposition parties, which, after the catastrophe of September 1939, were to preserve its traditions through the Second World War.

Nevertheless, the death of many respected politicians in the years before the Second World War seemed to be a kind of indication that the Poland of the generation which had founded the State was doomed to disappear. Of those who had prepared the way for independence, Bobrzynski and the centenarian Limanowski had already died in 1935; Daszynski and Wasilewski followed in 1936, and Wladyslaw Grabski in 1938. 2 January 1939 saw the death of Roman Dmowski, the thinker who had done most to develop Polish political thought, and Wojciech Korfanty, who had won Upper Silesia for Poland, died seven months later. But the public was shocked most of all by the suicide of Walery Slawek, who shot himself on 2 April 1939 in front of a picture of Pilsudski with the very same pistol with which he had fought in the ranks of the PPS in 1905. Slawek had been commissioned by Pilsudski to take over the presidency, and the impossibility of carrying out this task weighed on him heavily. He felt near to Pilsudski when he wrote as a farewell message, 'God will forgive me this last sin too'. What primarily drove Slawek to suicide was probably that he saw Poland's horizon clouded over all round, and that the constitution on which he had worked had become a reality which was repugnant to its creator. Thus his death symbolized the defeat of a concept of the state which Pilsudski had always sought, even if with inappropriate methods, to uphold.

Poland as an Authoritarian State (1935–1939)

THE POLICY OF THE 'THIRD EUROPE'

After Pilsudski's death Poland's foreign policy was confronted with the problem of orientating itself anew in face of the Franco–Soviet–Czech alliance created in May 1935. It was in Poland's interest to go on cultivating the old alliance with France as a safeguard against Hitler without, however, endangering the officially friendly Germano–Polish relationship or, on the other hand, letting the political influence of the Soviet Union in central Europe grow too powerful. Colonel Beck, who as Pilsudski's heir in foreign affairs swiftly attained a large measure of independence in the conduct of foreign policy, tried first to consolidate the friendly relationship with Germany by a visit to Hitler on 3 July 1935. However, he had continually to take account of the French bias of the generals, who, like the German military staff, wanted to continue older traditions in foreign policy without modification. When the German Government started a European crisis on 7 March 1936 by sending troops into the Rhineland and at the same time unilaterally denouncing the Locarno Pact, Polish foreign policy seemed to be faced with the necessity of choosing between a German and a French orientation. Beck's analysis of the situation – one later confirmed by the behaviour of the French Government – was that France would not take military action; thus, with the help of a purely formal offer of alliance to France on the one hand and pacificatory explanations to Germany on the other, he was able to steer the Polish Republic through the threatening conflict unscathed, without affecting relations with either of the two powers. Since the collapse of the Locarno treaties of 1925 had also nullified the Franco–Polish guarantee pact, in April 1936 Beck managed to have the old bilateral pact of 1921 regarded as unreservedly valid again. Rydz-Smigly's subsequent visit to Paris secured the Rambouillet Agreement of 3 September 1936, by which Poland received a loan from France. Even though this financial help was to mean little in practical terms owing to the devaluation of the franc, it did signify that a certain degree of political *rapprochement* between France and Poland had been achieved.

The conflict between Germany and Russia, or National Socialism and Bolshevism, which culminated in the summer of 1936 in the Spanish Civil War, the Soviet Popular Front policy and the intensification of German re-armament through Göring's 'Four Year Plan', seemed to Beck to be irreconcilable, to be in fact a sort of religious war. Simply because of the huge Soviet armaments he cultivated relations with Germany; but on the other hand he firmly refused to join the Anti-Comintern Pact of 25 November 1936 – with which Hitler, unknown to Beck, was playing a secret double game – in order to preserve the balance, at any rate formally, between the two powerful neighbouring powers and to give the Government of the USSR no excuse for unleashing a conflict. To Hitler, the fundamentally anti-Soviet attitude of the Polish Government was extremely valuable, since Poland covered the eastern flank of the German Reich while he was applying pressure – as he had been since November 1937 – against Austria and Czechoslovakia. Moreover, Hitler always hoped to be able to win over Poland one day as an ally for an anti-Soviet crusade, as was shown by his continually repeated, though always rejected, overtures to the Polish Government. For this reason he put a stop to the attempts of Forster, the Gauleiter of Danzig, to achieve unification of the Free City with the Reich; Hitler's declarations of 5 November 1937 and 20 February 1938 that he was willing to respect the *status quo* in Danzig were only comprehensible as moves in his long-term policy of winning German living-space in the east. These declarations confirmed Beck's view that, in spite of the internal *Gleichschaltung* of the city, Polish rights in Danzig were safe because of the importance of Poland to Hitler.

The apparently axiomatic nature of the antagonism between Hitler and Stalin, and also the further complication of German policy towards Austria and the Czechoslovak Republic, caused Beck to conceive the plan of creating an eastern central European bloc in the form of the so-called 'Third Europe'. Alongside the traditional Franco–British entente and the newly-created Rome–Berlin Axis, an alliance of the smaller States of eastern central

Europe was to be constructed, combining the Baltic countries with the Danubian and Balkan countries in a neutral bloc under Polish leadership; this bloc seemed suited to the preservation of neutrality in the expected Germano–Soviet 'religious war'. It was true that, owing to their hostility to Poland, the Czechoslovak Republic and Lithuania opened breaches in this projected system; however, Beck believed that the Czechoslovak problem would solve itself through the break-up of the Czechoslovak Republic, which he discreetly furthered. When, with the German annexation of Austria on 11–13 March 1938, a development long foreseen and secretly supported by Polish diplomacy finally took place, he forced Lithuania to open diplomatic relations with Poland; he was thus able to put a formal end to a seventeen-year-old conflict without fundamentally removing the cause of the quarrel about the Vilna region. The renewal of economic links and of communications with Lithuania took place step by step in the summer of 1938, even though this process created a new potential source of conflict between Poland and Germany because of Polish economic interests in Memel. When the so-called 'May crisis' of 20–22 May 1938 arose, with the Czechoslovak mobilization and Hitler's resulting decision to crush Czechoslovakia that same autumn, and the very serious nature of the Germano–Czech conflict became clear, Beck saw the situation as a confirmation of his thesis that the Czechoslovak Republic was bound to break up. He made use of the crisis to force the Prague Government to promise on 24 May that it would solve the problem of the Polish minority in Teschen on the same basis as it solved the Sudeten German problem. Beck had obviously recognized by then that Hitler was only using the annexation of the Sudetenland as a pretext and was really concerned to destroy Czechoslovakia. Beck used this situation without a second thought to press specifically Polish claims against a still unsuspecting Prague Government. Behind his demand for autonomy for the Poles of Teschen was the expectation that the Czechoslovak Republic was going to disintegrate, with the consequence that Slovakia would split off and the desired Polish–Hungarian frontier would be created.

155

Beck had been in contact with the Hungarian Government since February about the form in which Slovakia could be attached to Hungary in the future.

The Munich decisions of 29 September 1938 brought the annexation of the Sudetenland by Germany, but also the progressive disintegration of Czechoslovakia and the complete break-up of the Franco–Soviet–Czech alliance of May 1935. Beck exploited Czechoslovakia's difficult position to extort the cession of Teschen in accordance with the promise of 24 May. The cession actually took place on 1 October 1938, in accordance with the terms of the Polish ultimatum, although the Munich decisions had provided for a delay of three months. This territorial acquisition, which was complemented during the course of the next few weeks by the annexation of a few border districts in the Carpathians, brought Poland a considerable addition to her industrial potential and strengthened her strategic position in the Moravian gate; Beck had thus gained a substantial, if only superficial, triumph. Quite obviously he underestimated the fundamental importance of the post-war treaties on which the territorial integrity not only of Czechoslovakia but also of Poland rested. Moreover, he cannot have realized the full significance of the weakening of Czechoslovakia and of the huge increase in Hitler's power; this was made clear by the irrationality of his own political manœuvres after the Munich crisis. No one paid any attention to the prophecy of the Czech general who handed over the city and region of Teschen to the Polish forces and remarked as he did so that he was convinced that Poland would soon have to give up her new acquisition to Hitler.

With the Teschen question settled, Beck saw the way clear for the establishment of the common Polish-Hungarian frontier which he regarded as the first essential of a 'Third Europe' and for which he had been secretly working for years. He tried to forward this aim by actively supporting the Slovakian nationalist movement – on 6 October it had decided in favour of remaining within the Czechoslovak Republic for the time being – and by energetically combating Ukrainian nationalism in the autonomous

Carpathian Ukraine (Ruthenia), especially as this was affecting the Ukrainians of eastern Galicia. His plan envisaged the incorporation of Slovakia and the Carpathian Ukraine in Hungary, apart from frontier corrections in Poland's favour, or else nominally independent Slovakian Republic under Polish–Hungarian protection. In Berlin Beck described the Polish–Hungarian north-south axis, which was to be extended to include Rumania, Yugoslavia and Italy, as a protective wall against the intrusion of Soviet influence into the Balkans; in London and Paris he turned the argument round and claimed that the new axis would act as a barrier against German expansion in the Balkans. However, immediately after Munich Beck came up against the all-embracing policy of Hitler, who took over the protection of the whole of Czechoslovakia – if only provisionally and for tactical reasons – and in the Vienna award of 2 November 1938 assured the republic's continuance for the time being at the price of the cession of territory to Hungary. The Czechoslovak cross-bar, so inconvenient for Beck's plans, continued to exist in the form of a German-protected State. In spite of the collapse of his plans for Czechoslovakia, Beck tried to ensure the military occupation of the Carpatho-Ukraine by Hungary, but Hitler abruptly put a stop to this idea on 19–20 November 1938. In this way Hitler used his supremacy in the Danube and Balkan region to block the conception of a Polish-led 'Third Europe' in favour of his own plans for central Europe. Beck met similar opposition from Hitler in the Baltic area. It became quite clear that Beck was inclined to overestimate the political power of Poland, not least because of the exaggerated importance attached to geo-political considerations in the period between the wars. Although his master Pilsudski had often warned him of the danger, declaring that he had enough ideas for ten Polands, but not the means, Beck let himself be carried away by a misplaced romanticism which made a particularly painful impression because in his choice of methods he was often downright cynical.

THE RETURN TO GERMAN–POLISH HOSTILITY

Like Beck, Hitler saw in the Munich decisions a chance to acquire the hegemony of central Europe. By creating an association of States with a common purpose in eastern central Europe, he sought to gain a politico-military base for operations against the ussr. During this period immediately after the Munich conference he employed a policy of 'defensive cover in the west' towards England and France. In Hitler's view, the heart of this German-led eastern central Europe was Poland, and this is the key to the famous suggestions which he made to Poland for the first time on 24 October 1938. This 'global solution' envisaged the reintegration of Danzig in Germany in return for the safeguarding of Polish rights in Danzig through a free port and an extra-territorial access to it; and, vice versa, the 'Corridor' was to be bridged by a likewise extra-territorial traffic artery. In addition, Poland was offered the prospect of an extension of the validity of the 1934 Germano–Polish pact to 25 years, formal recognition of the Germano–Polish frontiers and concessions in the question of the Polish–Hungarian frontier. So far Hitler's proposals seemed acceptable, indeed more moderate than Stresemann's plans; but the most important condition, and to Poland the most critical one, was the demand that she should join the anti-Comintern pact. Such a step was calculated to compromise Poland hopelessly *vis-à-vis* the ussr, whereas Hitler, as a result of the secret agreement with Japan (an agreement unknown to the Poles), possessed the possibility of renewed co-operation with the Soviet Union. Even though the Warsaw Government could not yet take into account this aspect of a possible fresh partition of Poland, nevertheless it regarded Hitler's proposals as suspect and in the last analysis unacceptable; the enormous superiority in political power of Germany, whose satellite Poland would have become had she accepted Hitler's proposals, the resulting loss of prestige by the insecurely based Polish Government, the warning example of the eighteenth-century partitions, which had likewise begun with small concessions, and finally the insistence by the Germans on linking the question of the 'Corridor' with that of the anti-Comintern pact, all pointed in one direction.

Beck at first regarded the German demands as suggestions, not as a firm programme, and on 19 November 1938 declined them in veiled language. The earnestness of Hitler's conception only became clear to him during the Berchtesgaden conversations of 5–6 January 1939, when both Hitler and Ribbentrop insisted on the principle of 'all or nothing'. With the agreement of Marshal Rydz-Smigly and President Moscicki, Beck finally rejected Hitler's offers during Ribbentrop's visit to Warsaw on 25, 26, and 27 January 1939. Even – or perhaps precisely – the compensations which the German foreign minister offered in the still-to-be-conquered Soviet Ukraine could not make the leaders of the Polish State change their minds. Although Hitler now turned away from the Polish question and again actively set about destroying Czechoslovakia, the materials for future conflicts and the beginning of a war of nerves were now at hand.

The partition of Czechoslovakia, which Hitler achieved on 14–15 March 1939 contrary to Germany's real interests, was at first welcomed by the Warsaw Government, since with the splitting off of Slovakia and the occupation of Ruthenia by Hungary Beck's long-held political aims seemed to have been fulfilled. However, when only six days later, on 21 March 1939, Ribbentrop repeated the German proposals to Poland in a form which really amounted to an ultimatum without a time limit, the mood in Warsaw changed as rapidly and completely as it had in London. The re-incorporation of Memel in Germany on 22 March, the creation of a German protectorate over Slovakia on 23 March and the Germano–Rumanian trade treaty of 23 March showed very clearly that Poland was surrounded by the power of Germany both in the north and the south and that consequently all attempts to create a Third Europe had been nipped in the bud. But the really decisive point was that Hitler had broken only a few months later the solemn assurances which he had given at Munich and thus revealed the unscrupulous Machiavellianism or pseudo-Machiavellianism of his policy. When he now suddenly remembered the sufferings of the German minority in Poland, which he had intentionally disregarded for five years for the sake of larger political aims, he revealed to everyone that fundamentally it was not a question of this minority's rights but of making use of it to destroy Poland from within. It seemed clear that the methods used so successfully against Czechoslovakia were now to be turned against Poland. The first victims of these machinations were the Germans in Poland, who from now on were persecuted more and more.

In this desperate situation Poland acquired an unexpected ally in the shape of British public opinion. It too took the view that the point had now been reached when it was essential to say 'thus far and no further'. On 21 March, under the pressure of British public opinion, and in response to a call for help (for which there was in fact no reason) from the king of Roumania, Neville Chamberlain suggested a consultative pact to include England, France, the USSR and Poland. Beck agreed to this on 23 March, but at the same time requested the swift conclusion of a bilateral pact between Poland and Great Britain. On the same day, disturbed by German interference in Lithuania and Slovakia, Rydz-Smigly ordered a partial mobilization; four divisions were moved up to the East Prussian frontier. In view of these precautionary measures and of the news – which had no foundation in fact – that Germany intended to attack Poland at the end of March, the British Government decided to give a guarantee to Poland, especially as it had already decided in principle to assist Poland. Chamberlain gave this guarantee on 31 March 1939. Contrary to all previous diplomatic practice it guaranteed not the frontiers but the national integrity of Poland in the case of direct or indirect aggression. This elastic formula was intended to prevent the destruction of the Polish State from within by the German minority, but at the same time to leave open the possibility of a peaceful compromise in the form of frontier adjustments. However, the decision as to when the *casus foederis* had arisen was left to the Warsaw Government. This amazing renunciation of the right to decide between peace and war – a renunciation quite unique in the annals of British diplomacy, usually so cautious – could only be explained by the precedent of the occupation of Czechoslovakia and by the feeling in London that Poland was exposed to an acute military threat. On 2 April Beck travelled to London to replace the unilateral British guarantee, which seemed out of keeping with Polish prestige, by a bilateral treaty of assistance. Although he had been commissioned to conclude only a secret agreement, so that Hitler should not be unnecessarily provoked, on 6 April 1939 he signed the provisional Anglo–Polish treaty of assistance as a public pact.

The news of the signing of this treaty provided Hitler with the final motive for unleashing an open conflict. The partial Polish mobilization of 23 March had already irritated him in the same way as Benes' mobilization of 24 May 1938 had; the abrupt rejection of his proposals angered him still more, especially as it was accompanied, on 26 March, by the observation that any German attempt to seize Danzig would mean war. Hitler regarded the guarantee of 31 March as *carte blanche* for Poland to start a war whenever she pleased; he was incapable of realizing to what extent he himself had been responsible for bringing the Anglo–Polish alliance into existence. His hatred of England, nourished by Ribbentrop, was transferred to Poland, and on 3 April he gave orders – at first still intended to provide only for a contingency – to prepare for a military attack on Poland. The conclusion of the Anglo–Polish pact of 6 April finally convinced him that he was right in thinking that England was trying to 'encircle' Germany. So German military planning began on 11 April. On 28 April Hitler renounced the Germano–Polish pact, after convincing himself that it was in formal contradiction with the Anglo–Polish one. The era of illusory Germano–Polish friendship was at an end.

Beck replied to Hitler's acts on 5 May with the remark that peace was a valuable possession but the honour of the Polish nation was still more valuable. The open break with Germany was all the more critical for Poland because the Soviet Government, which had already hinted on 10 March at its readiness for negotiations with Germany, made its attitude quite clear on 3 May through the dismissal of the Foreign Minister, Litvinov, who was

friendly to the West. Beck failed to attach sufficient importance
to this warning sign, although it indicated a development which
could lead to a fresh Germano–Soviet entente. Moreover, this
new grouping was no longer comparable with the superficially
similar situation in the 'twenties, since both Germany and the
Soviet Union were now heavily armed and far stronger than
Poland. With Hitler and Stalin governing as pure dictators, the old
conceptions of a 'double frontier revision' or even of a new
partition revealed new and dangerous aspects. This new alliance
could certainly not be prevented by the Warsaw Government, but
owing to the prevailing idea that Bolshevism and National
Socialism were axiomatically opposed to each other its full significance was not even appreciated. This miscalculation revealed how
far Beck had departed from the sober judgements of Pilsudski.

WAR AND COLLAPSE OF THE REPUBLIC

Since the crisis which had begun on the Ides of March 1939 the
Polish public was aware of the acute danger of a military conflict
with Germany. Hitler's formal denunciation of the five-year-old
treaty with Poland was greeted with anxiety but also with a certain
relief. Open hostility was regarded as preferable to false friendship,
as it was in Germany too at that time. If war should turn out to
be unavoidable, both Government and nation felt that they could
accept it in the conviction that their cause was a just one. Considerable overestimation of Polish military strength and consequently of the country's power of resistance led not infrequently to
prognoses that were rather too optimistic.

The outbreak of the latest Germano–Polish conflict, papered
over since 1934, led to a clarification of the diplomatic situation in
central and eastern Europe. Up to March 1939 Poland's security
had been based almost exclusively on the traditional alliance with
France of 1921, and she now tried to consolidate it by negotiations
for the final confirmation of the British alliance and above all by
the conclusion of a new Franco–Polish military convention on
19 May; this convention obliged France to open an offensive
against the German forces with the bulk of her troops not later

than fifteen days after the mobilization of the French army. The Warsaw Government also negotiated with London and Paris for the provision of immediate financial, technical and operational assistance, but did not succeed in obtaining any binding assurances since the Western Powers wanted to avoid any definition of their obligations to provide direct help because of their own military weakness and their unfavourable geographical position. Hitler for his part, after making known to his close advisers his final decision to resort to war if Poland proved recalcitrant, tried to involve his allies, Italy and Japan, in the hostilities, but in both cases the invitation was rejected. The two Foreign Ministers, Beck and Ciano, had until now been united by common interests in the Danube area and by a similar approach to politics, while Poland and Japan had always maintained very friendly relations because of Soviet Russia. As a result of the division of Europe into Hitler's anti-Comintern group, consisting of Germany and Italy (this anti-Soviet coalition had by now become an anti-British one), and the Anglo-Franco-Polish alliance, the USSR enjoyed a key position. In fact it had been wooed since the spring of 1939 by the Western Powers, who tried to exploit the ideological conflict between National Socialism and Bolshevism, whereas Hitler only decided after a good deal of hesitation to enter into close contact with Soviet diplomacy. Nevertheless, he held the advantage in this diplomatic competition, since he was prepared to offer the Soviet Union territorial gains in eastern Poland, while the Western Powers were simply concerned to preserve existing frontiers. The Soviet choice of sides came in the middle of August 1939; the Government of the USSR, which had already more or less reached an understanding with Hitler, crippled the English and French efforts to obtain its support by making what was – as it knew very well – a demand unacceptable to the Polish Government of that day, namely that in the event of war Soviet troops should be allowed to march in to 'help' Poland through Vilna and Lwow. It was the news of this demand which first brought home to the Polish Government the mortal danger of a new partition of Poland.

How little the Polish leaders had so far reckoned with the military opposition of the USSR was shown by the nature of their operational preparations. The Polish plan of operations known as 'West', which was worked out hurriedly and never fully communicated to the army commanders, envisaged the massing of every conceivable fighting unit along the western frontiers. In face of the huge German superiority, the length of the Germano–Polish frontiers and the inclusion of Slovakia in the German superiority, the Polish staff was confronted with an almost insoluble task; it was hardly possible to counter the German strategy of encirclement in any effective way. Nevertheless, the evacuation of western Poland and the use of the Rivers Narew, Vistula and San as impassable anti-tank obstacles could have thwarted the German encircling move and created the possibility of a war of position, or at any rate gained a certain amount of time until English and French help became effective. However, this plan seemed unacceptable to Marshal Rydz-Smigly, since it would have presented the Germans straight away with the most important industrial regions and the best reservoirs of recruits. The suggestion of one of his army commanders that massed cavalry units should be sent into wooded Upper Silesia on the preventive mission of breaking up German troop movements was also ruled out by Rydz on moral grounds. Other factors which helped to tip the scales were a considerable overestimate, dictated by historical reasons, of the operational role of East Prussia, the aim of keeping a watch on Danzig with a special intervention corps, and finally a fatal underestimate of German operational possibilities in the area of the Moravian gate and the West Beskids.[1] Rydz-Smigly decided in favour of the plan to defend all frontiers; in other words, he chose a conception which dispersed the already weak Polish forces far too much and left only a minimum of reserves. Consequently, in spite of the bravery of the troops and the exceptional tactical skill of the regimental commanders, the Polish armies' defensive battle was lost before it began. But the Polish army command's greatest disadvantage was that it was necessarily behindhand in

[1] Mountains in south-west Poland.

the operational preparation of its units; it could hardly be made responsible for the fact that Hitler kept secret his decision to attack without any declaration of war and ordered that German troop movements should be carefully concealed. In addition, well-intentioned but militarily fatal interventions by Western diplomats led to a decisive delay in general mobilization. As a result of all this, when the German attack began, only about a third of the Polish army was ready for battle.

As well as making all necessary military preparations Hitler intensified his diplomatic preparations for the destruction of the Polish Republic. After a Press campaign – which drew a powerful response from the Polish side – had accumulated inflammatory material, and persecution of the Germans in Poland had reached such a pitch that the camps carefully prepared in Germany began to fill with fugitives, he arranged for a customs dispute to break out in Danzig, which had been secretly militarized. This made the Polish Government think that there might be an isolated *putsch* in Danzig and caused it to strengthen its troops in the corridor. Through C. J. Burckhardt, the German High Commissioner in Danzig, Hitler once again made a big effort, disguised as an attempt at mediation, to separate the Western Powers from Poland. That he already thought at this point that he could be sure of Russian support is shown by his words to Burckhardt on 11 August: 'If the Poles refuse to agree to my proposals, I shall destroy and partition Poland in concert with the USSR; but in the not-too-distant future I shall also attack the Soviet Union and take the east Polish territories away from it again; I need the Ukraine!'

August 23 saw the conclusion of a Germano–Soviet non-aggression pact and of a partition agreement – described as a 'secret additional protocol' – which defined the spheres of interest of Germany and the Soviet Union if the Polish Republic were obliterated; the dividing line ran 'roughly along the Rivers Narew, Vistula and San'. The Polish Government, which now became aware of the main outlines of the Germano–Soviet entente, was able to reply to it on 25 August with the formal signing of the treaty of assistance with Great Britain; the British Government was all the more ready to sign this pact because it wished to publish openly its decision to give military support to Poland, and thus to deliver a warning to Hitler. The German reproach that Great Britain had not made her participation in the First World War sufficiently clear in advance and had consequently contributed to the 'slide' into this war was not to be allowed to raise its head again. In fact, by concluding this treaty, the Governments of Poland and Great Britain did cause Hitler to withdraw on the evening of 25 August the order he had already given that hostilities were to begin on 26 August. However, this pause sprang only from temporary reflection, not from a fundamental renunciation by Hitler of military solutions. After a proposal for mediation cast in the form of an ultimatum, intended as a sort of alibi and communicated only by word of mouth to the British Government, and a supposedly Polish attack on Gleiwitz (Gliwice) radio station which was meant to serve as the *casus belli*, Hitler ordered that the invasion should begin on the morning of 1 September.

In contrast to the unfavourable military and political conditions for waging war with which Poland had to cope, for Germany the Polish campaign amounted to little more than the execution of a well-prepared plan. In spite of heroic stands by individual units, the deployment of the Polish armies and hence their defence plans were shattered in the first five days of the campaign. When on the night of 5–6 September Marshal Rydz-Smigly gave his army commanders the long-delayed permission to withdraw behind the Vistula, the German armoured columns were already in a position to enclose the bulk of the Polish field armies in a huge double pincer movement. The bitter counter-attacks of the Poznan and Pomorze (East Pomeranian) armies, which on 3–4 September could have still seriously endangered the German advance, were no longer capable of affecting the course of operations in the period from 9 to 11 September. Thus the battle on the Bzura formed the climax but not the strategic turning-point of the campaign. By 16 September the German columns advancing from north and south were able to join hands to the east of the Bug and thus encircle the still unbroken Polish field armies. When the last big units – the Poznan and Pomorze armies – capitulated on 19–21 September the campaign was operationally over, in spite of continued resistance in the fortresses of Warsaw, Lwow, Modlin and Hel. If what the Germans called 'the eighteen-day campaign' became the 'September catastrophe' for the Poles, this only endorsed the judgement of Pilsudski, who had regarded the high command as the weakest point in the Polish army. Even more telling was the technical and numerical inferiority of the Poles, and above all the absence of any help from the Western Powers; the French army fulfilled its obligation to open a general offensive within fifteen days by making a local and symbolical attack, although it outnumbered the German divisions confronting it by at least five to one.

The swift withdrawal of the Polish civil and military authorities before the advancing German army had tragic results during the early days of the campaign for the Germans living in Poland; many of them were deported, shot out of hand or murdered in the wave of national hatred which arose. If we include the victims of the so-called 'Bloody Sunday of Bydgoszcz' (3 September), the dead amounted to some 7,000. The widespread view that the Germans in Poland had formed a 'fifth column' corresponded to the truth in only a few cases; on the other hand, a considerable number of Germans serving as loyal Polish soldiers were killed by the bullets and shells of the German army. The murders occasioned by anti-German rioting were important in that they provided the German propaganda machine with material for its official description of the reasons for the war and contributed to Hitler's decision to punish the Polish people mercilessly after its defeat.

The Polish Government, which retreated step by step into eastern Galicia as the campaign developed and sent numerous calls for help to the Western Powers, was unable to prevent the collapse of the Republic. Impressed by the Polish defeat and urged on by Hitler, the Government of the USSR decided to occupy the sphere of interest conceded to it. On the night of 16–17 September it informed the Polish Government that it regarded the Polish Republic as defunct and was therefore compelled to order Soviet troops into eastern Poland to protect the White Russian and Ukrainian population. After the incursion of two Soviet army groups had demonstrated the futility of further resistance, the highest authorities of the Republic – President, Government and high command – all crossed over on the same day into the territory of Poland's ally, Roumania. There, contrary to the provisions of the treaties in force, they were interned; the Roumanian Government feared German or Russian intervention. Thus although according to the Polish view and the provisions of the constitution the international survival of the Republic seemed to be assured, and although even the victorious powers never issued a formal statement proclaiming the disappearance of the Polish State, 17 September saw the *de facto* collapse of the Republic after an existence of just twenty years.

After the Soviet invasion, which reached the western border of the Soviet sphere of influence at most points by 21 September, the military resistance of the remaining Polish troops entered its last agony, although there were many isolated deeds of bravery. From 21–23 September the German divisions withdrew to the pre-arranged line, but were not followed immediately by the Soviet forces, and at this point the Polish will to resist inspired many smaller units to fight on again. However, Lwow had to capitulate on 21–22 September, after being besieged first by German and then by Soviet troops; Warsaw fell on 28 September, and the forts of Hel on 2 October. The capitulation of the last Polish field units at Kock on 5 October ended organized resistance, although guerrilla warfare went on until the spring of 1940. A large number of Polish soldiers went into hiding and were able to join the ranks of the military resistance movement later on; about 100,000 men managed to reach Lithuania, Latvia, Roumania or Hungary, and to escape from these countries to France. There they formed the backbone of the future army in exile.

The unexpectedly swift demise of the Polish Republic made people ask what had caused the collapse. Social tensions and national antagonisms, the incongruity of state and society, of people and nation, were frequently cited as decisive reasons, and the description of Poland as a 'seasonal state' seemed to be justified. But the 'September catastrophe' was no criterion of the country's inner vitality. In spite of widespread hostility to the minorities and of nationalistic tendencies, the core of this multiracial state was not so rotten that the minority problem alone would have sufficed to cause it to break asunder. More serious were the questions of agrarian over-population and inadequate economic strength, which produced serious social and political tensions and unsound dictatorial forms of government, although it is true that these problems could never have been solved from Poland's own resources. Consequently the Poland of the inter-war period offered the picture of a state which burdened itself with heavy mortgages, especially at the time of its foundation, and in the twenty years of its existence sometimes exceeded the bounds of political prudence. Nevertheless, it displayed a creative strength which formed an excellent testimony to the talents of a nation that had been without a state for a hundred years, and certainly did not deserve to be destroyed from outside. In particular, it should always be remembered that in spite of an authoritarian government, nationalistic excesses and the Bydgoszcz murders, the Polish Republic belonged in the autumn of 1939 to the ranks of those who defended European democracy against Hitler and Stalin. On this occasion, too, Poland played the part of a champion of European freedom, as it had in 1794, 1831 and 1863.

CHAPTER VI

Poland in the Second World War
(1939-1945)

THE FIFTH PARTITION OF POLAND

The military collapse of Poland in September 1939 gave the victorious forces a formal excuse to divide up its territory. According to older theories of international law – the Polish thesis was based on a newer conception of the continuance of an exiled authority exercising all extra-territorial public power – the conquerors were entitled, after defeating the country, to undertake its legal reorganization. This territorial redivision of Poland was the subject of the negotiations which Hitler and Stalin conducted in the last few days of September. Discussion of the question of a possible continuance of Polish sovereignty was avoided by both sides.

In the Moscow agreement of 28 September the experienced diplomacy of the Soviet Union succeeded in having the whole of Lithuania made part of the Russian sphere of influence. In return, Russia renounced any claim to the territory between the Vistula and the Bug. The frontier thus established along the Rivers Pissa, Narew, Bug and San gave the Soviet Union a piece of territory which certainly included some solidly Polish regions, such as the Bialystok area, and also many scattered Polish settlements, but on the whole exhibited a Ukrainian or White Russian majority. The Soviet Government thus substantiated its claim to have done no more than effect the liberation of two 'sister peoples' from the 'Polish yoke'. It left the German Government with the responsibility for the Polish problem in the narrower, ethnic sense. This territorial decision must have seemed all the more dubious to the

German side since Hitler still had no clear ideas about the political future of the German sphere of influence.

The establishment of a German military administration under Colonel-General von Rundstedt and Chief Administrator Hans Frank, which Hitler ordered on 25 September, did not prejudice the situation according to international law. Obviously Hitler was toying with the idea of a residual Polish State of roughly the same size as the Kingdom of Poland set up in the First World War. This state would be demilitarized and adapted to fit into the Germano–Soviet alliance. In his radio talk of 6 October Hitler offered the Governments of the Western Powers 'the foundation of a new Polish State' in return for the cessation of hostilities. In fact, at this period the German Government was considering trying to induce Polish politicians such as Prince Janusz Radziwill, Count Adam Ronikier, Professor Wladyslaw Kucharzewski and the publicist Wladyslaw Studnicki – who had all collaborated with the Germans in the First World War and were therefore regarded as friendly to Germany – to form a Quisling Government. These ideas reached few of those at whom they were aimed, and Poland was to be the only 'country without a Quisling' in the whole of the Second World War. Naturally enough, the Western leaders did not find Hitler's proposals acceptable. On 8 October Hitler therefore annexed, by his decree on the 'division and administration of the eastern territories', the whole of western Poland up to the extreme limit of the scattered German settlements, that is, up to a line which ran roughly midway between the frontiers of 1795 and 1815 and for the time being was kept secret. These 'Incorporated Eastern Territories', although almost purely Polish in population, were marked out for future Germanization. When Chamberlain rejected Hitler's proposals on 12 October, pointing to the untrustworthiness of National Socialist statements, Hitler finally adopted the idea, favoured particularly by Frank, of turning the territory of the residual Polish State into a kind of German colony under German administration. On the very same day, 12 October, he issued his decree 'on the administration of the occupied Polish territories'; this decree formed the basis of the

PARTITION OF POLAND
1939

Occupied by Nazi Germany

Occupied by Soviet Russia

Polish Frontier ·1919 ----·-·-

W. Bromage

MAP 6

future 'Government General for the Occupied Polish Territories', of which Frank was put in charge. The military administration came to an end on 25 October, and the new administrative and customs boundaries came into effect on 20 November. With the return to Slovakia on 21 November of the border strips in the Carpathians acquired by Poland in 1920, 1924 and 1938, the territorial partition of German-occupied Poland was for the time being concluded. Germany now controlled a vast body of Polish citizens, amounting according to the official Polish figures for 31 August 1939 to some 21,200,000; of these, about 10,568,000 lived in the 'Incorporated Eastern Territories' and about 10,610,000 in the General Government.

The Russian annexation of eastern Poland formed the antithesis of Hitler's mode of behaviour, in so far as the Soviet Government did not base its claim on the right of the conqueror but tried to give the impression that it was paying due regard to the right to self-determination. In the interests of a policy of moral conquest, on 10 October the Moscow Government ceded the city and region of Vilna to the Republic of Lithuania, which took over this territory on 27–28 October. The Soviet Government thereby put into effect again the provisions of the Russo–Lithuanian peace treaty of 1920. It was able to do this without hesitation because Hitler had abandoned the whole of Lithuania, and in fact nine months later it was to occupy the whole country. In all the rest of eastern Poland, Moscow held on 22 October pseudo-democratic elections for 'West Ukrainian' and 'West White Russian' National Assemblies, in which previously designated groups of candidates were elected with majorities of 90·9 per cent and 90·7 per cent respectively. The two bodies thus created, which sat in Lwow and Bialystok, requested on 27 and 29 October respectively that the territories which they represented should be incorporated in the Soviet Union. At the same time both bodies, by making fundamental decisions on the expropriation of landowners and the nationalization of industry and banks, adopted constitutions easily adaptable to the Soviet system and intended to affect the predominantly Polish property-owning class. The Supreme Soviet admitted the West Ukrainian and White Russian regions to the corresponding Soviet republics on 1 and 2 November respectively. The Soviet Union thereby acquired a slice of territory inhabited according to the Polish figures for 31 August 1939 by some 13,200,000 persons. Of these, 5,274,000 spoke Polish, 1,109,000 spoke Yiddish or Hebrew, 4,529,000 spoke Ukrainian–Ruthenian and 1,123,000 spoke White Russian. However, according to the assertions made by Molotov on 31 October 1939, more than seven million Ukrainians and three million White Russians were involved.

The historical importance of the annexation of eastern Poland by the Soviet Union was far greater than that of the partition of the purely Polish-speaking territory administered by the Germans. It was Hitler who threw away the fruits of Pilsudski's victories of 1920 and gave the Soviet Union the access to central Europe for which the Red Army had striven in vain at the end of the First World War. He thereby created the factual – not the legal – basis of the Soviet claim to eastern Poland, and in the last analysis – if involuntarily – the delicate situation of the Western Powers with regard to Polish–Soviet territorial disputes, which finally gave rise to the idea of compensating Poland with German territory. At any rate, the Moscow Government had now achieved that 'reduction of Poland to its narrowest ethnographical boundaries' of which Foreign Minister Chicherin had spoken to Stresemann as early as 1925, and it was to insist right up to the present day on the legal validity of this annexation based on ethnic ties and apparent self-determination.[1]

[1] If in the following pages the fate of the non-Polish population of eastern Poland and the occupation policy pursued there are not described, that does not imply recognition of the Soviet thesis. In the view of the Polish Government-in-exile, the disputed territories remained Polish until the end of the war, and in the view of a considerable number of Poles they still are today. Thus it is due simply to considerations of space that only the Polish racial groups in eastern Poland can from now on be considered in this book.

Poland in the Second World War (1939–1945)

POLAND DURING THE PERIOD OF GERMAN–SOVIET CO-OPERATION

In the late autumn of 1939 most of the Polish nation felt little regret that the régime of Rydz-Smigly and Moscicki had collapsed so abruptly. The 'September catastrophe' was certainly regarded as a national disgrace and the foreign rule of the occupying powers seemed like the imposition of a hard and undeserved fate, but the stunning shock of the unexpectedly swift collapse and disappointment at the failure of the Polish Government led to sharp criticism or else to apathy. In general, people's sympathies turned to the four big parties of the pre-war opposition, that is, the National Party (SN), the Peasant or Populist Party (SL), the polish Socialist Party (PPS) and the Labour Party (SP), especially as these parties strove to carry on Polish political traditions in the country.

In these circumstances, the Government which had fled to Roumanian territory and been interned there was recognized as legitimate but could only count on enjoying real authority in the country if its personnel was completely changed and the Opposition allowed to participate in it. Consequently the illegal internment was almost a stroke of luck, for it enabled President Moscicki and the Prime Minister, Slawoj-Skladkowski, to resign on 30 September 1939 in accordance with Article XIII b of the constitution of 1935, on the grounds that their authority had been obstructed, and to hand over the presidency to Wladyslaw Raczkiewicz, the Speaker of the Senate, who was in Paris. On that day Raczkiewicz swore the oath to uphold the constitution and thus assured the political continuance of the Republic. Although he was a supporter of Pilsudski he appointed as Prime Minister, in accordance with the country's wishes, General Wladyslaw Sikorski, the dead marshal's great opponent.

Sikorski formed in Paris a Government of politicians from the four big opposition parties who had either been living abroad or had succeeded in escaping from Poland. The new Cabinet was quickly recognized by Great Britain, France and the United

States; in November 1939 it moved to Angers. In December of the same year a Parliament in exile was also formed; it was known as the 'National Council' (RN) and comprised nineteen politicians belonging to the four parties. The old man Ignacy Paderewski, who as a living political symbol of a generation of Polish history was chosen as president of the Parliament, could carry out his duties only seldom from reasons of health, so that in practice the office was filled by Stanislaw Mikolajczyk, the secretary-general of the Populist (Peasant) Party and Witos's appointed representative.

Both Government and Parliament regarded it as their most important task to create without delay new forces to carry on the war against Germany. Soldiers of the old army who had escaped, Poles living abroad who were conscripted and volunteers all helped to build up an army which by spring 1940 already numbered 84,000 men; three divisions were incorporated in the French army, while the mountain brigade (Brygada Podhalanska) distinguished itself in the fighting round Narvik. The possession of her own troops formed the decisive criterion for the recognition of Poland as a fighting ally, and above all it enabled the commander-in-chief, Sikorski, not only successfully to postulate the existence of the Republic in international law but also to advance its claims with some emphasis.

Besides the 'army-in-exile', a 'home army' was created. As early as the end of September 1939, when Warsaw was capitulating, General Michal Karaszewicz-Tokarzewski, in agreement with the four political parties and with the support of the old army, formed the organization 'Service for the Victory of Poland' (SZP), which was to become the nucleus of the future underground forces. On 13 November, in the name of the Government-in-exile, Sikorski gave his deputy commander-in-chief, General Kazimierz Sosnkowski, command of the military resistance in Poland itself; however, control from exile proved unsatisfactory, and on 15 January 1940 the ZWZ appointed Colonel Stefan Rowecki ('Grot') as its commander. After fairly long negotiations this appointment was accepted by the Government-in-exile and Grot was promoted to general. The command in southern Poland was taken over by the well-known cavalry colonel Count Tadeusz Komorowski ('Bor'). The extension of the szp – which now changed its name to the 'League for Armed Struggle' – in the parts of western Poland annexed by Germany and also in the eastern regions under Soviet control met considerable difficulties; General Tokarzewski, commander designate of eastern Poland, was arrested by the Soviet authorities in March 1940 on his way to Lwow, while the cadres of the zwz there were disrupted again and again by the deportations of Poles carried out from February 1940 onwards. Nevertheless, Rowecki was able to unite numerous spontaneously created combat groups under his command and by the middle of 1940 the strength of the zwz had risen to about 100,000 men. Its groups did not yet undertake any armed actions but concentrated all their energies on developing the organization of sabotage, propaganda and military intelligence, which was passed on to France and England by wireless or by couriers.

Together with the underground army an 'underground' civil authority, organized on the same lines as the old administration, was brought into being. It was to be subject to a 'local delegate' of the Government-in-exile; at the start, this office was held by the pps politician Mieczyslaw Niedzialkowski, who had also played an influential part in the foundation of the szp. However, the organization of this underground state did not make much headway at first, since the peasants in particular held back owing to the shock of the September catastrophe and the unlikelihood of a swift liberation of Poland. In addition, disputes broke out between the military and civil leaders on the question of spheres of jurisdiction; these disputes were to last for years.

In general, at the end of 1939 and the beginning of 1940 the population of German-occupied Poland was not too ill-disposed towards the German occupation régime. Even though any kind of political collaboration with the occupation authorities was almost unanimously rejected, it was expected that German fairness and administrative ability, with which the Poles had become acquainted during the First World War, would keep the country in order. However, although the German administrative machine quickly came into play and took measures to look after the population, Polish hopes of fair treatment were soon completely dashed by Hitler's racial and resettlement policy and by Himmler's police terror. The arrogance of the National Socialist leaders awoke a profound national hatred which from early 1940 onwards affected the relations between the occupying power and the population to an increasing degree.

Out of the bulk of the 'Incorporated Eastern Regions', together with the towns of Danzig, Torun, Bydgoszcz, Poznan and Lodz, the *Reichsgaue* (i.e. provinces) of 'Wartheland' and 'Danzig-West Prussia' were formed, while large strips of territory were added to the provinces of Upper Silesia and East Prussia. According to Polish calculations, the population of this west Polish region as a whole consisted of 9,221,000 Polish-speaking persons, 622,000 who spoke German, 582,000 who spoke Yiddish or Hebrew and 71,000 who spoke Czech; the figures arrived at by the Germans were 7,864,000 Poles, 559,000 Jews and 161,000 other non-Germans. In spite of the predominantly Polish character of these territories, Hitler decided on a policy of universal Germanization. He entrusted its execution to the head of the s s, Heinrich Himmler, who on 7 October 1939 was appointed 'Commissioner for the Consolidation of German Nationality'. Himmler's programme aimed at Germanizing the new territories of Upper Silesia, West Prussia and East Prussia mainly by assimilation of those groups in the population whose nationality was undetermined, that is, the Cassubians, Masurians, Upper Silesians, Slonzaks and Germano–Poles; the purely Polish inhabitants of Wartheland, the East Prussian district of Zichenau (Ciechanow) and the Polish areas of Upper Silesia and West Prussia were to be driven out, physically annihilated or sent away into Germany itself. The work of Germanization was to be completed by the settlement of Germans from the territories which Hitler had abandoned to the ussr on 23 August 1939, in other words mainly the Baltic States.

In the execution of his terrible task Himmler worked on purely physical and biological principles, in accordance with National Socialist racial theories; 'blood, race and mother-tongue' were to be the criteria for the division into master-race and helot-race. The basis of this policy was the decree of 25 November 1939, which gave German citizenship only to those inhabitants of the 'Incorporated Eastern Territories' who were incontestably German. The Polish intelligentsia and all officials, politicians and leaders of Polish associations were eliminated or killed as early as the late autumn of 1939 by mass arrests carried out in three stages and based on local investigations, police court hearings and the use of Polish files and card-indexes. A mass deportation of Polish families was intended not only to weaken the Polish element in the population but also to make room for the Germans brought into the area in accordance with the Germano–Soviet resettlement treaty. The main weight of this policy of expulsion fell on Wartheland, which by 31 March 1941 had lost 100,000 inhabitants through flight and 280,000 through deportation. That section of the population which was half German and half Polish was prepared for gradual assimilation by means of the 'ethnic list', a device which was developed in Wartheland and was later – on 31 March 1941 – to be more precisely defined in a special law; those on the list were granted German citizenship either unconditionally or subject to revocation, according to their classification. The Poles not included in this scheme, in other words the majority of the population, ranked merely as 'people under German protection' and had almost no rights at all.

German economic and social policy was also designed primarily to assist the process of Germanization, since the Poles were not only subject to special regulations but were also kept far below the German level in conditions of work, pay and rations. The State funds and a huge quantity of private property were confiscated and used to assist the German colonists. Culturally, efforts were made to blot out the Polish character of these territories by means of the extermination or deportation of the intellectual and cultural *élite* – in the town of Torun alone, more than 2,000 people were arrested in one night and sent off to concentration camps – by the halting or Germanization of secondary and higher education, the confiscation of the contents of Polish archives and libraries, the separation of the churches into Polish and German ones, and finally by the total suppression of the Polish Press. Even elementary education in the primary schools was restricted to a bare minimum. The full weight of this 'denationalizing' policy was already beginning to make itself felt by the end of 1939, although Hitler had not yet finally decided on the territorial limits of the 'Incorporated Eastern Territories'. He caused the new eastern frontier of Germany to be kept secret until the French campaign.

The Government General, which according to Polish sources contained in autumn 1939 about 9,863,000 Poles, 61,000 Germans, 1,225,000 Jews and 357,000 Ukrainians and Ruthenians, was given a colonial-type Government under Governor-General Hans Frank, in accordance with the basic decree of 26 October 1939, and divided into the four 'districts' of Warsaw, Cracow, Radom and Lublin. The seat of the exclusively German Cabinet appointed in November 1939 was Cracow. At first there was something of a dichotomy in the exercise of power. On the one hand, the Governor-General implemented ruthlessly the hard demands of Göring's war economy, but on the other defended the interests of the Poles, even if partly for propaganda reasons, as in the case of the provision of food for the population of Warsaw in the winter of 1939–40. To start with, the sole aim of German economic policy was the ruthless plunder of the country, since the German Government still entertained the idea of a 'residual state' and reckoned on the possibility of an eventual return of the Government General to a Polish régime. The German authorities therefore arranged for the dismantling of valuable industrial plant and for the confiscation of State property and a small proportion of private property. The police, who were quite independent of Frank and responsible to Himmler alone, certainly went about their work with a view to the brutal suppression of all things Polish. Clear proof that Himmler's aim was the destruction of the Polish intelligentsia was provided by the arrest of the whole teaching staff of the Jagellon University at Cracow on 6 November 1939. Although German university teachers protested against this act of barbarity, they could not prevent the death of numerous Polish professors in Sachsenhausen camp.

The German victory in France in May and June 1940 brought significant changes in the fate of Poles at home and abroad. Sikorski's Government was involved in the collapse of France and fled in several stages to the Bordeaux area; from Libourne[1] it hastily recognized, on 18 June 1940, the leaders thrown up by the resistance movement in Poland itself. Sikorski refused to let the Polish troops be involved in the French capitulation and with British help was able to evacuate at least 17,000 men to England. After stormy discussions with Reynaud, the French Prime Minister, and encouraged by the promise of help from Churchill, Sikorski also transferred his Government and the National Council to London on 20 June 1940. On 5 August he reached an agreement with the British Government allowing him to station Polish troops on British soil; among the newly-created units, the air force in particular distinguished itself, playing a valuable part in the defeat of the German air offensive against England. In addition, Sikorski reached a good understanding with President Roosevelt, thanks largely to the skill of the Polish ambassador in America, Jan Ciechanowski. Roosevelt agreed to supply the Polish army in England with American weapons, and Sikorski was allowed to recruit American citizens of Polish birth as volunteers.

The German victory in France resulted in an intensification of the German occupation policy, since with the collapse of France any hope of a swift liberation of Poland disappeared and it no longer seemed necessary to show any consideration at all. On 8 July 1940 Hitler defined the territorial limits of the 'Incorporated Eastern Regions', and at the same time central Poland under Frank (which will henceforward be referred to as the Government General or G G) became a protectorate or, to use Hitler's definition, a 'subsidiary country of the Reich'. Although this consolidation of German possession put an end to the period of dismantling and pure plunder, immediately after the French campaign a liquidation operation was set in motion which accounted for the

[1] A town fifteen miles east of Bordeaux. (*Trans.*)

fine flower of the political intelligentsia of Poland, including such men as Mieczyslaw Niedzialkowski. In the Incorporated Eastern Regions in particular, the concept of denationalization was put into effect over a wider and wider field by means of a cleverly thought-out series of new regulations.

On the other hand, from 8 July 1940 onwards the GG was regarded by the German Government as the 'Polish homeland', in which the Poles were to be allowed to have a certain cultural and economic life of their own, but one with a strong German tinge. At first there was no more thought of Germanization or 'de-Polonisation' than of real autonomy. For the duration of the war at least, the Poles were to be kept on the level of a half-free, politically unconscious, auxiliary people with only a vocational education. All the universities and secondary schools remained closed; only the technical schools and the research institutes were allowed to function. Technical talent was utilized, but the intellectual and political *élite* was suppressed by the same methods as those used in the Incorporated Eastern Regions, and the highly developed party political life of Poland was driven underground. In accordance with Goebbels's directives, the whole opinion-forming Press was liquidated, all writing that referred in any way to national traditions – in other words, almost all the Polish classics – was suppressed, and all public art collections, together with some private ones, were confiscated. Only purely factual or technical publications were permitted.

Economic policy now tended to spare and exploit the country's modest industrial capacity, mainly, it is true, in the interests of the German war economy and the build-up against the USSR, a process now beginning. Capital was spent on improving the transport system, again mainly for strategic reasons. Agricultural production was raised by the regrouping and improvement of land, the importation of breeding stock and seed and the construction of sheds for agricultural machinery and the storage of crops; collection and distribution were looked after by the swift reconstruction of the co-operatives under a newly-founded agricultural centre. Here again the same utilitarian considerations were at work on the German side as in their industrial policy; nevertheless, the result was that the situation of the farmers was relatively favourable, and this was another reason why their attitude to the resistance movement was somewhat reserved.

However, the main reason why the rural population and part of the urban population hesitated to join the civil and military underground movement was the fall of France, which seemed to destroy any chance of national liberation for years. The Poles certainly felt a certain satisfaction at the swift collapse of France, which made their own defeat look less shameful, but at the same time it caused them to fall a prey to a certain despondency; in autumn 1940 the numbers of the zwz fell to 70,000. However, the ss terror instead of frightening people only aroused their hostility, and with it their readiness to join the underground movement. Consequently, from spring 1941 onwards there could be no further question of any understanding between Poles and Germans.

POLAND IN THE FIRST YEARS OF THE WAR BETWEEN
GERMANY AND THE SOVIET UNION

Hitler's invasion of the Soviet Union on 22 June 1941 completely changed the political situation of the Polish Government-in-exile and with it that of the underground movement in Poland itself. In itself, the alienation of the two partitioning Powers might well have made it possible for the Poles to opt for an anti-Soviet attitude; such an option could at the same time have formed the basis of a *modus vivendi* with Germany. However, Hitler set his face against this possibility, although so far as the war against the Soviet was concerned he must have wanted the alliance with the Poles to gain which he had made so many concessions from 1934 to 1938. By continuing the same form of government, which suppressed all national movements, he not only threw away any chance of Germano–Polish co-operation but also helped to harden the hostility between Germans and Poles. There were certainly strong groups in the country, particularly among the National Radical Right, which considered the might of the Bolsheviks more dangerous than that of the National Socialists, groups which were

183

ready to drop their struggle against the occupying power and which, to gain support for their conception, strove for a revision of the Germans' policy towards Poland. They were not only rebuffed but in many cases actually persecuted. The real reasons for this incredible hubris lay no doubt in the belief in the invincibility of German arms, and above all in the National Socialist concept of a German *Herrenvolk*, a concept which simply did not permit the renunciation of colonial methods and the recognition of the Poles as equals.

For Sikorski's Government, which resided in London and was dependent on British policy, the new path to be taken in its own foreign policy was clear. After Paderewski had indicated on 26 June 1941 (three days before his death) that the basis of the discussions must be the return of eastern Poland and the liberation of the million and a half Poles captured or deported by the Russians, Sikorski started negotiations, under pressure from the British Foreign Office, with the Government of the USSR. These negotiations finally led, on 30 July 1941, to a Polish–Soviet agreement which was signed under Churchill's chairmanship. This agreement declared the Germano–Soviet partition treaties of 28 September 1939 invalid and provided for the resumption of diplomatic relations and mutual support in the struggle against Germany. It also made provision for the raising of a Polish army in the USSR and a general amnesty for all Polish prisoners in Soviet custody. At the same time it did not give any guarantee – and the British Government expressly adopted this interpretation, on the basis of the guarantee formula of 31 March 1939 – that Poland's pre-war eastern frontiers would be restored, although in itself the annulment of the partition treaties would have demanded this. Even in the autumn of 1941, that is, at a time of extreme military difficulty, the Moscow Government was unwilling to modify in any way the claims to eastern Poland which Hitler had enabled it to make good. Sikorski, who was subject to strong British pressure, had to be satisfied with the hope of a future 'gentlemen's agreement'; he was not in a position to re-establish Poland's rightful claims. It is difficult to judge how far he himself, as a soldier and a man of honour, believed in promises, and how far he underestimated the perfidy of Soviet methods or else, as a native of Galicia, was incapable of seeing through them. At any rate, here lay the germ of that unfortunate development which was finally to lead, through the Polish–Soviet estrangement at the end of the war, to the drawing of the frontier along the Curzon Line. Perhaps the two ministers Zaleski and Sosnkowski, both supporters of Pilsudski, who resigned when the treaty was concluded, foresaw more clearly than Sikorski the significance of Russia's failure to recognize the old frontiers. In fact, the signing of the treaty and the ministerial crisis provoked such serious conflicts in the National Council that on 3 September 1941 President Raczkiewicz was forced to dissolve it.

Thus the problem of the ownership of eastern Poland – which from autumn 1941 onwards was for the time being under German control – affected Polish–Soviet relations from the start. On 3 December 1941 there took place in Kuybyshev that memorable conversation between Stalin and Sikorski in which the Soviet leader suggested 'very small alterations' in the Polish–Soviet frontier; Sikorski refused to discuss this question, so that Stalin's aims could not be clearly discerned. Nevertheless, it seemed highly significant that even at a moment when the USSR was in extreme danger – the German armies were then fighting near Moscow; that was why the Soviet Government had fled to Kuybyshev – Stalin was unwilling to abandon his claim to eastern Poland. That the Russian Government looked upon eastern Poland as fundamentally a Soviet province was also clear from the fact that the Polish ambassador to the USSR, Professor Stanislaw Kot, had been told on 1 December that Poles of Ukrainian, White Russian or Jewish nationality were to be regarded, in principle, as Soviet citizens. Only a few days after the Kuybyshev conversation official Soviet demands for the Curzon Line were heard, in other words demands for a frontier which had been discussed in December 1919 and July 1920 in completely different conditions and even then had not been meant by its Western authors to represent a definitive eastern frontier of Poland. All the same, it is interesting to note that the Soviet Cabinet refrained from basing its demands to Roosevelt, Churchill and Sikorski on the partition arrangements made with Hitler and was able to support its claims, although this meant giving up the regions of Przemysl and Bialystok, on an apparently legal frontier proposal whose author was supposed, if wrongly, to be a British Foreign Minister. As a result, Sikorski, who was dependent the whole time on Churchill, got into such difficulties that on 30 January 1942 he issued a secret order forbidding any mention of Polish–Soviet differences. His worries were somewhat lessened when the Soviet Government declared in Article V of the Anglo–Soviet Treaty of Alliance of 26 May 1942 that it sought no territorial aggrandisement; however, this assurance was really worthless so far as eastern Poland was concerned, since the Soviet Government regarded this region as an integral part of its territory in just the same way as the Russian Government and public had done up to the First World War, and Stalin himself had always taken the same view.

The question of the recruitment of a Polish army on Russian soil was affected by the territorial dispute. In accordance with the provisions of the pact of 30 July 1941, a start had been made on the creation of cadres in autumn 1941. Command of these troops was assumed by General Wladyslaw Anders, once an officer in the Imperial Russian army. However, the Polish soldiers and officers who had been in captivity since September 1939 and had been 'amnestied' since 12 August 1941 were in very poor physical condition, especially as the Soviet authorities did not make sufficient rations available. Some 10,000 officers were still missing and could not be found. Finally, in accordance with the basic attitude of the Soviet Government, Polish citizens of Ukrainian, White Russian or Jewish nationality were not allowed to join this Polish army; two leaders of Polish Jewry, Henryk Erlich and Wiktor Alter, who wanted to create their own Jewish units within Anders's army, were executed by the Soviet authorities at the beginning of December 1941, just when Sikorski was trying to clear up these questions in Kuybyshev in connection with the creation of an army. Since on 22 January the Soviet Government limited the maximum size of the Polish army to

96,000 men (it actually numbered about 70,000 at this time), demanded that smaller units should be quickly sent into action, and when the Poles refused to do this reduced the maximum to 44,000 (20 March 1942), the Polish leaders decided to carry out a plan they had long been considering and to move the army to Persia. Between April and August 1942 General Anders's army was transported in stages to Persia and thus removed from Soviet jurisdiction. Thus the army question too ended in a serious Polish–Soviet disagreement. The fundamental reason for this was undoubtedly Stalin's demand that the Poles should send into action small, scattered units which would soon suffer losses and cease to constitute any danger in the question of eastern Poland; Sikorski and Anders, on the other hand, for the same political reasons, wished to send into action a compact, thoroughly trained army. With the removal of Anders's troops to Persia and subsequently to the Middle East and North Africa, any chance of a liberation of Poland from the east by a land army independent of the Soviet had of course disappeared. This circumstance too was to be of great significance for the future fate of Poland.

For the time being the whole territory of Poland was still firmly occupied by the Germans. In the course of the swift conquest of eastern Poland and the western part of the USSR by the German army in autumn 1941 Hitler had peremptorily divided up these territories in a way which paid no heed at all to their history or natural structure. In spite of its purely Polish population the region of Bialystok was not united to the Government General but christened 'Bialystok district' and placed, on 17 July 1941, under Gauleiter Erich Koch, who undertook large-scale deportations with a view to the eventual annexation of the region to East Prussia. However, the legal status of the region was influenced less by memories of the Prussian 'Crown Department' of Bialystok of 1795–1806 than by Koch's wish to possess a private empire stretching uninterruptedly from Königsberg to Kiev. On the other hand, on 17 July 1941 Hitler put eastern Galicia, in spite of its predominantly Ukrainian population (the Poles there had suffered serious losses through Soviet deportations) under

Governor-General Frank, because the region was an 'old Austrian province'. Although they had been under Soviet control for scarcely two years, all the other territories, like the conquered Soviet regions, were placed on 17 July 1941 under the jurisdiction of Alfred Rosenberg, the 'Reich Minister for the Occupied Eastern Regions' (RMO). This arrangement was felt to be anti-Polish and in many respects certainly was so; it was reminiscent of the German policy of 'buffer states' in the First World War and further intensified Polish hostility to the Germans.

Quite apart from the territorial questions of the eastern border lands, the Poles in Poland itself had long made up their minds against taking an anti-Soviet attitude. The deciding factor here, in view of the country's loyalty to the London Government, had been the Polish–Soviet Treaty of Alliance of 30 July 1941. In addition, the German occupation policy, which in the first year or two of the Germano–Soviet war reached the highest pitch of severity and megalomania, made the decision easy. The deep mistrust of Soviet intentions had by no means disappeared, but emotional hatred of the Germans, intensified by the interplay of anti-Polish measures and Polish underground activities, obscured the question of what was going to happen in the more distant future; the struggle against National Socialism seemed the first essential if life was to be preserved.

In the Incorporated Eastern Regions Germanization made considerable progress. The existing regulations required only few additions; of these, the decree issued in Wartheland on 10 September 1941, which forbade Polish men under twenty-eight and Polish women under twenty-five to marry, was of particular importance from the point of view of racial politics. The deportations and colonization went on, although the Poles concerned were no longer transferred to the GG but sent to Germany itself to work in munition factories or moved to the interior of the Incorporated Eastern Regions. By January 1944 245,000 Germans had been settled in Wartheland alone, and only 103,000 in all the rest of the Eastern Regions put together. In Upper Silesia, Danzig–West Prussia and the administrative district of Ciechanow the main policy pursued was racial assimilation, and this did not in fact result in any very considerable ethnic mutations, while in Wartheland, thanks to the big deportations carried out there, the nationality structure was fundamentally changed. Altogether, from 1939 to 1945, Wartheland probably lost, through murder, resettlement and deportation, some 390,000 Polish and about 380,000 Jewish inhabitants, or in other words a sixth of its 1939 population. On the other hand, the number of Germans living there had risen by 1943 to about a million, so that the proportion of Poles to Germans changed from 13:1 (August 1939) to 4:1 (January 1944). In addition, the German authorities sought to split up the remaining Poles politically by special measures, such as the foundation of the 'League of Polish Achievement' in Wartheland on 20 December 1942. Such attempts were not very successful, even though the power of the underground movement in the Incorporated Eastern Regions was severely limited; from 1941 onwards Polish propaganda even succeeded to an increasing degree in dissuading the half-German, half-Polish section of the population from applying for inclusion on the list of persons desiring German nationality.

The German occupation policy met still stiffer resistance from the 90 per cent Polish population of the GG. As the intellectual *élite* of the country had been decimated since the middle of 1940 and the leaders of a possible resistance movement consequently seemed to have been eliminated, the Government General was administered more as a war economy than as a political unit. It was regarded as particularly valuable because it was one of the most important supply areas for the eastern front and also formed a rich reservoir of men and material. By the middle of 1944 a million and a quarter persons had been recruited or rounded up to work inside Germany. The amount of raw materials, cattle, horses and especially food removed from the country became enormous; in some places the local population was left with only a third of what it needed and the townspeople in particular suffered great hardship. The rural population, which was given preferential treatment in the supply of consumer goods in order to secure the highest possible production of food, and therefore offered less resistance to the measures of the German authorities, was exasperated by the colonization policy of the ss. November saw the start of an operation designed to remove 110,000 Polish and Ukrainian farmers from the district of Zamosc, which was to be settled by German farmers and become a colonial link between Breslau (Wroclaw) and the Crimea. This disregard of private landed property, which had previously been regarded as safe from interference in the GG, played an extremely important part in driving the mass of the peasants into the arms of the underground movement. In the woods of Zamosc the Resistance organized for the first time armed combat groups – the so-called 'Kedyw' units – to attack the police and the new settlers, and towards the end of 1943 actually succeeded in forcing the ss to halt the colonization. Thus in circumstances like these the very harshness of the German occupation policy developed an attitude of mind in the Poles which made them ready to join the underground movement.

Probably the strongest impulse to resist was provoked by the physical destruction of Polish Jews; this began in the middle of 1942 and soon became known all over Poland. The Jewish citizens of the Polish Republic, who from 1939 onwards had been shut up together in numerous ghettos – the biggest were in Warsaw, Lodz, Cracow, Lublin, Czestochowa, Kielce, Lwow and Vilna – and compelled to work for the Germans in inhuman conditions, were able to offer little resistance when they were shipped off to be exterminated at Auschwitz, Treblinka or Belzec. It was only when the transportation to the death camps became a mass affair, when the daily quota for deportation from the Warsaw ghetto rose in October 1942 to about 10,000, that a specifically Jewish fighting organization came into being. The Polish resistance movement helped it by providing weapons and by carrying out diversionary activities. After some 300,000 of the 360,000 inhabitants of the Warsaw ghetto had been murdered at Treblinka the Jewish combat groups staged a desperate uprising between 19 April and 16 May 1943 against the German police troops and those in the service of the Germans. From the start it was doomed to failure. Similar, smaller revolts in Bialystok and Vilna in September 1943 also failed. The losses suffered during the war by the Jews of Poland, who numbered about 3,500,000 in August 1939, were reckoned by Jewish authorities at between 2,350,000 and 3,000,000 persons, and there can be no doubt that the figure was at least 2,500,000. This policy of mass extermination made a deep impression on the Polish inhabitants of the Republic. Although anti-Semitism, widespread before the war, had by no means completely disappeared, the methods of the ss were universally regarded as abominable. Moreover, certain utterances of the Governor-General and of senior ss officers led the Poles to fear that after the Jews had been exterminated they themselves might suffer partial liquidation and would in any case certainly be deported in large numbers.

Thus the swift recrudescence of the national resistance movement after the start of the Germano–Soviet war was mainly due to the German occupation policy itself, in so far as it was not a mere act of self-defence. In 1941–2 the underground army zwz under General Rowecki was able to add to its ranks the combat units of the pps, the National Democrats and the Peasant Party which had sprung up spontaneously all over the country, and when on 14 February 1942 it assumed the title 'Home Army' (ak) this was no more than an accurate reflection of its – so to speak – legitimate status as a military underground movement under the orders of the exiled Government in London. By the end of 1943 its numbers had risen to nearly 350,000; when General Rowecki was arrested on 30 June 1943 the leadership was taken over by General Count Tadeusz Komorowski ('Bor'). Alongside it was a firmly constructed civil underground organization based on the four big pre-war opposition parties, which were all represented on the central 'Political Committee' (pkp). In accordance with the Polish–Soviet treaty of 30 July 1941 and the exiled Government's order of 27 April 1942, both underground movements, civil as well as military, regarded it as their main task to hinder the German war effort in the east in every conceivable way, but above all by sabotage, spying and propaganda.

Their greatest successes consisted in the large-scale destruction of German supply lines and transport and the discovery of German military secrets, such as the development of the V-weapons. As a result of the extension of the German sphere of influence to Kiev and Smolensk the conditions for universal underground activity embracing the territory of eastern Poland as well had improved considerably. The Polish resistance movement mainly benefited the Soviet armies, although by 1942–3 the leaders of the A K were well aware that collaboration with the Soviet could have only tactical significance and would not affect the final outcome of the war. However, the German reprisals, which started in earnest in summer 1943, were so brutal that they generated an overpowering desire for revenge on Germany and temporarily drove mistrust of Soviet policy into the background. Thus in those years most Poles were bound to regard National Socialist Germany as enemy number one.

The very wide scope of the underground movement in Poland enabled the London Government to consolidate its position among the nations fighting against Germany. The exile Cabinet signed the Atlantic Charter and – on 2 January 1942 – shared as an equal partner in the Proclamation of the United Nations; on 1 July 1942 it was able to conclude a Lend-Lease agreement with the US A. But if Sikorski's Government could count on the firm and true friendship of Roosevelt and Churchill, its relations with Stalin were a source of permanent disquiet, mainly because of the frontier question. In October 1939 Lord Halifax, in the name of the British Government – if only in the stress of a situation provoked by Hitler – had related the dividing line of September 1939 to the Curzon Line, thus presenting a splendid argument to Stalin, who made known his aims in this quarter in December 1941. Ever since then this frontier question had poisoned Polish–Soviet relations. It was true that by Article V of the Anglo–Soviet treaty of alliance of 26 May 1942 the Soviet Government proclaimed in principle that it sought no territorial changes; but as early as October 1942 it was admitted by the journalist Ksawery Pruszynski, one of a group of Polish communists and left-wing socialists in the USSR, that their aim was the Poland of Boleslaw Chrobry, that is, a Poland cut back in the east to the San and the Bug, but extended in the west to the Oder. This was the first time that the idea of territorial compensation at the expense of Germany was publicly mooted. It was an idea which was to become all the more significant in the future since the British guarantee to Poland of March 1939 – formulated, it is true, in completely different circumstances – allowed a territorial shift of Polish sovereignty, and the Curzon Line, originally conceived purely as a kind of internal, administrative frontier, now began to assume in Soviet diplomatic memoranda the character of a real political frontier. Moreover, since January 1942 a small pro-communist party, the 'Polish Workers' Party' (PPR), had been formed in the Polish underground movement; this party, as mouthpiece of the Polish communists in Moscow and consequently of the Soviet Government, adopted this 'shift to the west' as part of its programme. It remained an extremely weak party but gained a certain influence thanks to its gifted leaders, Pawel Finder and Wladyslaw Gomulka, to its fighting organization, the 'People's Guard', under Marian Spychalski and above all to the energetic support of the Soviet. The Russian Government waited only for the victory of Stalingrad, which gave it a certain freedom of movement in the diplomatic sphere, to announce officially its demand for that part of Poland which lay east of the Curzon Line. There was an exchange of notes between the Soviet and the Polish Government in-exile on the frontier question. Beginning in January 1943, it led finally on 2 March 1943 to a note from Moscow in which the Polish claim to the eastern part of the country was expressly rejected. Relations between the two Governments took their final turn for the worse with the German announcements about the discovery of the corpses at Katyn. The fears long entertained by the Poles about the fate of the officers captured by the Russians in September 1939 were now confirmed. When the Polish Government-in-exile asked on 20 April 1943 for definitive information about the officers who had been missing in the USSR since May 1940, the Russian Government refused to take part in any further discussions. On 25 April 1943 it announced that it regarded relations with the Polish Government-in-exile as broken off.

This break put an end to two years of difficult diplomatic co-operation between unequal allies; obviously the Moscow Government believed that it no longer needed Polish support now that the tide of war had begun to turn against the Germans. On 8 May came the foundation of the 'League of Polish Patriots' (ZPP), which formed the embryo, as it were, of a future Soviet–Polish satellite State and began to create its own fighting forces in the shape of the 'Kosciuszko' division under General Zygmunt Berling. Almost simultaneously with the organization of Soviet–Polish civil authorities and troops – whose activities were, it is true, confined for the time being to Soviet territory – and with the arrest of Rowecki, commander-in-chief of the Home Army, General Sikorski was killed in an aircraft accident near Gibraltar (4 July 1943). This series of events seemed to symbolize the turn in Poland's fate. After midsummer 1943 events in Poland would be controlled primarily by the Soviet, in whose theatre of operations the country lay, and only secondarily by the Government-in-exile. Hence the curious paradox that the German forces whose attack on Poland had unleashed the Second World War, and whose arrogant occupation policy had necessarily been opposed by the Polish resistance movement, now protected the sphere of influence of the legitimate Polish Government-in-exile, since for the time being they were keeping the Soviet armies out of Poland.

THE FRUITLESS VICTORY OF THE POLISH NATION

In accordance with the distribution of strength in the Polish exile Parliament Sikorski was succeeded by the former vice-premier Stanislaw Mikolajczyk, a politician who was more at home in internal than external affairs and certainly possessed little experience of Soviet diplomatic methods. He formed his Cabinet on 14 July 1943; the post of commander-in-chief of all Polish forces, which had also been filled by Sikorski, was taken over by General Kazimierz Sosnkowski, once the intimate friend of Pilsudski. The new Government took the helm at a moment when, through the break with the Soviet Union, Poland was in a difficult diplomatic position, but at the same time, thanks to its military achievements, was playing a fairly important part in the Allied war effort. Apart from the 'Home Army', which had already gone over to open guerrilla warfare with its 'Kedyw' units, the forces-in-exile – which at that time comprised 150,000 men and by the end of the war had risen to nearly 200,000 – were distinguishing themselves in the operations in Africa and in the air battles over western Europe.[1] Their finest deeds were performed in the Italian campaign, in which the Second Polish Corps under General Anders was to succeed in storming the key point of the German line in central Italy, the monastery of Monte Cassino (18 May 1944). Polish units – in particular the First Armoured Division – also played an honourable part in the invasion of northern Europe. These military achievements undoubtedly won sympathy for the Poles in the USA and Great Britain, a sympathy which carried political weight; but it was questionable whether this capital would be sufficient to ensure that the exile Government would receive the unconditional support of the Western Powers even in the face of Soviet claims. Autumn 1943 saw the start of powerful Russian offensives whose aim, apart from the destruction of the German forces, was the conquest of eastern Poland. These attacks were at first held up on the eastern frontiers of White Russia, but in the Ukraine they quickly led to the forcing of the Dnieper and an advance towards the Polish–Soviet border of 1939, which was crossed on 4 January 1944 at Sarny in Volhynia. The question of the Polish–Soviet frontier and the dispute over the relative validity of the Curzon Line and the Treaty of Riga now became really acute. The Western Powers were confronted here with a real dilemma, especially as the frontier problem had been so fatally prejudiced by the Hitler–Stalin pact of 1939. On the one hand they had to consider the morally and legally well-founded claims of a Poland for whose sake they had entered the war, and on the other the more questionable demands of

[1] A number of Polish ships – destroyers and submarines – also fought with distinction with the British navy throughout the war. (*Trans.*)

Soviet Russia, whose military achievements were far more important to Allied strategy than those of Poland. The unravelling of this Gordian knot depended solely on the result of conversations between the 'Big Three', Churchill, Roosevelt and Stalin; thus the attitude of Mikolajczyk and Sosnkowski to the frontier question, which was an absolutely decisive one for the Poles, was of only secondary importance.

Polish–Soviet differences were one of the more important subjects discussed at the Conference of Tehran (28 November to 1 December 1943). Stalin was able to sustain his thesis that the Curzon Line was 'ethnographically right' without any real argument from Churchill or Roosevelt. The British premier demonstrated with his well-known match-stick method how he envisaged the compensation of Poland with German territory (this proposal had been in the air for a year) and Poland's consequent 'migration to the west'. In harmony with the British guarantee of March 1939, Churchill clearly felt obliged to meet Stalin's demands, if these could not be refused, with corresponding counter-proposals. Compensation with the wealthy territories of eastern Germany seemed important to him because he wanted a strong post-war Poland to counterbalance the Soviet Union; it was at Tehran that his plan for an invasion through the Balkans was finally rejected. The problem of the exchange of population necessitated by 'shifting Poland to the west' seems to have worried only Roosevelt. Probably the only transfer of population which would have seemed permissible to him was one dictated by genuinely humanitarian considerations, such as the Greco–Turkish exchange after the First World War, which really did remove a source of strife from the world. To Stalin, who had been brought up in the Russian tradition of big shifts of population and as recently as 1941 had had all the Volga Germans deported, utilitarian considerations were no doubt decisive, while Churchill probably attached little importance to mass migrations of East Germans because he had been influenced by the deportations undertaken at that time by Hitler and Himmler and perhaps also by certain suggestions of Benes, in whose view the Sudeten Germans – if

only as passive tools of Hitler – had destroyed the first Czechoslovak republic. In these circumstances the Big Three agreed on
a westward shift of Poland, without defining its new western
frontiers or discussing in detail the necessary transfer of population. This arrangement was not binding in international law, but
it was nevertheless decisive.

After Tehran Churchill in particular exerted himself to gain
the agreement of the Mikolajczyk Government by emphasizing
the necessity of making concessions to the USSR. But the scheme
was rejected by almost all the exiled politicians, especially
Sosnkowski, and the British Premier failed completely to achieve
his aim. On 14 February 1944 the Polish Cabinet-in-exile agreed,
as an extreme concession, to accept a demarcation line to the east
of Vilna and Lwow, but it absolutely refused to accept the Curzon
Line and consequently any big shift of Poland to the west. The
big non-communist parties in Poland itself adopted the same
attitude. Churchill went on negotiating with Mikolajczyk about
this question until the latter resigned in November 1944, but in
spite of the application of considerable pressure the only result he
achieved was to cause continual internal crises in the exile Parliament and consequently in the Government as well.

The problem of relations with the USSR formed a kind of
watershed dividing the political forces in Poland itself as well.
The legitimate resistance movement, whose civil organization
owed allegiance to the 'Delegate of the Government-in-exile', Jan
Stanislaw Jankowski, and since the middle of 1943 had been
controlled by a 'Representative Political Committee for Poland'
consisting of members of the four old parties, continued to
recognize the policy of the Government-in-exile as lawful. The
AK (Home Army) therefore continued its unconditional struggle
against the occupying power – which, in spite of the German
defeats, with almost incredible hubris made no fundamental
change in the severity of its policy but only minor tactical alterations – although little sympathy for the aims of the AK could be
expected from the future Soviet conquerors. On the other hand,
the Moscow-controlled PPR and some allied left-wing splinter

groups organized themselves more firmly; on 1 January 1944 the fighting organization of the PPR was converted from the 'People's Guard' into the 'People's Army', but even after this change it never numbered more than a few thousand. Inside the PPR and the People's Army there were two groups: the officials schooled in the USSR and headed by Boleslaw Bierut, who had been flown into Poland in August 1943, and the 'native communists' led by Wladyslaw Gomulka, who in November 1943 had become secretary-general of the PPR. On 1 January 1944 all parties in agreement with Soviet policy and the Curzon Line formed a conspiratorial parliament, the 'National Council of Poland' (KRN) under the presidency of Boleslaw Bierut. This new foundation stimulated the creation of an underground Sejm by the old parties, which on 9 January 1944 formed a representative body known as the 'Council of National Unity' (RJN). The relationship between these two big underground movements was not unlike that between Mihailovich's camp and Tito's partisans in Yugoslavia; and bearing in mind the civil war in Yugoslavia the London Government gave express orders that the AK, though twenty times stronger, was not to interfere with the activities of the PPR and the People's Army. However in 1943 a third underground movement was formed, the 'National Fighting Force' (NSZ). It sprang from the right-wing radical 'Lizard League', and declined to fight against the German occupation authorities because it regarded the USSR as the more dangerous adversary. These forces, a good 30,000 strong, were under the nominal leadership of General Czeslaw Osiewicz, but were actually controlled by Colonel Tadeusz Kurcjusz, who had been a staff officer in the AK and was able to use his knowledge of the organization and planning of the AK for the benefit of his own troops. The proposed amalgamation of the NSZ with the AK, which Sosnkowski in particular would have liked to achieve, came to nothing precisely because of the different attitudes of the two organizations to the USSR. In the decisive negotiations of 7 March 1944 only a part of the NSZ agreed to take orders from the leaders of the AK.

The advance of the Soviet troops into Polish Volhynia at the end of 1943 and the beginning of 1944 confronted the big underground movements in Poland with the question of co-operation with the Soviet army in a practical form. The general staff of the AK had made plans for this eventuality; in accordance with the instructions of the Government-in-exile they provided for tactical co-operation with the Soviet forces so long as these respected Polish sovereignty over the territory to the west of the Riga frontiers. The order *'Burza'* ('tempest'), issued on 20 November 1943, was to be the signal for a general uprising, with intensified sabotage and diversionary activity, while at the same time selected combat groups were to be mobilized in the forests of Poland. In accordance with these orders the AK troops in Volhynia organized themselves into the 27th Polish division; they had hitherto been fighting the German occupation troops, isolated groups of Soviet partisans and the 'Ukrainian Rebel Army' (UPA) for control of the province. In March and April 1944 this 27th division took a hand in the fighting for Kowel; at first its efforts were successful, but through lack of support from the Soviet troops -- at first they even fought the AK units -- it was later almost completely annihilated. The spring fighting in Volhynia thus provided a sombre overture to the coming struggle for the mastery of Poland.

June 21–23 1944 saw the start, on the eastern borders of White Russia, of a Soviet offensive which led in a few weeks to the complete collapse of the German central army group and cost nearly twenty-five German divisions. During the advance of the Soviet armies the AK units – which in eastern Poland could call on at least 50,000 men – rose in local revolts. From 7 to 13 July 1944 they were fighting round Vilna, most of which was in their hands when it was occupied by Soviet troops on 13 July; they also took part in the fighting round Lwow from 23 to 27 July. The Soviet commanders gladly made use of this extremely valuable military help, but only a few days later they suppressed the AK units and had their leaders deported. It thus became quite clear to the Poles that the Soviet authorities had no intention of recognizing Polish sovereignty to the east of the Curzon Line.

The Soviet summer offensive, which on 14 July spread to the Ukrainian front as well, soon disclosed that the Soviet Government had still more extensive political aims. Scarcely had the Soviet spearheads succeeded in crossing the Bug – in these battles the A K troops captured, either alone or with Soviet help, eighteen towns in the Lublin region and were thereby largely instrumental in preventing the consolidation of the German front behind the Bug – when they set up in Chelm (21–22 July 1944), and later in Lublin, an opposition Government amenable to their own wishes. This was the 'Polish Committee of National Liberation' (P K W N); it was headed by the left-wing socialist Edward Osobka-Morawski and consisted predominantly of communists trained in the Soviet Union. This so-called 'Lublin Committee', which was officially recognized by the Government of the U S S R on 27 July, took over the administration of all Polish territory west of the Curzon Line conquered by Soviet troops; it also claimed to be the lawful organ of government for all the areas still to be wrested from the German occupation troops. Since most of the population it controlled, including the bulk of the socialists, continued to remain loyal to the London Government, its political basis was limited to a small 'popular front' alliance of left-wing splinter groups. For this very reason it tried to gain greater popularity by announcing a programme of general land reform. But even popular measures like this could not hide the fact that the authority of the satellite Government really rested on its executive power, which was supported by the Soviet. The committee therefore hastened to build up its own police force, which, with the Soviet security units, began to destroy ruthlessly the civil and military organizations of the national resistance movement. In addition, by amalgamating the 'People's Army' with the units of Berling's army, which had been raised in the Soviet Union, it created its own defence force, the 'Polish Army', which was quickly strengthened by conscription. The Lublin Committee thus served mainly to establish a barely-veiled Soviet supremacy over the whole of Poland. This *fait accompli* of 21–22 July 1944 served the interests of the Soviet

Union alone, since it called into being an amenable puppet Government which could be set up against the Governments of the Western Powers and the exile Government they had hitherto supported, and which also recognized the Curzon Line and westward shift of Poland as legitimate.

The disintegration of the German central army group, which could only manage to form an emergency defence line on the Vistula, the silent annexation of eastern Poland by the USSR and finally the proclamation of the Lublin committee decided the general staff of the AK to start a rising in Warsaw, the key point in the German Vistula line. Such an uprising had not been envisaged in the original plans. Bor-Komorowski's decision, which was fully approved by Jankowski, the vice-premier and the London Government's representative in Poland, was decisively influenced by the consideration that the Soviet troops – on 30–31 July 1941 Rokossovsky's army group was already advancing on Praga – ought to be welcomed as guests in an already liberated capital, not as conquerors; the tragedy of Vilna, Lwow and Lublin was this time to be avoided. In view of the collapse of the German troops, who by 31 July had had to abandon to the Soviet army the towns of Bialystok, Przemysl, Deblin and Pulawy and also some bridgeheads over the Vistula, it seemed possible to liberate Warsaw in a few days, especially as the AK had 50,000 men at its disposal in its Warsaw corps. On 29–30 July the Soviet broadcasting stations repeatedly called for a rising, referring to the help in the way of arms which could be expected from the Soviet, and on 1 August Bor-Komorowski gave the order to attack; by 4 August his units had captured most of the city, but then had to surrender the initiative to the German forces newly brought up from outside the city under the SS General Erich von dem Bach-Zelewski, and confine themselves to defence. The staff of the German Ninth Army, which was defending the Vistula on both sides of Warsaw, was informed of the plan for an uprising by its intelligence agents, but lacked the strength to prevent it; it was concentrating all its available units against Rokossovsky's army group, on which it launched one last great successful counter-attack on 3 August. All the same, this temporary defeat was not enough to explain why Rokossovsky let his troops stand idle in front of the German bridgehead at Praga until 10 September, that is for a good five weeks; by this time the insurgents had been split up into several small pockets and had started to negotiate a surrender. Soviet troops to the north and south of Warsaw were certainly in a position to force their way across the Vistula. That the inactivity of the Soviet units before Warsaw was intentional became fairly clear from the attitude of Stalin, who in conversation with Mikolajczyk – in Moscow since 30 July for negotiations – refused to accept responsibility for the 'senseless adventure' of the rising and in particular successfully delayed granting the Western air forces the right to land on Soviet aerodromes. The attempts of the US Air Force and the RAF to fly in supplies for the insurgents from England and Italy consequently remained completely inadequate; the use of the Polish parachute brigade, which had been specially trained to support insurrections in Poland, was not permitted by the British Government. In these circumstances small-scale attempts to cross the Vistula by Berling's army, which had been incorporated in Rokossovsky's army group (18–19 September 1944), and a simultaneous supply flight by 250 US bombers came too late. On 2 October, after all military possibilities had been exhausted and pockets of his men had already capitulated, Bor-Komorowski and the rest of his troops had to lay down their arms. The Soviet Government's passivity, indeed even obstructiveness, which was the primary reason for the tragic end of the revolt, made it seem probable that the Russians were more concerned with the destruction of the Polish *élite* than with strategic considerations. If they spared themselves the necessity of taking their own measures to suppress the national resistance, as they had in the area to the east of the Vistula, and left this task to Germans, it was nevertheless apparent that they had taken to heart the lessons of Tsarist policy towards Poland, especially those of the rebellion of 1794.

The Warsaw rising formed the turning-point in the struggle between the communist or communist supporters and the anti-communist forces among the Poles; the defeat of the latter was largely due to the poor support received from the Western Powers. It was in vain that under pressure from Churchill Mikolajczyk displayed the utmost readiness to meet the Soviet half-way. Even the resignation of Sosnkowski, which the Russians secured on 30 September, was of no avail. He was replaced as commander-in-chief by Bor-Komorowski, now a prisoner of the Germans. When Mikolajczyk asked the British Government for support it informed him in the 'Cadogan letter' of 2 November 1944 that it would favour the Curzon Line and the Oder as the frontiers of a future Poland, but could only guarantee the independence of Poland in conjunction with the USSR. Mikolajczyk also turned to Roosevelt, whose support seemed still more important, but the American President waited until he had been re-elected on 7 November 1944 before giving an evasive reply (on 17 November) couched in very general terms. It thus became clear that Churchill still hoped to be able to make a Poland reinforced by eastern Germany into something of a counterpoise to the USSR, while to Roosevelt the military defeat of Germany and Japan still took precedence over the political problems of the post-war period. Both these attitudes were quite unacceptable to the Polish Government-in-exile and Mikolajczyk took the only course open to him: on 24 November 1944 he resigned. His successor, who in view of the situation in Poland was faced with an almost impossible task, was Tomasz Arciszewski, the old leader of the PPS and an irreconcilable opponent of the Bolsheviks. Arciszewski eventually took office on 29 November, but he too was unable to convince Churchill, who was very much in favour of the cession of eastern Germany to Poland and the transfer of the German population, that the cession of eastern Germany would in itself make the future Poland inescapably dependent on the USSR.

In Poland itself especially, the turn which the Warsaw rising had given to events became clear to all the political parties. Under its new commander, Leopold Okulicki, the AK continued operation 'Burza' against the German troops to the west of the

Vistula, particularly in the Kielce-Radom area, where the AK troops for a time tied down several German divisions. Not until the onset of winter 1944 was partial demobilization ordered, and even then headquarters staffs were kept together. In itself the continuation of the struggle against the declining German power had little point, since the Soviet authorities had shown clearly enough their readiness to destroy the national underground forces. Nevertheless, even the last measures of the occupying power were calculated to perpetuate the bitter enmity of the Poles for everything German, particularly Hitler's order of 1 August 1944 that Warsaw was to be razed to the ground as a punishment for the rising and that if need be not even its civil inhabitants were to be spared. As a result of this command thousands of women and children and tens of thousands of non-combatants had been killed in the first few days of the revolt, and after it had been suppressed there began, on 3 October 1944, a systematic process of demolition – quite unnecessary from a military point of view – which involved the destruction of almost all Warsaw's important buildings, its palaces, museums, archives and art collections, and thus finally turned the city into a wilderness. This last act of National Socialist barbarity induced not only the AK units but even a number of NSZ groups to combat the German domination in its last hour. The Lublin Committee made a great deal of capital out of the devastation of Warsaw; it tried to represent itself as the real opponent of the Germans by taking over Soviet slogans about the unrealistic character of the AK's efforts. By 1 January 1945 the PKWN was able to proclaim itself the 'Provisional Polish Government' (PRT) and thus consolidate its claim to all Polish territory still to be liberated.

The final collapse of the German occupation was effected by the long-prepared Soviet winter offensive, which began on 12–14 January 1945 and by the middle of March had brought under Soviet control the whole of western Poland and eastern Germany as far as the Oder. Warsaw and Cracow – where Governor-General Frank had officiated until the end – fell into the hands of the Soviet armies, and hence into those of the Provisional Government, on 17 and 18 January respectively. In accordance with the exile Government's instructions of 8 December 1944 the AK tried to go underground; on 19 January 1945 General Okulicki ordered the dispersal of AK units, while the officers remained bound to silence and conspiracy. The NSZ troops started guerrilla warfare against the Soviet army in the Holy Cross mountains and the Beskids; some of their units even joined up with the retreating German troops. The NSZ soldiers and those of the AK who made themselves known were persecuted so mercilessly by the Soviet and Polish security units that in the Sandomierz area, for example, between 18 August 1944 and 13 February 1945 more persons were arrested than in the previous four years of German occupation. The civil and military leaders of the AK resistance movement, who had already begun to create a new underground organization called 'Independence' (NIE) to outlast the Soviet occupation, were enticed to Warsaw on 27–29 March 1945 by the assurance of a safe conduct and from there were taken to Moscow, where fifteen of them, including Okulicki and Jankowski, were condemned to long terms of imprisonment. About 50,000 members of the AK and an unknown number of NSZ soldiers were also deported to Russia. Under Soviet protection the authorities of the Provisional Government took over the administration not only of Poland but also of the already conquered east German territories and of the free city of Danzig, which was converted on 30 March into a Polish voievodeship. Thus the Provisional Government already regarded Danzig and eastern Germany up to the Oder as Polish territory; in this way future international agreements were prejudiced.

At the Yalta Conference (4–11 February 1945), which took place just at the time of the huge Soviet advance from the Vistula to the Oder, the Big Three took further important decisions about the internal and external form of post-war Poland. The already mortally sick Roosevelt – he died on 12 April – was interested in the question of the Polish frontiers only from the point of view of possible effects on American internal politics, and therefore offered little opposition to Stalin, although the State Department, in a number of excellent memoranda, had drawn his attention to the serious consequences which the deportation of East Germans would have in so far as it would make the future Poland dependent on Soviet supremacy; in addition, he probably overestimated the military requirements for the defeat of Germany and Japan, and hence the consideration due to the USSR, just as he certainly attached too much value to the compensating effect of the United Nations in the post-war period. As for Churchill, since the formation of the Polish Provisional Government he had obviously seen that his secretly pursued intention of creating a strong Poland to counterbalance the Soviet Union had become unreal, and that consequently the policy he had followed since Tehran of forcing eastern Germany on Poland was based on a miscalculation. However, owing to the positions he had taken up earlier, especially in the Cadogan letter, he was unable to secure any changes in the frontier question, hard though he tried at Yalta. Stalin therefore had a fairly easy time at the conference; the Curzon Line was finally adopted on 6 February 1945, while no definite decision was taken about the extent of the territorial compensation in the west. Although the whole of Poland was now occupied by the Russians, Roosevelt and Churchill tried to ensure that its government would be democratic in the Western sense of the word, and to this end they insisted on linking the frontier question with that of free elections, to be held at once; however, in the decisive question, that of a fresh Government, they accepted the Soviet view that this must be based on the Provisional Government, with a few London politicians participating as individuals. This decision meant the cool sacrifice of the London Government, which for more than four years had been accepted as the legitimate Government of Poland. Thanks to the *de facto* power which it exercised in Poland and to its apparent indispensability to Allied strategy, the Soviet Government had achieved its fundamental aims.

Since Arciszewski's Government had lost its last footholds in Poland the enforcement of the Yalta decisions caused no serious difficulties, but the negotiations over the composition of the new 'Government of National Unity' dragged on for some months. Although Poland had belonged to the United Nations since

1 January 1942, she was not invited to the first conference at San Francisco on 25 April 1945, since the exile Government was not acceptable to the USSR and the Provisional Government had not yet been recognized by the Western Powers. The arrest of the political leaders of the national underground movement by the Soviet authorities on 29 March 1945 led temporarily to a sharp controversy with the State Department, but the American ambassador-at-large, Harry Hopkins, finally succeeded in effecting an agreement about the formation of the new Polish Government, even though he was unable to prevent the trial of the arrested AK leaders (18–21 June 1945). So the Government of National Unity (PRZN) came into existence on 28 June 1945; in the end only two members of the exile Government participated in it, one of the two being Mikolajczyk. On 5 July 1945 the new Cabinet was recognized by the Governments of the USA and Great Britain, and this finally rendered it futile for the exile Government to make any further claim to international recognition.

At the Potsdam Conference (17 July to 2 August 1945) Poland was represented from 24 July onwards by a delegation headed by Bierut and Mikolajczyk. The Polish delegation pushed hard for a new Polish western frontier along the Oder and the western section of the Neisse; it thus strengthened the Soviet diplomatic position, although in fact its decision on the frontier question had been made for it long in advance. So far as Polish affairs were concerned, the declaration of 2 August 1945 corresponded in general to Soviet expectations. Polish sovereignty over the eastern parts of Germany, including southern East Prussia and Danzig, was recognized in the form of an administrative mandate, and the Polish authorities received the power to deport the German inhabitants of the region. These Potsdam agreements also obliged Poland to hold free elections for a constituent assembly as soon as possible. Thus the decisions of the three Heads of Government embodied only one of the original Western postulates, in the shape of certain obligations, postponed to the future, on the part of the Polish Government, while the Eastern demands were in practice already fulfilled. The whole work of the Potsdam

A History of Modern Poland

Conference bore a provisional character, since the final solution of all frontier and resettlement questions was to be reserved for a future peace treaty. This very decision gave rise to a long-standing controversy, since in the view of many Western statesmen – particularly German ones – the Potsdam conference prejudiced nothing, while in the Eastern view its decisions constituted a genuine preliminary peace settlement. At all events, for Poland – and also for Germany – the Potsdam Conference became in practice the concluding diplomatic event of the Second World War, since it settled for a sizeable period of time territorial and national questions in the Germano–Polish frontier area, if only in a forcible and inorganic way.

The Potsdam decisions set the seal on the paradoxical historical fact that the result of a universal war originally begun to preserve Poland's integrity was the partitioning of the country's territory and population and the imposition of a régime rejected by the majority of Poles. The responsibility for this certainly lay to a large extent with the Western Powers, whose policy of compromising with the USSR forced this fate on Poland; on the other hand Churchill and Roosevelt had their hands forced by the concession which Hitler had made to the Soviet Union in August 1939. If Soviet policy was able in 1944–5 to set up the satellite Government and create the Soviet Poland which Stalin had visualized in 1920 and Pilsudski had prevented by the victory on the Vistula, it was fundamentally indebted for this success to National Socialist hubris. It was Nazi arrogance which had thought it could heedlessly tear down central Europe's bastion against the Bolsheviks. This considerably reduces the responsibility of Western statesmen for the indubitably wrong decisions of Tehran, Yalta and Potsdam. Moreover, Western statesmen's lasting sense of guilt towards Poland provided Poles both in exile and at home with a piece of moral capital which could be made to pay a handsome political dividend, especially after the upheaval of October 1956.

CHAPTER VII

Poland After the Second World War
(1945-1956)

POLAND ON THE MOVE

The fate of Poland in the post-war period was to be moulded by the advance of the Soviet armies into central Europe and the decisions of the great powers at the conferences of Yalta and Potsdam. The geographical shift of the Polish state to the west, the loss of almost half its old territory in the east and the allocation to it of parts of eastern Germany destroyed the basis of the Jagellonian Poland which had been the object of such bitter struggles from 1916 to 1921 and even from 1939 to 1944. The expulsion of the old-established Polish population from the historical eastern marches, a process which corresponded to the expulsion of the Ukrainians and White Russians from Congress Poland and central Galicia, and the numerically far more important eviction of the East Germans, broke up structures that had existed for centuries. It ended the mixture of nationalities and religions which had long been so typical of eastern central Europe and finally turned not only Poland but also the Lithuanian, White Russian and Ukrainian nations, which had arisen on the soil of the historical Polish empire, into purely national states. It was only the forcible division of peoples which ensured the incorporation of the Lithuanian, White Russian and Ukrainian linguistic areas in the Soviet Union and transformed the long-disputed Curzon Line into a real national frontier. At the same time the removal of the Polish frontier to the Oder and Neisse, which was effected through the flight, resettlement or expulsion of the East Germans, created a compact, national Polish State in territory which had after all been ruled by the Piast dynasty in the Middle Ages.

MAP 7

Poland after the Second World War (1945–1956)

The agreements of Yalta and Potsdam laid heavy burdens on the Polish nation. In the east Poland lost about 70,000 square miles out of its pre-war area of 150,000 square miles; in return it took over the administration of some East German provinces and the free city of Danzig – altogether some 39,610 square miles. Indeed if we take into account the old Polish realm of 1772, the loss of surface area amounted to more than 180,000 square miles, that is, a slab of territory as big as the Germany of 1937. Only about 80,000 square miles of the old State – 28 per cent of the area of the Republic of 1772 or 54 per cent of the territory of 1921 – were unaffected by the frontier changes. Thus the State created in 1945, consisting of what was left of the old Poland plus Danzig and the East German territories, covered about 120,000 square miles, 39,000 of which had been German up to the end of the Second World War. The great powers had therefore moved the home of the Polish nation some 150 miles, on an average, to the west.

This decision was all the more painful for Poland since these territorial changes did not mean simply a change of ruler, as would have been the case in the eighteenth century, but on the contrary brought with them the expulsion and resettlement of huge numbers of people The Polish nation had already suffered heavy losses of population during the war; one in five of the citizens of the pre-war republic had fallen in battle or been killed in some other way, and there was scarcely a family which did not mourn the loss of one of its members. In the remaining part of the country alone the population, which had amounted on 1 January 1939 to about 23,210,000 had fallen to some 18,840,000, as was shown by the 'summary census' of 14 February 1946. This figure corresponded fairly closely to the census figure of 1910, so that the Second World War had consumed the population increase of thirty-five years. Apart from the numerical aspect, the loss was a terrible one from the qualitative point of view, for the liquidation operations of both the Germans and the Russians – apart from the general destruction of the Jews by the Germans – had been aimed primarily against the Polish intelligentsia. For this reason the westward emigration of the Poles which began in 1945, and the corresponding expulsion of the German, Lithuanian, White Russian and Ukrainian population, took place in circumstances which, in spite of many isolated acts of reconciliation, revealed the general desire for revenge and reparation. The methods introduced into central Europe for the first time by Hitler – transplantation of whole national groups, manipulation of 'racial raw material', contempt, repeatedly shown, for the rights of the native population – now impinged on the non-Polish inhabitants, especially the East Germans and Danzigers.

These forced migrations began in eastern Poland, which was finally allocated to the Soviet Union by the frontier treaty signed in Moscow on 16 August 1945. The Curzon Line, with a few minor alterations, became the frontier between Poland and Russia; this was a clear victory for Soviet diplomacy, which had thus made good its defeat in 1920–21. By this settlement Poland lost territory which had been inhabited at the beginning of the war by nearly twelve million people. The two parties to the negotiations also established a provisional demarcation line in East Prussia running almost due east from the Frischer Haff at Braunsberg to the point near Suwalki where the former German, Lithuanian and Polish frontiers had all met; the process of marking it out precisely was concluded on 7 May 1947 by a 'demarcation protocol'. The exchange of population, which had been arranged in principle as early as 9 and 22 September 1944, was governed by the agreement of 6 July 1945. It is true that the official transfer of the three million Poles who had lived in the ceded area brought only about a million and a quarter under Polish sovereignty, but those who had fled in 1939–40 and 1944–5 swelled the number of Poles from the east to be found on Polish soil in 1950 to about 2,180,000. Although these figures indicate that hundreds of thousands of Poles remained – unwillingly, for the most part – in the lands to the east of the new frontier, the Polish character of the Eastern Marches was so thoroughly obliterated that in future it would be quite hopeless for Poland to make any claim to these regions on ethnic grounds. After all, back in 1921 more than a million Poles had emigrated westward from the territories to the east of the frontier established by the Treaty of Riga. To counter-balance this expulsion of Poles, most of the Lithuanians, White Russians and Ukrainians living west of the new frontier were sent off to the east. About 520,000 inhabitants of the regions of Suwalki, Chelm and Przemysl thus came under Soviet rule, while about 120,000 were moved out of former German territory. As the Poles did not succeed in resettling these regions fully, thinly populated areas came into existence; for example, the once thickly populated region of Przemysl lost – compared with the figure for 1931 – 54 per cent of its inhabitants. Transfers of population in the east came to an end for the time being with the Polish–Soviet frontier correction treaty of 15 February 1951, by which Poland ceded about 180 square miles of border territory on the upper Bug and received in return the same amount of land to the east of the upper San. The populations of these two areas were also ex-changed.

The exchange of population in the East German–Danzig mandated area was a much more serious affair. Article XIII of the Potsdam Agreement of 2 August 1945 had given the Polish Government the right to expel all Germans from 'Poland' in an 'orderly and humane fashion'. Taken literally, this decision applied to the 1,300,000 Polish citizens who, according to the pre-war census and counts made by the Germans themselves, reckoned that they were of German nationality. However, the Warsaw Govern-ment interpreted their powers as extending to the ex-German territory under their administration. This region, as far as the Oder and Neisse, had also been handed over to them by the Potsdam agreement (Article IX b). In the Polish view the Warsaw government was thereby entitled to expel a population of about 8,400,000 German citizens – this did not include the northern part of East Prussia, ceded to the Soviet Union – and about 400,000 citizens of Danzig. This interpretation was tacitly approved by the Allied Control Commission for Germany in so far as the Polish authorities had begun the expulsion in June 1945 and on 17–20 November a plan was drawn up by the Commission for the reception of fugitives. A considerable proportion of those affected had fled or been evacuated during the Soviet offensives of 1944–5, but had no wish to bid farewell to their homeland for ever; this was shown by the fact that by the middle of 1945 about a million Silesians and a quarter of a million other East Germans had returned from evacuation. There can be no doubt that the Polish interpretation of the Potsdam decisions corresponded to the intentions of the great powers at the end of 1944, even if these intentions had perhaps changed by the time of the Potsdam conference itself. On 15 December in the House of Commons Churchill had deplored the resistance of the Polish Government to the partition of eastern Germany and had given this assurance: 'So far as Russia and Great Britain are concerned, Poland is at liberty to extend her territory to the west at the expense of Germany.' He had also pleaded in favour of 'the complete eviction of the Germans from the territories which Poland gains in the west and north.' Recognizing providentially that fundamentally such a solution would benefit only the Soviet Union, and that it would prolong Germano–Polish enmity for as long as could be foreseen, Arciszewski, the Polish Prime Minister at that time, had replied to Churchill that Poland did not wish to push her frontier so far west that it enclosed eight or ten million Germans. The Polish Government desired 'neither Breslau nor Stettin'. Now this solution which they had fought against for so long was imposed on the Poles just as forcibly as on the Germans. There was a very curious dichotomy in the Potsdam agreements: on the one hand Poland was expressly granted only administrative authority over eastern Germany, but on the other hand the expulsion of its inhabitants which had been encouraged by the Governments of the three Great Powers themselves was tacitly permitted and the administrative mandate was thus robbed of its essential content. In this way a *fait accompli* of scarcely imaginable proportions was effected, but at the same time the injured party was assured of a legal claim against this *fait accompli*, a claim whose validity in international law could hardly be doubted. By taking over eastern Germany and driving out the majority of its inhabitants Poland put herself in a position, *vis-à-vis* revisionist policy, of almost unavoidable dependence on the Soviet Union; Stalin's great counter-stroke against the Hitlerian conception of a combined Germano–Polish invasion of the Soviet Union had succeeded all the more in so far as from now on millions of East Germans who had been driven from their homes were bound to become, for objective reasons, the exponents of anti-Polish revisionist ideas. It is by the hold thus gained over the whole Polish nation even more than by the acquisition of eastern Poland that the extent of the Soviet triumph at Potsdam should be measured.

The transfer of eastern Germany and Danzig to the Polish state began as early as 30 March 1945 with the creation of the voivodeship or province of Danzig (Gdansk), but dragged on – especially in Silesia – until September. The Government formed the three big 'administrative areas' of Masuria, Pomerania and Silesia, which were put under the control of 'plenipotentiaries of the Polish Government'; smaller pieces of territory were administered from the neighbouring provinces. On 29 May 1946 these administrative divisions were confirmed by law and the administrative areas were converted into provinces; the additional border strips to the west of the Oder near Stettin acquired in October 1945 and October 1947 were incorporated in them. Since 13 November 1945 all the 'recovered western territories', usually called later on simply 'the recovered territories', had been under the control of a special ministry headed by Wladyslaw Gomulka, the Deputy Prime Minister and secretary-general of the PPR. His chief task was to ensure, in accordance with Prime Minister Osobka-Morawski's proclamation of 3 May 1945, that the administrative area was 'handed back to Polish culture and settled by Poles'.

The eviction of the Germans was carried out in several stages between 1945 and 1949. According to the German census of 13 September 1950 and the Polish census of 3 December 1950, flight and expulsion, including all losses, accounted for about 7,200,000 German citizens and 380,000 citizens of Danzig; of these about

1,200,000 Germans and some 90,000 Danzigers perished. About 880,000 former Polish citizens of German nationality were expelled from Polish territory; roughly 200,000 of these died, many of them in Polish internment camps. Among those not evicted were about 1,190,000 Germans, 30,000 Danzigers and 430,000 Polish citizens who before the war had mostly classified themselves as German but now opted in large numbers for Polish nationality. Those German and Danzig citizens who stayed where they were – there were nearly 1,260,000 of them on 3 December 1950 – were divided by the Polish administration into 'autochthonous natives' and 'recognized Germans'. The main reason why the quarter of a million 'recognized Germans' were exempted from expulsion was that until 1947 they were working for the Soviet occupation troops and afterwards had no opportunity to leave. Like all Germans not expelled from Poland, until 20 July 1950 they were placed under separate laws and to a large extent lacked any German cultural facilities. The million or so 'natives' – Polish estimates of their numbers varied from 992,000 to 1,075,000 – were mostly bilingual and had predominantly Polish names; the bulk of them – about 750,000 – were Upper Silesians, and most of the rest Masurians. Although before the war a large number of these 'natives' had embraced German nationality, the Government attached particular value to looking after them since they were regarded as really Polish and only superficially Germanized, and therefore well adapted to demonstrating the original 'essentially Polish' character of the 'administrative area'. For this reason they were verified as Poles, mainly in 1945–6, by specially appointed commissions, which employed purely material, pseudo-objective criteria. The results by no means always corresponded to the wishes of those 'verified', but in the last analysis profession of German nationality meant expulsion. After the verification 'natives' were not allowed to use the German language in school, church, the Government service or the law courts. But these very measures and others dictated by an impatient nationalism led quickly to a fresh consolidation of the German position among the 'natives'; in Upper Silesia a German underground organization was even formed. There was certainly a grain of truth in the bitter observation of a Polish superintendent of the Evangelical Church who before the war had striven tirelessly in German Upper Silesia for the preservation of Polish nationality and now came to this conclusion: 'Ten years under the Polish People's Republic have succeeded in doing what six hundred years of German rule could not accomplish – turn the native Poles into Germans.' Nevertheless, the strength of Polish culture was also demonstrated by 'natives' who later emigrated to West Germany and there sometimes became defenders of Polish civilization. On the whole the official thesis that the region was fundamentally Polish found little support among the mass of ordinary Poles, since the Poles' traditional sense of justice often opposed interpretations which did not fit the more recent history of eastern Germany. All the same, outwardly the nation shared the Government's attitude to the question of eastern Germany, for it was always conscious that the Government could not adduce the real reasons for the partition of eastern Germany out of deference to the Soviet Union, and was consequently in a somewhat embarrassing situation.

The settlement of Poles went on hand in hand with the expulsion of the German population. In summer 1945 'indiscriminate settlement' was still the order of the day, although in June 1945 the CC of the PPR had drawn up a detailed colonization plan. The activity of the 'First Brigade' – this was the Poles' nickname, borrowed from the Pilsudski period, for adventurers and plunderers – together with the bonfires of the Soviet occupation troops added a good deal to the damage caused by the war. However, from winter 1945–6 onwards settlement went on for the most part in an orderly fashion and under the control of the 'National Repatriation Ministry'. At the census of 12 February 1946 the number of new settlers amounted to about 1,850,000; by 31 December 1947 another 2,346,000 had immigrated into the area. The census of 3 December 1950 showed that the 'administrative area' already had a population of about 5,900,000, or almost two-thirds that of 17 May 1939; this figure included, besides the

1,260,000 indigenous inhabitants, about 1,500,000 new settlers from eastern Poland. Seeing that one Pole in every four now lived in the 'administrative area' (i.e. that part of Poland which had been German territory before the war) and that the latter had become a region inhabited predominantly by Poles, the Government felt that it could abolish its special administrative status. After the 'Ministry for the Recovered Territories' had been wound up on 21 January 1949, a number of administrative changes took place which were intended to bind the ex-German territories more closely to the State. An effort was made to secure diplomatic confirmation of Polish sovereignty over these regions by means of two agreements with the Government of the East German Republic. The combined Polish–East German declaration of 6 June 1950, in which the Oder-Neisse line was described as the 'final frontier' between the two countries, was complemented by the frontier treaty of 6 July 1950. However, so far as validity in international law was concerned, neither pact was recognized outside the eastern bloc.

The political and ethnic 'Polonization' of the ex-German territories was accompanied by a similar process in the ecclesiastical sphere; Poland's churches too had to emigrate to the west with their members. In the Catholic Church the complete or partial loss of the eastern Polish dioceses was followed by the creation of the five apostolic administrations of Breslau, Offeln, Allenstein, Landsberg and Danzig which Cardinal Hlond – primate of Poland and papal legate – set up on 15 August 1945. However, in accordance with the wishes of the Vatican the new order did not affect the continuance in ecclesiastical law of the province of Breslau; it was simply designed to create provisional arrangements for the spiritual care of the newly-arrived Catholics. By 1950 the build-up of the Catholic Church in the ex-German territories was almost complete; over 3,000 priests looked after the six million or more Catholics who were then living in the newly-created administrative districts. By a State decree of 19 September 1946 the 300,000 or so members of the Evangelical Church who remained in the region were put under the control of the Polish

Evangelical Church. In general, the State was anxious to stabilize the ecclesiastical situation in the ex-German territories in accordance with its own policy. After the frontier treaty of 6 July 1950 had been signed the Government therefore pressed the Catholic authorities to replace the provisional administrative districts by permanent bishoprics. Since the Vatican and the Polish episcopate refused to comply with these wishes, on 26 January 1951 the Government deposed the apostolic administrators and had capitular vicars acceptable to itself elected by so-called 'diocesan councils'. This arbitrary solution was to last for more than five years, and formed one of the causes of the conflict between Church and State which came into the open a little later. There could be no doubt that up to then not only purely spiritual but also patriotic motives had been involved in the Polish episcopate's efforts to build up the Church's organization swiftly in the ex-German territories. Primate Stefan Wyszynski, Hlond's successor, described the re-establishment of Catholicism in eastern Germany as an act of 'the justice of God, the lord of history'.

Compared with the great problems of Poland's westward shift, smaller frontier conflicts with Czechoslovakia dating from the pre-war period possessed, as it were, only episodic importance. The long-standing dispute about Teschen, occupied in the name of Poland by Marshal Michal Rola-Zymierski's troops on 19 June 1945, was checked by Soviet intervention. The restoration of the frontiers of 1920–1938 did not rob the conflict of its sharpness, as was shown by the repeated failure of negotiations on the subject. Not until the signature of the Polish–Czech assistance pact on 10 March 1947 was tension relaxed in accordance with Soviet wishes, both sides tacitly renouncing any further attempts at frontier revision.

On top of its problems at home the Warsaw Government had to cope with the question of the *émigrés* who during the war had supported the London Government and for the most part were still loyal to it, although the Great Powers had ceased to recognize it since the end of the war. The existence of a competing Government based on the exile army seemed all the more threatening to the Warsaw régime since this government continued to maintain that it was the only legitimate government of Poland and was in fact still recognized by the Vatican, Spain, Ireland and a few smaller States. International, political and ideological differences between the two Governments seemed to rule out any possibility of an agreement. These differences helped considerably to worsen relations between the Warsaw Government and those of the Western Powers; the British Government in particular was not ready to accede to Warsaw's demands that the Government-in-exile should be liquidated and the army repatriated. The question of the Polish gold reserves in Great Britain was finally settled by the financial agreement of 24 June 1946; so far as the return of the army was concerned, the London Government guaranteed every soldier, contrary to Warsaw's wishes, the right to make a free choice. In fact only 55,000 out of the 228,000 members of the Polish forces returned home; the rest remained abroad. In the end, on 13 September 1946, the Warsaw Government deprived all those unwilling to return of Polish citizenship. However, it could not prevent the formation among the proved leaders of the Second World War of a young political *émigré* movement which strove to continue the tested traditions of the 'Golden Emigration' of 1831. After the death of President Raczkiewicz, the resignation of Prime Minister Arciszewski in June 1947 and the flight of Mikol-ajczyk in October 1947, the *émigré* movement split into a number of political groups, some of them at loggerheads with each other; nevertheless, all these intertwined bodies formed a sort of 'substitute State'. Finally the 'Council of Three', set up on 8 August 1954, to which Anders, Arciszewski and Edward Raczyn-ski belonged, was recognized by the majority of Poles in exile as their political hub. The Government in Poland was unable to convert the *émigrés* to its own way of thinking, although from July 1955 onwards it made great efforts to win them over, especially by founding the 'Polonia' society, and did succeed in inducing a few individual politicians to return home. The *émigrés* were very active in the worlds of scholarship and public life and sought to help metropolitan Poland, often to the detriment of their own political interests. Thus the new *émigrés* of the Second World War remained what their predecessors of 1831 had managed to be for generations, a living branch of the Polish nation.

THE REPRESSION OF NON-COMMUNIST FORCES IN THE POST-WAR REPUBLIC

After the end of the war, in accordance with the expectations of the Soviet Government, the logic of Poland's geographical and ethnic shift to the west began to affect the Poles' political thinking as well. The Jagellonian tradition certainly remained alive in their historical consciousness, and so did the memory of the centuries-old struggle with Russia which had not been decided until 1921. Similarly, the feeling that they were culturally superior to the Russians was not entirely forgotten. Nevertheless, the majority of Poles became convinced that after the transfer of population there could be no question of winning back the eastern territories. Views like those of the old man Studnicki, who demanded the moving back of the eastern Poles and a revisionist policy in the east, were regarded as hopelessly impractical and won little or no support. On the other hand, the German territories taken over as compensation in the west could obviously be retained only by close collaboration with the Soviet Union, especially as historical experience showed that the Poles would certainly have to reckon with an energetic German revisionist policy. Unpleasant as many people found the decision in favour of Germano–Polish hostility forced on them by the Great Powers because of the frontier question, reasons of state necessitated a policy of good neighbourliness with the Russian people, whatever kind of government it might possess. Thus even non-communist Poles had to adopt a policy which since the unsuccessful revolt of 1863 had been foreshadowed in the positivism of Swietochowski and developed in the political thinking of Dmowski. Thus through an objective change in all the political circumstances, a change for which Pilsudski's political activity could certainly not be made responsible, the marshal's mode of thought had lost its chance of exerting any further influence.

As a matter of fact, traditional historico-political conceptions provided a good touchstone by which to measure the extent to which the compromise decisions of the Great Powers had affected the internal politics of Poland. Without doubt Poland's future destiny was decisively affected by the fact that in practice the Government of National Unity and the National Council (KRN) controlled the country. A historical lesson on this point had been provided by the struggle between Pilsudski and Dmowski after the First World War, even if this struggle had been conducted on different lines. Nevertheless, on that occasion the opposition forces had finally won the day, and this lent hope to the large number of Poles who felt bound to the old pre-war parties and their exiled leaders or to the returned Mikolajczyk. After all, the example of Finland seemed to show that incorporation in the Soviet bloc need not necessarily entail an internal social transformation on the pattern of the Soviet State. People felt that they could rely on the proved strength of political and purely spiritual resistance, which had saved the national soul even in the period of Russification from 1864 to 1905, and above all on the Catholic Church, which seemed called in a special way to be the protector of the Polish way of life. On the other hand, no open political opposition could be attempted simply because, thanks to the existing legislation and methods of government, the legal possibilities were far more limited than after the First World War. Loyalty to the former Pilsudski camp or to the National Party, especially the National Radicals, was regarded as high treason. These assumptions, in conjunction with the fact that those of the old parties which were permitted only gradually lost their conspiratorial character while those not permitted remained underground, led in the first few years after the war to that curious hovering between semi-legality and semi-illegality which characterized the political activity of the opposition. This was far more pronounced in Poland than in other eastern European countries. Likewise, the fact that the opposition parties were rooted in underground movements, while lending them additional powers of resistance, also made it easier for the Government to take action against them under the criminal code. In view of this situation the State could reckon on being able to make a good start at suppressing non-communist forces and forcing the country into the Soviet mould.

The influence of the communists in the State was based primarily on the fact that, with the Lublin socialists, they had a majority in the National Council. More important still, the Government of National Unity was dominated in practice by the PPR (Polish Workers' Party), although on the surface it contained only six PPR ministers. For example, by the side of the Prime Minister, Edward Osobka Morawski, stood Wladyslaw Gomulka, the secretary of the PPR, in the post of Deputy Premier; and even those ministers who did not belong to the PPR were for the most part assisted by loyal party members who, as Secretaries of State, materially helped to determine Government policy. In addition, some of the nominally independent ministers such as Michal Rola Zymierski, the officially non-party Minister of War, were at least outwardly in sympathy with the aims of the PPR. Finally – and this was to be as decisive in securing the triumph of communism in Poland as it was in other countries of the eastern bloc – the police forces (known as the MO or 'Citizens' Militia'), the 'Internal Security Corps' and various special troops were under the command of the Security Minister, Stanislaw Radkiewicz (PPR), who thereby had at his disposal at first larger forces than the War Minister. By the decree 'For the Protection of the State', issued as early as 30 October 1944, the Security Minister was empowered to take action against the steadily growing political movements which rejected the Government of National Unity and had remained underground in the middle of 1945.

These resistance groups represented a number of very different political tendencies. Besides the successors of the AK, namely the NIE units, which soon assumed the collective title 'Freedom and Independence' (WIN), groups of the right-wing radical 'National Forces' (NSZ) were still operating, and so were units of the 'Ukrainian Rebel Army' (UPA), especially in the area round Przemysl and Chelm. An amnesty announced by the Government

on 2 August 1945 for all underground fighters who came into the
open and handed in their weapons within a month had little
success; for example, according to official figures only 9,450 men
of the former AK had laid down their arms by 12 October 1945.
The security troops therefore waged guerrilla warfare against 'the
men from the forest' more energetically than before, and in
November 1945 they registered their first big success by arresting
the headquarters staffs of the WIN and NSZ. Nevertheless, the
'Joint Committee of Underground Organizations' (PKOP),
founded on conspiratorial lines in December 1945, continued to
wage the politico-military struggle so long as there seemed to be
any chance, from a diplomatic point of view, of preserving a
bourgeois, democratic form of state. With the consolidation of the
communist régime after the elections of January 1947 active
resistance gradually petered out. Nevertheless, on 28 March 1947
Ukrainian UPA partisans succeeded in shooting the Deputy War
Minister, Karol Swierczewski, in the Sanok area.

The gradual suppression of the national underground forces
was accompanied by action against the legal opposition. The
Government regarded the crippling of the opposition as a particularly urgent necessity because the Government party proper,
the PPR, had a relatively small number of adherents; between
April and June 1945 its membership had sunk from 300,000 to
160,000. The main reason for this drop was that Zhdanov's policy
speeches at that time and Mikolajczyk's participation in the
Government had led many Poles to believe in the possibility of
an 'individual Polish way', a 'middle way' between Eastern and
Western forms of government, and made them think that it
was possible to avoid a purely Soviet brand of communism. The
other Lublin parties were in the same position of weakness as
compared with the older parties of the same name in Poland, and
could count only on a small following. In this situation the actual
or supposed participation of members of the Opposition in the
underground movement gave the Government a ready means of
getting rid of individual politicians or even whole groups, and
the security minister did not fail to make use of it. The Govern-

ment also tried, although with only moderate success, to broaden the base of the *bourgeois* and socialist Lublin parties by amalgamating them with the corresponding traditional parties.

The Government regarded it as particularly important to enlarge and strengthen the Lublin PPS under Osobka-Morawski. This party had already been joined at the beginning of 1945 by the left wing of the PPS, which had broken away from the older PPS, and at the end of the war a number of well-known pre-war left-wing socialist leaders also joined it when they returned from imprisonment in Germany. Among them were Jozef Cyrankiewicz, who took over the post of secretary-general on 1 July 1945, and Adam Rapacki. Julian Hochfeld and a few other members of the exile PPS also joined the party. Nevertheless, its membership was still small, for the great majority of socialists remained loyal to the traditional PPS (PPS–WRN) under Zygmunt Zulawski, a party which even in the Second World War had been for the most part anti-Bolshevist. Negotiations for amalgamation were at first unsuccessful; the foundation of a Polish Social Democratic Party (PPSD), which Zulawski attempted on 14 October 1945, was prevented by means of arrests and the KRN's decree of 4 November. Zulawski and his followers were now ready for unification – in the hope of being able to infiltrate the Lublin PPS – and this took place in December 1945. In January 1946 the united PPS already had 200,000 members; Kazimierz Puzak, a man of inflexibly anti-Soviet views, who was released from Soviet custody in November 1945, formed a second, semi-secret centre of leadership within its ranks. However, in October 1946 tensions between the 'Lublin' section and the 'old' section led to the withdrawal of Zulawski's group from the party. Although the right-wing socialist traditions of the inter-war period lived on in the PPS, through the agreement which it made on 28 November 1946 with the PPR it gradually sank into dependence on this party. The subsequently created 'organic unity' of the two parties entitled the PPR to control even the inner structure of the PPS.

Of the *bourgeois* parties, the Lublin 'Democratic Party' (SD) remained small and almost without influence. In contrast, the

'Labour Party' (SP), reorganized by Karol Popiel, who had returned to Poland from exile in London, succeeded in attaining a certain importance; however, its first congress, arranged for 19 July 1946, was prohibited and Popiel was forced to give up his party activities. The requisitioning of its buildings and newspapers and the exclusion of seven SP members from the KRN made the Labour Party so docile that in September 1946 it chose Feliks Widy-Wirski, a figure acceptable to the Government, as its chairman. With that its role as an Opposition party was finished. In general, the middle class and the former landed nobility were able to exert little influence on the struggle between the various political parties because their erstwhile political representatives, in particular the National Party and the Pilsudski camp, remained underground.

In these circumstances the Peasant Party (SL), which dropped its conspiratorial character at the end of the war and changed over again to mass agitation, acquired a key position among the Opposition parties. The SL had represented the interests of the peasants for decades and its aged leader, Wincenty Witos, enjoyed deep respect in all quarters. In autumn 1945 Stanislaw Mikolajczyk, who actually led the party in place of Witos, now seriously ill, tried in vain to absorb the Lublin SL by amalgamation. After this, in September 1945, the SL changed its name to PSL (Polish Peasant Party). Mikolajczyk, who had become the formal head of the party after Witos's death on 31 October 1945, renewed his efforts to secure an amalgamation. However, the counter-measures of the Government, which in the winter of 1945–6 arrested numerous members of the Peasant Party – including some of the Lublin SL who were ready for union – prevented such an amalgamation for the second time. Nevertheless, in spite of all administrative obstacles, by January 1946 the membership of the PSL had risen to about 600,000; the first PSL Congress in Warsaw (19–21 January 1946) proved that, because of its extensive roots in the peasantry and the removal of the older middle-class parties, the PSL would in future be the Government's main adversary.

In view of the promised 'free, unhindered elections', the party political spectrum, in which towards the end of 1945 four Government parties – the PPR, PPS, SL and SD – were lined up together against the Opposition PSL, was of considerable importance. At Potsdam Bierut had promised Ernest Bevin that these elections would take place 'at the beginning of 1946', but he had later postponed them several times; at the first congress of the PPR (6–12 December 1945) Gomulka demanded the formation of a 'democratic bloc' as a united front of all permitted parties. Lengthy negotiations on the participation of the PSL were finally broken off on 25 February 1946, so that the democratic bloc remained an alliance of the four Lublin parties, including the PPS. The executive committee of the PPS now suggested (on 31 March 1946) postponing the elections yet again and first holding a referendum in which the electorate should give their views on these questions: the abolition of the Senate, the agrarian reform and the nationalization of heavy industry, and the Oder–Neisse frontier. This plan was approved by the KRN. The Government and the PPR obviously thought that by putting these questions they could achieve considerable majorities independent of party political affiliations.

At Mikolajczyk's instigation the PSL decided to try a test of strength against the democratic bloc's 'triple affirmative' propaganda, and to express its opposition by a 'no' to the first question. However, the PSL's electoral propaganda was severely hindered by arrests. A left-wing group under Tadeusz Rek split off from the PSL – obviously at the suggestion of the PPR – and set up on 12 June 1946 as an independent party under the name 'PSL–New Liberation'; it too favoured the triple affirmative. In spite of blatant interference with the voting and all kinds of facilities for voting 'yes', the result of the referendum, which was held on 30 June 1946, was a clear defeat for the Government. In those electoral districts in which trusted supporters of the PSL had taken part in the counting the leaders of the PSL were able to ascertain that 83·5 per cent of the voters had said 'no' to the first question as opposed to 16·5 per cent who had said 'yes'. However, the official result – which was not announced until ten days after the voting – declared that of the 11,530,000 valid votes cast 68 per cent had said 'yes' to the first question, 77·2 per cent had said 'yes' to the second question and 91·6 per cent had said 'yes' to the third question.

Now that the democratic legitimacy of the Government's policy seemed to have been formally demonstrated to the world by the plebiscitary character of this referendum, the Government and the PPR felt that they could at last arrange the long-delayed elections for a constituent Sejm. On 21–22 September the KRN accordingly passed an electoral law. In form, this law was modelled on the decisions of 1921, particularly in its retention of the 'five adjective' suffrage, but it left the Government considerable opportunities for manipulation. These lay primarily in the division into electoral districts of the still thinly populated East German territory and the possibility of disfranchising whole groups of voters. In fact, during the election campaign – in which once again the PSL provided the only opposition to the democratic bloc – the Government made plentiful use of its powers. In the second half of 1946 nearly a million voters were disfranchised;[1] and in ten out of the fifty-two electoral districts the PSL candidates were struck off the lists. These ten districts, containing about a quarter of the total population of Poland, were for the most part ones in which the influence of the PSL was particularly strong. Finally, the electoral committees all over Poland were so constituted that the PPR or its allies were assured of the decisive influence. Mikolajczyk's protests about this were just as ineffective as those made by the United States Government on 5 and 9 January 1947.

As a result of all this manipulation and the open voting employed in some areas, the elections of 19 January 1947 resulted in a victory for the democratic bloc. It obtained 80·1 per cent of the 11,244,873 valid votes cast, while the PSL obtained only 10·3 per cent, the SP 4·7 per cent and the other groups, including the PSL–New Liberation, 4·9 per cent. According to the information supplied by trustworthy representatives of the PSL, who had taken

---

[1] On the pretext that they had collaborated with the Germans or with 'Fascist' organizations.

part in the counting in 1,300 out of 5,200 constituencies, in these constituencies 60–80 per cent of all the votes had actually been cast for the PSL. The PSL's objections based on this information, like those of the USA (28 January 1947) and Great Britain (3 February 1947), had no effect at all. When the seats were allotted, the democratic bloc received 394 out of 444, and the PSL only 27, or 6 per cent.

The constituent Sejm met on 4 February and on the next day chose Boleslaw Bierut, hitherto president of the KRN, as President of the Republic. On 19 February it approved a new constitutional law, the so-called 'Little Constitution'. This law defined the powers of the Sejm, of the Government, of the newly created Council of State and of the President in accordance with the division of functions enshrined in the constitution of 1921, but made frequent exceptions to this principle, especially by transferring legislative and controlling functions to the Council of State. The new Government formed on 7 February 1947 under Jozef Cyrankiewicz was similar in composition to the previous one, but was much more under the influence of the PPR, especially as Mikolajczyk no longer belonged to it. It was soon to become clear that the most powerful members of the Government were those who also belonged to the Politbureau of the PPR, namely the deputy prime ministers, Wladyslaw Gomulka, Aleksander Zawadzki and Hilary Minc; the Under-Secretary of State in the Prime Minister's office, Jakob Berman; and the Security Minister, Stanislaw Radkiewicz.

With the elections, the adoption of the new constitution and the formation of the Government, the role of the PSL as an Opposition party was to all intents and purposes played out. Opposition forces therefore came to the conclusion that their only remaining chance of taking legal political action lay in the PPS. However, the government took measures against the PPS, especially as it sought to tone down the PPR's nationalization programme and was therefore regarded as a quasi-opposition. In May and June 1947 the PPS lost about 200 leading politicians belonging to the WRN wing, including Kazimierz Puzak, through

arrest; and at the same time through 'organic unification' with
the PPR it was so thoroughly 'purged' by the latter that in the
first half of 1947 it lost about 150,000 members and thereby
forfeited its numerical lead among the parties to the PPR, which
by the middle of 1947 already had about 850,000 members.

The forcible alteration of Poland's internal political structure
was paralleled by a decision affecting external policy which made
plain the country's gradual withdrawal from the Western world:
on 7 July 1947 Poland declined to take part in the conference on
the Marshall Plan in Paris. This decision meant that in future
the Polish Government not only wished to renounce the USA's
welcome economic assistance but was also prepared to incorporate
the Polish national economy in the Soviet-controlled economic
system of the Eastern bloc. In addition, this step also destroyed
the last chance of assistance from outside for an internal anti-
communist opposition. This circumstance was keenly appreciated
by the PSL in particular. Faced with the impossibility of maintain-
ing any kind of legal opposition and threatened with arrest,
Mikolajczyk made up his mind to flee the country. On 21 October
1947, with the help of the American ambassador, he left Poland;
he was followed by his party colleague, Stefan Korbonski, and
the erstwhile leader of the SP, Popiel. This meant that the attempt
of former exile politicians to influence the political life of a
communist-controlled State by collaboration could be regarded
as a failure. The PSL, led from November 1947 onwards by Jozef
Niecko, was brought into line with the parties of the democratic
bloc. The period of the 'individual path to socialism', of the
'Polish pattern', and of its application to state, economy and
society, was over. The road to assimilation to the Soviet system
of government, and thus to the real 'Sovietization' of Poland, was
now open.

THE DEVELOPMENT OF THE POLISH 'PEOPLE'S
DEMOCRACY'

By the final reduction of all the opposition parties to impotence
the PPR had become the sole decisive political power in the

country, and henceforth turned to the resettlement of internal ideological struggles within its own ranks. The real motive force for such struggles sprang in the first place from Stalin's intention to convert the countries of the Eastern bloc into 'People's Democracies', an intention which was made particularly clear in the Prague revolution of 25 February 1948. Sovietization obviously had to proceed in two directions: on the one hand it seemed necessary, by amalgamating the Communist and Socialist Parties, to produce that 'unity of the working class' which was an essential condition for the remodelling of the State as a whole; on the other, it was necessary to suppress or remove the 'National Communist' section of the PPR in favour of the group trained in the Soviet Union and therefore regarded as absolutely loyal to the Soviet. These two tendencies were intertwined in Poland in a particularly curious way.

The secretary of the PPR, Gomulka, had already (1 May 1947) called on the leaders of the PPS for negotiations on the unification of the two parties; and the arrests of May–June 1947 had contributed to the victory in the supreme council of the PPS of the section which was ready for amalgamation. After the Prague *putsch* Cyrankiewicz, the secretary of the PPS, began to push for amalgamation; it was a sign of the internal changes in the PPS that soon after the ejection of the WRN wing – on 23 March 1948 – it withdrew from the Socialist International. However, unification was held up by the struggle inside the PPR, the so-called Gomulka crisis.

In the PPR there had long been opposition between those communists who had taken part in the underground struggle in Poland during the war, thought primarily on national lines and defended the possibility of a 'Polish path', and the Soviet-trained erstwhile Comintern officials, the 'people of the Oka'. While the 'Nationalists' favoured a conciliatory attitude to the PPS and of communism on the Tito model, their opponents wanted to enforce as faithfully as possible an imitation of Soviet models. The most important members of the first or nationalist group, besides its leader, Gomulka, were Marian Spychalski, Wladyslaw

Bienkowski, Zenon Kliszko and Ignacy Loga-Sowinski; the second included – in addition to Bierut – Jakub Berman, Hilary Minc, Aleksander Zawadzki, Edward Ochab and Stanislaw Radkiewicz. The overture to the struggle between the two factions was formed by the address on the 'historical traditions of the Polish workers' movement' given by Gomulka at a meeting of the Central Committee of the PPR on 3 June 1948; this address was violently criticized by the opposing group. The decision was taken at the Central Committee's meeting of 31 August to 3 September 1948, which was almost entirely devoted to Gomulka and his 'deviations to the right'. As a result of this meeting, Gomulka resigned from the post of party secretary and Bierut took over the leadership of the party as 'Chairman of the Central Committee'. By his self-criticism Gomulka saved his membership of the Central Committee and also retained his ministerial positions, but in practice he was put into cold storage. Most of his followers went into the wilderness with him; only Spychalski – obviously under pressure – went over to the Stalinist side.

Now that the 'Moscow group' had gained sole control of the PPR they felt that they ought to take up once more the idea of an amalgamation with the PPS. They found Cyrankiewicz more than ready to meet them half-way; at the conference of the supreme council of the PPS (18–21 September 1948) he expressed thoroughly Stalinist views and started a purge which did not spare even the earlier exponents of collaboration with the PPR. Boleslaw Drobner and Osobka-Morawski had to resign from the supreme council, and Julian Hochfeld's group was pushed into the background; the tone was now set by the 'Leftists' led by Stanislaw Matuszewski and Adam Rapacki. The repeated purges and voluntary resignations reduced the size of the PPS to such an extent that its membership, which had been 800,000 in December 1946, had shrunk to 450,000 by December 1948. This made it only half as strong as the PPR. The final unification of the two parties into the 'Polish United Workers' Party (PZPR) was completed on 15 December 1948. Party offices were filled in proportion to the numerical strength of each party at the time of amalgamation. The new

Politbureau contained eight representatives of the PPR and three representatives of the PPS; it included Bierut, Cyrankiewicz, Berman, Minc, Radkiewicz, Rapacki and Spychalski. Spychalski was the only member who was not an unconditional supporter of the 'Moscow line'.

After the amalgamation of the two workers' parties there seemed to be no point in showing any further consideration for the Gomulka group. Gomulka himself lost his ministerial posts on 21 January 1949. At the third plenary session of the PZPR's Central Committee (11–13 November 1949) Bierut finally had Gomulka, Spychalski and Kliszko excluded from the Central Committee and from all party offices both then and for the future. However, it said a good deal both for the weakness of the accusations and the nation's sensitive feeling for justice that none of the three was arrested until much later; Bierut did not dare to subject them to a public trial, although 'show trials' of 'national communists' were the order of the day in other eastern European countries at that time.

The formation of one united workers' party set the pattern for the amalgamation of the peasant parties, an operation which had been the subject of negotiations since May 1948. After the PSL had been thoroughly purged of Mikolajczyk's supporters, and 'reactionary' politicians – including Jozef Putek, hitherto the party's chairman – had also been removed from the Lublin SL, the amalgamation could be completed. The official inauguration of the 'United Peasant Party' (ZSL) took place at the unification congress of 27–29 November 1949. The leadership of the new party was taken over by Jozef Niecko and Wladyslaw Kowalski, marshal of the Sejm. The party structure of Poland had now fallen into a rigid pattern which did not undergo any further changes; by the side of the ruling PZPR there were from now onwards only two satellite parties, the ZSL and the SD.

At the same time as the Gomulka crisis and the unification of the parties a crisis arose over the army. Up to autumn 1949 the Polish armed forces had been weak both in numbers and equipment and had possessed little importance. For this reason the gradual replacement of Russian officers by Polish ones – including many pre-war officers – carried out by Marshal Rola-Zymierski and his Deputy War Minister, Spychalski, had met no opposition from the Soviet Government. However, the intended transformation of the State could not be attempted unless the Soviet-trained PZPR and the security forces had the backing of a reliable army. In view of the largely Polish-nationalist character of the army and the past history of its commander – Rola-Zymierski had after all once been an officer in Pilsudski's Legions – the Moscow Government felt that it could not be relied on. In addition, considerations dictated by external events were obviously at work: the North Atlantic Treaty was signed on 4 April 1949 and the Federal Republic of Germany was set up on 7 September.

Marshal Bulganin had already expressed his dissatisfaction with the Polish army in Warsaw in spring 1949, and as a result of this the Deputy Minister for War, Spychalski, had been replaced on 7 April by Edward Ochab as First Deputy Minister and by Stanislaw Poplawski, a Soviet general of Polish descent, as Second Deputy Minister. Then, on 6 November, the Soviet Marshal Konstantin Rokossovsky was suddenly – and rather surprisingly – appointed Minister for War and commander-in-chief of the Polish forces. Rokossovsky, who, like Poplawski, was of Polish descent, had hitherto been supreme commander of the Soviet occupation troops in Poland. He began the complete transformation of the Polish army. By linking it closely to the PZPR and by intensifying its political indoctrination – which was safeguarded by the foundation of the Feliks Dzierzynski Military Academy on 22 March 1951 – he sought to make it into a politically reliable instrument. At the same time he had Polish officers of the pre-war army removed from all high commands and once again replaced by Soviet ones; four generals – Stefan Mossor, Stanislaw Tatar, Jerzy Kirchmayer and Franciszek Herman were prosecuted in a 'show trial' (31 July–13 August 1951) which attracted a good deal of attention. Finally, Rokossovsky re-equipped the army and increased its numbers to 500,000, a figure achieved mainly by the re-introduction of conscription on 4 February 1950. The extent to which Rokossovsky also took over political functions in the Government as a whole became clear when on 10 May 1950 he was admitted to the Politbureau of the PZPR.

The linking of all the leading positions in the state, economy and army, often on a personal level, to the Soviet Government, as demonstrated most clearly in the fall of Gomulka and Rokossovsky's take-over, was only the outward sign of the radical change brought about in Poland in the years 1949–50. The possibility of an individual political path, even within the framework of the United Workers' Party, had now been removed, and all that the future seemed to offer was complete assimilation to the Soviet pattern, that is, the transformation of Poland into an authoritarian state. For this very reason the easily inflamed patriotism of the Poles sprang to life again in spite of the outward rigidity of the country's political forms. The occupation of all important positions in the Government by henchmen of the Moscow Government, the influx of so many Soviet 'advisers', produced the impression that Poland was being treated as a dependency. People became aware that the leading figures of the Stalin era were no longer the socialist revolutionaries who in 1905 and even in 1917 had collaborated with the Polish revolutionaries and demanded the independence of Poland. The way in which the Soviet Union was now exercising power in Poland was more reminiscent of Catherine II's diplomats or of Senator Nowosiltsow, who as the governor's adviser had in practice ruled the Kingdom of Poland. Fed by historical memories of this sort discontent increased; it affected not only the traditionally anti-Russian circles of the former middle class but also the workers, among whom the traditions of the older PPS had not yet died out. As well as this patriotic resentment among the Poles there was also the feeling that the orthodoxy of their socialism had been impugned. Particularly among the left-wing intelligentsia people felt that they possessed an older and more direct Marxist tradition than the Russians and they consequently failed to see that the Soviet pattern of complete nationalization or socialization of the economy was necessarily superior to the Polish concept of an economy with three sectors. In addition, Marxist political theory too gave rise to strong patriotic impulses, for it had long been known in Poland how enthusiastically Marx and Engels had championed the idea of an independent, anti-Tsarist Poland with the frontiers of 1772. In these circumstances the internal cleavage between people and Government began to grow more marked just at the time when the conversion of the country into an authoritarian state on the Soviet pattern was being completed.

At first this kind of mood was certainly not calculated to deter the leaders of Poland from continuing along their chosen path towards the totalitarian state. The main emphasis in state planning lay on economic policy, which was directed by Hilary Minc, head of the state planning commission set up on 10 February 1949. The outbreak of the Korean War on 21 June 1950 hastened the formulation of a six-year plan, which was adopted by the Central Committee of the PZPR on 15–16 July 1950, became law on 21 July 1950 and was to complete the 'transformation into a socialist economy'. It was also intended to make Poland into a highly industrialized state by neglecting consumer needs, to some extent in favour of armaments. At the same time the collectivization of agriculture was to be pushed on. That Bierut and Minc – probably on Soviet instructions – sought to ensure by every means in their power the early fulfilment of this very far-reaching plan was certainly connected with the tension between East and West caused by the Korean War.

Simultaneously with the tightening up of economic policy, and indeed partly to assist it, a comprehensive reorganization of the administrative and constitutional machinery was undertaken. The People's Councils set up in 1944, which had hitherto carried out legislative tasks in municipalities, districts and provinces, were endowed by the law of 20 March 1950 with executive power as well. The classic division of powers was thereby abolished and by means of this chain of councils the omnipotence of the PZPR-dominated state was assured right down to the smallest parish. Administrative reform was only the prelude to the adoption of the new constitution which the constituent Sejm produced at this end of its labours on 22 July 1952. Modelled on the Soviet pattern, this constitution carried through to its logical conclusion the abolition of the division of powers throughout the State. Theoretically the Sejm, as the chief assembly of the State, possessed both legislative and executive authority. To carry out the functions of Head of the State the Sejm elected a committee of fifteen, the Council of State, whose chairman was to officiate as the formal Head of State. It was also the Sejm's task to appoint the Government. However, the extensive powers of the supreme authorities remained without any very great practical importance since vital decisions continued to be taken, as before, in the Politbureau or the Central Committee of the PZPR, and the corresponding resolutions of the State organs were little more than formalities.

In accordance with the provisions of the new constitution, elections for the Sejm were held on 26 October 1952. There was just one single list of candidates, those of the 'National Front', which embraced the PZPR, the ZSL, the SD and alliances of these parties. The result of the elections was therefore no surprise: 99·3 per cent of all valid votes cast went to the National Front. In accordance with the scheme arranged before the elections the PZPR provided 273 of the 425 members of the Sejm, the ZSL 90 and the SD 25; 37 were officially independent. The Sejm met on 20 November and chose Aleksander Zawadzki as chairman of the Council of State. Bolesław Bierut was given the task of forming a Cabinet, and presented his Government to the Sejm on 22 November. As a result of the progressive nationalization of industry the number of ministries had grown since 1949 to thirty-five; consequently the importance of the Cabinet as a whole had declined. This only gave more influence to the 'inner Cabinet', which had come into existence in 1949 and from now onwards was formally distinguished from the Government as a whole by the appointment of eight Deputy Prime Ministers. The most important of these, besides Bierut, were Cyrankiewicz, Minc, Zenon Nowak, Berman and Rokossovsky, who were all at the same time members of the Politbureau of the PZPR. These personal links demonstrated more clearly than ever the dependence of the Government on the PZPR.

The new Government regarded the execution of the economic plans as its main task and concentrated all the nation's energies on this. However, fairly big individual successes such as the development of the new industrial town of Nowa Huta near Cracow could not hide the fact that supplies of consumer goods and food were growing scantier. The country regions and the small towns often remained without local supply services, since most investment went into the newly created 'giants'. The lack of consumer goods, the very low real incomes and finally the currency reform of 30 October 1950 quickly gave rise to discontent caused by economic factors. This discontent was particularly rife in the broad strata of the workers and peasants, while the intelligentsia was upset by the methodical 'Sovietization' of cultural life. The reorganization of higher education on the Soviet pattern, which reached its climax in the creation of the 'Polish Academy of Sciences' (PAN), offended native academic tradition no less than the 'First Methodological Conference' of Polish historians (28 December 1951 to 12 January 1952), which introduced the application of Soviet–Marxist categories to historical research. So far as the arts were concerned, writers in particular were irritated by attempts to regiment them in accordance with the principles of 'socialist realism'. From 1950 to 1953 the discontent spread through all classes of the population. The expectations of the opposition intelligentsia, of the bulk of the peasants and of many of the workers, too, now turned to the only institution which had been able to preserve an intellectual life of its own, namely the Polish Church.

For the Catholic Church in Poland the years from 1945 to 1949 had been a period of post-war healing and thus of a sort of renascence. In spite of its unilateral denunciation of the Concordat of 1925 (16 September 1945), the Government had made no serious attempt to interfere with the internal life of the Church during this period. The basic reason for this tolerance was that the migrations of 1945–9 had effected an almost perfect identity between nation and Church; apart from a few small remnants, religious minorities had been excluded from the State with the national minorities. Thanks to its historical function as protector of Polish nationalism against Russian and German culture, the Catholic Church had far closer ties with the nation as a whole than in other countries of eastern central Europe, and its suppression would therefore have seemed like an attack on patriotism. In addition, the swift build-up of ecclesiastical organization in the former German territories, more or less completed by 1950, corresponded on the whole to the wishes of the Government. It was obviously sound politics for the State to try to preserve a tolerable relationship with the Church in the period before the establishment of a pure communist state, and the Government's attitude was reflected in President Bierut's attendance at church on special occasions.

Thus it was not until the Pope issued his decree of 1 July 1949 excommunicating communists that the struggle between Church and State really began. In Hungary and Czechoslovakia this struggle had broken out a good deal earlier. In Poland the fight began with a sharp propaganda campaign against the Vatican and the Church; this was followed in January 1950 by the seizure of *Caritas*, the big Church welfare organization, which was now put under State control, and in March 1950 by the confiscation of Church estates. On 14 April 1950 the Government and the episcopate signed an agreement which safeguarded the spiritual activity of the Church within certain limits, while pledging it to support the State in temporal affairs, but this brought only a temporary relaxation of tension. The Government now tried to force the Church out of public life by administrative measures, in particular by arresting numerous clerics and laymen. In Article 70 of the new constitution of 22 July 1952 it created a further tool for use against the Church.

Open persecution of the Church began with the Cracow 'show trial' of 21–27 January 1953. At the same time there was a Press campaign aimed chiefly against the primate of Poland, Stefan Wyszynski, who had been made a cardinal on 12 January 1953.

On 9 February 1953 the Council of State issued a decree on ecclesiastical appointments, which gave the State full personal and institutional control over the Church and obliged the clergy to take an oath of loyalty to the Government. A fresh 'show trial' from 14 to 22 September 1953 ended in big jail sentences for Bishop Czeslaw Kaczmarek, arrested in 1951, and three other priests. Finally, on 26 September 1953, the primate himself was arrested, after refusing to issue the ecclesiastical condemnation of Kaczmarek demanded by Bierut. The Government could now assume that it had broken the Church's resistance. On 17 December 1953 all the bishops and vicars capitular still free – about a quarter of all the clergy had by then been arrested – took the prescribed oath of loyalty in the presence of the Premier, Cyrankiewicz. The Polish Church too now seemed to be marked out for the slow death to which the Church had already been condemned in other eastern European countries.

However, precisely because of this forcible take-over by the State the Church became endowed with new powers of resistance. The loss of traditional social positions brought moral conquests the like of which the Church had not registered for decades. Numerous opponents of the Government in the middle-class intelligentsia, among the workers and even in the PZPR – including groups who were traditionally anti-clerical – gave the Church their allegiance, at first for purely political reasons. Across this bridge of political opposition the Church was able to extend and deepen its spiritual influence. Moreover, it retained its traditional roots in the peasantry, which at that time was successfully resisting collectivization. So the proposals put forward with Government support in autumn 1953 for a schismatic national Church aroused little response. The federation of 'socially progressive Catholics' founded by the former National Radical Boleslaw Piasecki on 1 November 1945, the so-called 'Pax Movement', which since 1947 had been trying to reconcile Marxism and Catholicism in a sort of syncretism, had certainly achieved by 1953, with State help, considerable economic and spiritual influence; but it was opposed to a break with Catholicism in the rest of the world and always recognized the supreme teaching authority of the Pope. The group of 'patriotic priests', which collaborated openly with the Government and was amalgamated with Pax on 15 October 1953 under Government pressure, had no following of any significance. In these circumstances the Church was able to preserve its internal and external unity even in the period of the struggle with the Government. It said a good deal for its powers of spiritual resistance that it was even able to save the 'Catholic University' of Lublin, the only institution of its kind in the whole Eastern bloc. Finally, the steady growth of its roots in the nation as a whole was demonstrated by the fact that every measure taken by the Government against the Church resulted in a temporary fall in production. The relationship between State and Church in 1953 thus showed that the establishment of an autocratic totalitarian State had to be paid for with the progressive alienation of nation and Government.

FROM STALIN'S DEATH TO THE 'POLISH OCTOBER REVOLUTION'

Stalin's death on 5 March 1953 did not lead to any structural alterations in the totalitarian State. Bierut was able to retain his double position as head of the party and Prime Minister, although this position did not correspond to the division of power in other eastern European states. Neither the revolt in the Soviet zone of Germany on 17 June 1953 nor the fall and execution of Beria (10 July and 23 December 1953) threatened the continuance of his power; obviously Bierut was in a position to demonstrate both his adaptability to the system of collective leadership in the Soviet State and his indispensability as leader of the PZPR. The institutional framework of the People's Republic too, particularly those parts of it created by the constitution of 22 July 1952, proved its solidity in that it needed only small additions, such as the new municipal organization of 25 September 1954.

In contrast to the hardening of the apparatus of the State, Government practice in the three years by which Bierut was to outlive his master Stalin was compelled to adopt certain changes.

Soon after Stalin's death deficiencies in the supply of consumer goods, which were discussed at the plenary session of the PZPR Central Committee on 29–30 October 1953, made it necessary to cut back some of the very ambitious plans for industrialization. At the second congress of the PZPR, held between 10 and 17 March 1954 and attended by Khrushchev, the individual members, who included Bierut, Minc, Nowak and Ochab, presented an economic balance-sheet which, in spite of the progress made with industrialization, indicated failures in certain essential sectors. The shortfall in agricultural production and the setbacks in the collectivization policy became quite clear; so far it had been possible to collectivize only about a tenth of the land suitable for agriculture. What seemed particularly serious was that the membership of the PZPR, which had amounted to roughly 1,500,000 at the time of the first congress in December 1948, had fallen by February 1954 to about 1,297,000. If the number of new members was taken into consideration, the total losses through cancellation, expulsion, death and, in particular, 'loss through change of address' must have amounted to nearly half a million. Because of these warning signs alone the leaders of the PZPR emphasized – as they had already done at the October plenary session – that they were anxious to raise the living standards of the workers. This promise involved slowing up industrialization again and putting more emphasis on the production of consumer goods. However, the path towards the general development of industry, once taken, could not be totally abandoned without sacrificing the large investment already made. The leaders of the party and the State – obviously under Soviet influence – therefore decided in favour of a policy of 'half measures'. This decision was to govern the whole mode of running the State during the period of 1954–6.

At the second congress of the PZPR it was decided to introduce into the leadership certain changes aimed at producing a stronger resemblance to the system in force in other eastern European states. On 18 March 1954 Bierut was confirmed in his previous position as leader of the party with the title of First Secretary – the office of chairman of the CC now fell into abeyance – but at the same time he handed over the premiership to Cyrankiewicz. Government, Central Committee, Politbureau and party secretariat all underwent slight modifications; it was particularly significant that only two former socialists belonged to the new Politbureau (Cyrankiewicz as a member and Rapacki as a nominee). Soon afterwards, towards the end of 1954, the new leadership structure had to stand up to some nasty shocks as a result of the 'disclosures' made by Jozef Swiatlo, a lieutenant-colonel in the security service who had fled to the west in December 1953. Swiatlo's disclosures related to antagonisms within the ruling circle. The most seriously compromised department was the Ministry of Security. On 7 December 1954 it was abolished and the Minister of Security, Radkiewicz, was demoted to Minister for State Farms. Most of his assistants were arrested or at any rate dismissed. At the same time the Ministry for Home Affairs, abolished since 4 May 1950, was re-established; its new head, Wladyslaw Wicha, also took over the command of the Militia, the Frontier Guard and the Security Corps. The powers of the new 'Committee for Security' under Wladyslaw Dworakowski were restricted to control of the secret police and the counterespionage service.

The liquidation of the hitherto almost omnipotent Security Ministry, which at the time of its abolition had at least 100,000 people in custody for political or criminal offences, was only the overture to the concessions which the régime had to make from now on. It was true that the impulse to relax internal and economic policy had originally come from the Soviet Government, as the Second Congress of the PZPR in particular had made clear; nevertheless, since the creation of the totalitarian State round 1950 forces had made themselves felt which would demand a degree of liberalization going far beyond what was intended. The process of industrialization and bureaucratization had certainly started in Poland before the war, but it was later compressed into a few years, particularly the period round 1950–3. The newly-created 'third estate', that is the bulk of the old and new intelligentsia, of the Government, trade union, municipal and party officials, and of the managerial, technical and academic classes – altogether about a quarter of the total population – had not had the time which its equivalent in other European countries had had to adapt itself mentally to the new modes of life. Most of the members of this class were still very conscious of older private social distinctions, and the newly created omnipotent state – in contrast to the situation in Soviet Russia, for example – had no spiritual hold over them although it controlled them on the material plane. Among them were still a number of people with aristocratic names who had put themselves at the disposal of the post-war State from purely patriotic motives. The Government could not renounce their services, or those of the intelligentsia in general, because the mass annihilations of the war years, together with the emigration, had decimated the numbers of highly educated people in the country. The execution of the huge tasks imposed by a planned economy, by the development of industry and by export obligations necessitated a good deal of consideration for opposition tendencies, even if these resulted only in passive resistance. Such was the background to the curious alternation of half-concessions and more extensive demands which characterized the relations between State and nation up to the 'Polish October'.

The strongest undertone in the latent criticism – apart from general discontent at the low standard of living – was that of patriotic sensitivity, mixed with strong anti-Russian feeling. Czeslaw Milosz, the writer and diplomat, who like so many Polish intellectuals had learnt afresh during the German occupation to appreciate the value of the national tradition, expressed the views of large circles of the population when he compared Poland to a 'province of the great empire', a province 'ruled by edicts from the centre via a continually shrinking autonomy'. The compulsory sacrifice of so many things they had achieved themselves was all the harder to bear because in Polish eyes Polish culture had always belonged to the Roman area of civilization and Poles were accustomed to look 'towards the focal points of this old tradition – France, England, Italy – as though to a familiar home'. Of course, the Polish intelligentsia was realistic enough to come to terms on the rational plane with the *fait accompli* of Poland's incorporation in the Russian sphere, but it found it extremely painful 'to have to bow to the hegemony of a people that is still uncivilized and primitive, and to have to accept its manners and customs, its science and technology, its literature and art as unconditionally superior'. At times these anti-Russian feelings outweighed anti-German feeling. Jozef Mackiewicz, a leading *émigré* writer, could even say: 'Nevertheless Stalin's totalitarian tendencies went far further than Hitler's. The National Socialists only came into power in 1933; the Bolsheviks had been in power since 1917. The Bolsheviks were familiar with concentration camps, mass deportations and mass murders when Hitler's name was still unknown to most people.' Because Polish culture was so closely intertwined with European culture as a whole, patriotic feelings were shot through with anti-communist postulates from the realms of literature, music, art and law. It was the call for the restoration of the rule of law and violent anger at the infringement of the traditional sanctity of the law that contributed most to the abolition of the Security Ministry. The attempt to make literature serve particular ends was utterly rejected, especially since from the time of the partitions, when a spiritual Poland had replaced the missing political reality, literature had enjoyed unlimited, indeed absolute validity. The Polish public believed that it knew the reasons which drove many writers, historians and philosophers to take refuge in the past, and in face of the relativization of modern literary production it clung all the more firmly to the riches of the older literature. But the spiritual crisis of those years went much further than mere persistence in opposition or the effort to keep certain areas of life free from state interference. Quite a few members of the older generation had originally approved the establishment of the People's Democracy because they had been oppressed by doubts about the objective powers of resistance of Western modes of life. In spite of manifold links with the Poland of the pre-war period they felt they had to bow to the new world emerging from the east, whose victorious progress seemed irresistible, even if they could not assent to its social structure.

For young people the break with received traditions and the task of adapting themselves to the new universal view of life had been a good deal easier; thanks to the tension that always exists between one generation and the next the role of advance guard in the struggle to overturn *bourgeois* society had held a certain attraction for them. But now the young too felt disillusioned and tired of the continually repeated slogans and unimaginative solutions of the Stalinist era. If many of the older people had given up their previous notions and adopted the new ideology without really feeling at home with it, consequently falling victims to a resigned scepticism or even nihilism, the young were often liable to feel a conflict of conscience. The young poet Janusz Koniusz gave shattering expression to such feelings in a poem published in January 1955. Polish youth, brought up on the Soviet brand of socialism, did sometimes show signs of a crass materialistic positivism, but on the whole it had never forgotten that Polish socialism was traditionally based on idealistic and humanitarian concepts, and that the noblest task of this socialism had always lain in the liberation of man from any kind of slavery, not in the doctrinaire application of a particular economic theory. It is thus not surprising that it was a member of the younger socialist intelligentsia, Adam Wazyk, who on 21 August 1955, with his 'Poem for Adults', pilloried the naïve optimism and the untruthfulness of Government propaganda and thus achieved the final breakthrough to the Polish 'thaw'.

When the Twentieth Congress of the Russian Communist Party in Moscow (14–25 February 1956) gave the signal for energetic de-Stalinization, the intellectual evolution in the Polish intelligentsia had reached a critical stage. The PZPR was represented at this Congress mainly by supporters of a 'hard' policy, such as Bierut, Cyrankiewicz, Berman, Zawadzki and Ochab; it cannot have pleased Bierut in particular that the general revision of the history of communism included the rehabilitation of the KPP, in whose dissolution in 1938 he himself had shared. A fortnight after the end of the congress, on 12 March 1956, Bierut died quite unexpectedly in Moscow; he was buried in Warsaw

on 16 March with great solemnity. Thus the 'Polish Stalin' out-
lived the posthumous fall of his prototype by only a few days.
Many Poles had regarded him simply as a loyal Soviet official, a
mere viceroy ruling on behalf of the Moscow Government. The
exceptional severity of his régime and the splendour of the court
which he held in the palaces of Warsaw was scarcely calculated to
win him much affection. Nevertheless, during the twelve years in
which he had held power (1944–56) he had demonstrated a well-
developed feeling for the dignity of the Polish Republic.

On 20 March 1956, in the presence of Khrushchev, Edward
Ochab was chosen as Bierut's successor in the office of First
Secretary of the PZPR and hence as the real ruler of the country.
During the Stalinist period Ochab had had the reputation of being
'a Bolshevik with sharp teeth'. In face of the general discontent in
Poland his task was no easy one, especially as the Twentieth
Congress of the CPSU had had much the same effect as the bursting
of a dam. Ochab had to reckon with the emergence of a long-
present but latent opposition, marshalled mainly in three camps:
the intellectuals – especially the writers, historians and philosophers – were demanding greater freedom in their work; the
economists and commercial experts pressed for reforms, particularly the introduction of the profit motive; and the Church wanted
the removal of the restrictions hampering its spiritual, educational
and charitable activities. This intellectual opposition possessed a
broad foundation in all social classes; on every side there were
lively expectations of such things as a rise in the standard of
living, a stronger emphasis on Polish sovereignty *vis-à-vis* the
Soviet Union, the complete restoration of the rule of law and the
right of all workers to have a say in the enterprises in which they
were employed. Quite obviously Ochab could meet these wishes
only by considerable alterations of policy and by making radical
changes in the personnel of the Government. He therefore made
contact with Gomulka, who was related to him by marriage.
Gomulka had already been released from custody on 21 April
1955, and on 4 April 1956 his release was made public. However,
the former party leader, who enjoyed in some respects the support

of Khrushchev, posed demands which went considerably further than the measures which the Stalinist group was prepared to approve. As a result of the events of summer 1956, which partly confirmed his prognosis, Gomulka's position certainly grew steadily stronger; in the course of his six months in power Ochab was consequently forced to hold out to Gomulka the possibility of more and more concessions. Thanks to his letters to the party newspaper *Trybuna Ludu*, which became known though they were never published, Gomulka came to be regarded as a sort of tribune of the people. One of the results of this was that his readiness to abandon parts of the communist–socialist programme was certainly overestimated. All the same, Ochab's governmental policy and particularly his choice of personnel were already considerably influenced by Gomulka.

The 'new course' began with a series of changes in personnel which mainly affected the Stalinists. The most fundamental were the final fall of the former security minister, Radkiewicz, on 20 April 1956 and the resignation of Jakob Berman, the 'Grey Eminence' of the Bierut era, which was announced on 6 May 1956. A comprehensive amnesty, affecting about 100,000 persons, was a sign that the policy of releasing prisoners and of reducing the number of people in custody, which had been pursued tentatively since 1955, was now being speeded up. In spite of such attempts to win over the non-communist part of the population, the basic lines of economic policy and the low standard of living remained unaltered. These were almost certainly the most important reasons for the outbreak of the Poznan rising, which began on 28 June 1956 during the Poznan fair as a mere demonstration but quickly grew into an armed revolt. It was a few days before Polish and Soviet troops could overcome the resistance of some groups of fighters. According to official sources the casualties amounted to 48 dead and 270 wounded. The original official thesis that the revolt had been a planned action against the State could not be maintained; the inquiry made it quite clear that, at any rate at the start, the rising had been quite spontaneous. Consequently the sentences passed on the mainly youthful participants were fairly mild; in any case they were cancelled entirely after a few days.

Although the Poznan rising was a clear indication of the general mood of discontent the plenary session of the Central Committee of the PZPR from 18 to 28 July 1956 decided to continue along the middle path of half-solutions. The Stalinist group, which had already lost influence as a result of the events in Poznan, yielded still more ground. Their pre-eminence in the Politbureau was particularly inhibited by the appointment of Adam Rapacki, who had been made Foreign Minister on 27 April 1956, as a member and of Stefan Jedrychowski, the head of the planning commission, as a nominee. The new Government programme provided for limited liberalization without any radical reforms. The central direction of the national economy was to be relaxed by means of a certain degree of decentralization, a limited amount of self-administration for the workers and the encouragement of crafts. A politically significant revision of the recent history of Poland was also announced. This new attitude was expressed in the Warsaw People's Council's decision of 31 July 1956 to erect a monument to the 'Heroes of Warsaw', and thus to implement the removal, already announced in the spring, of the ban on recording the exploits of the Home Army. The final rehabilitation of Gomulka, Zenon Kliszko and Marian Spychalski on 5 August pointed in the same direction. But the growing criticism in the Sejm and in the Press showed that such concessions would no longer be enough. The tercentenary (25–26 August 1956) of the coronation of the Virgin of Czestochowa as 'Queen of Poland' developed unexpectedly into a powerful demonstration attended by more than a million people. It not only reflected the purely Catholic wish that Cardinal Wyszynski should at last be released from his internment in a monastery but also gave expression in silent form – and therefore all the more impressively – to the general political opposition to the régime. Thus even this popular gathering at Czestochowa helped to strengthen Gomulka's position. The erstwhile leader of the PPR could now really set himself up as the representative of popular feeling, which for its part was quite ready to forget the rigours of his earlier period of rule, which paled into insignificance in comparison with the general misery of the Stalinist era. The resignation, announced on 9 October 1956, of Gomulka's chief opponent, Hilary Minc, who for all his doctrinaire rigidity had shown considerable capacity for planning, but had also incurred objective responsibility for economic failures, thus fulfilled the main demands not only of Gomulka but also of the majority of the nation.

On 15 October the Politbureau of the PZPR met to prepare the ground for the Eighth Plenary Session of the Central Committee, a session in which Gomulka – contrary to previous practice – took part. The discussions at this plenary session caused disquiet among the population and there were stormy demonstrations in favour of a fresh take-over of power by Gomulka. It had become known that the still strong Stalinist group headed by Wiktor Klosiewicz, Zenon Nowak, Franciszek Mazur and Franciszek Jozwiak was trying to hinder Gomulka's return to power by every possible means, apparently even by the use of Polish and Soviet troops. The main reason why these plans foundered was probably that the Security Corps under the recently rehabilitated General Waclaw Komar, the students of Warsaw and the majority of workers throughout Poland made no secret of their support for Gomulka. As a result of the rumours of Soviet troop movements and of the reports that a Soviet delegation had arrived in the country all classes of people were exceptionally excited when the Eighth Plenary Session of the Central Committee of the PZPR began on 19 October 1956. At this meeting, particularly during the negotiations between Ochab, Gomulka and Khrushchev in the Politbureau, a compromise solution was finally achieved which gave the PZPR – and hence the Polish State which it ran – extensive internal independence while preserving its close links with the CPSU and the Soviet Union. This compromise was due partly to popular feeling, which regarded Gomulka – certainly to a greater extent than his aims justified – as a patriot and Khrushchev's opponent, to the attitude of the centre group and above all to Ochab, who declared himself in favour of Gomulka's taking over power. The elections of 20-21 October for places on the party's highest committees indicated the compromise nature of the new ruling circle. Gomulka took over the leadership of the party as First Secretary in place of Ochab, supported by a secretariat which included six of the previous seven secretaries, including Ochab. Cyrankiewicz, Ochab, Rapacki, Zambrowski and Zawadzki stayed on in the Politbureau; Rokossovsky, Zenon, Nowak and such dyed-in-the-wool Stalinists as Jozwiak and Mazur left it; and Gomulka and his henchman Loga-Sowinski rejoined it. Jedry-chowski was promoted from nominee to full member. As the new line-up of personnel indicated, there was to be no fundamental break with the previous mode of government, and certainly not with the basic principles of eastern European socialism. Never-theless, popular feeling regarded the expected changes of policy as important enough to be greeted with enthusiasm. That the changes seemed to have been forced out of a reluctant Soviet Union, that the future relationship between Poland and Russia was to be based on independence and equality, and that even the official party newspaper *Trybuna Ludu* announced that the sequence 'sovereignty, democracy, socialism' was the right order in which to place the aims of the new programme, all added a special lustre to the events of October. Gomulka's take-over was obviously the beginning of a new epoch in the post-war history of Poland and the change was due as much to the nation's own efforts as to the actions of the groups which had ruled the country until then; to that extent the extravagant slogan 'spring in October' seemed at the time to be justified, even if the extensive hopes of many Poles were not to be fulfilled in the future.

CHAPTER VIII

Poland Under Gomulka (1956-1965)

BASIC CHARACTERISTICS OF THE COUNTRY'S INTERNAL ORGANIZATION

Wladyslaw Gomulka was fifty-one when he took over the direction of the State for the second time. By this time his bitter experiences during the Stalinist persecution and his sufferings in prison had undermined his health, but at the same time they had also tempered the inexorable attitude of the militant communist which earlier on had often made his behaviour somewhat ruthless. His communist convictions remained as unshakeably firm as ever, and he still retained his ascetic determination to pursue them to their logical conclusion and a remarkable way of putting them into effect which combined rigorous disciplinary severity with fatherly care. He had a deep-rooted distrust of the ambitious and sometimes unpractical talents which had characterized the older ruling class, and a tranquil confidence in his own laboriously acquired and somewhat down-to-earth education. He may have lacked humour, imagination and wealth of ideas, but he was tough, industrious, persevering and convinced that the problems of the Polish nation could soonest be solved if one could succeed in 'teaching this people to do a decent job of work'. The specific virtues of the leaders of the older Polish socialism, particularly exceptional personal unpretentiousness, modesty and guileless-ness, disinclination for representational duties and a Spartan hatred for any form of corruption went without saying so far as he was concerned. Indeed, the solitary nature of the way he made decisions, the impatience of his directives and his occasional out-breaks of temper made him as uncomfortable a Head of the State as Pilsudski had once been, although he shared little more with the marshal than a common origin in the socialist movement.

Poland under Gomulka (1956–1965)

Thus the strict, almost Prussian discipline of his régime, his zealous and somewhat puritanical pursuit of practical socialism, which was aimed entirely at the present, reflected the sort of personality usually found only among hard-headed sectarians, trade union officials and primary school teachers. It was consequently certain that the rule of such a 'Praeceptor Poloniae', with its combination of robust feeling for power and paternal care, would produce groans not only from members of the administration but also from broad classes of the nation. It seemed as if with Gomulka's accession to power the age of the older aristocratic intelligentsia and its undisciplined mode of life was finally over, and the Stalinist period was to be succeeded by a new era dominated by class-conscious workers of peasant origin.

In these circumstances Gomulka's conception of government, in which he remained true to older ideas, was bound to prove a bitter disappointment to many enthusiastic supporters of the October 'revolution'; but at the same time it also meant a decisive and irrevocable renunciation of Stalin's dictatorial dogmatism. As early as 30 November 1946 Gomulka had asserted that there were 'fundamental differences' between the socialist development of Poland and that of the Soviet Union, and that in Poland 'the dictatorship of the proletariat was neither unavoidable nor useful'; ten years later, after the fiasco of Stalinist methods, he could reiterate his conviction with even greater emphasis. Since a socialist State had already been achieved, the creation of social unity and national solidarity seemed to him more important than continually harping on the class struggle. What he was primarily concerned to effect was not a radical break with older Polish traditions, but their organic transformation, and he therefore sought, in spite of the tenacity with which he clung to the idea of the PZPR's leading role, to get non-communist circles play a part in public life. To this extent the resolute renunciation of the remote and abstract ideal of the communist millennium, the pursuit of which had given rise to the over-exertions of the preceding years, was just as essential as an energetic onslaught on the many pressing tasks of the present. Thus the policy speech

253

with which Gomulka began his governmental activities on 20 October 1956 contained numerous indications that he intended to make a sound pragmatism the dominant theme of his administration. He sharply criticized rigid centralism, doctrinaire practices and rose-coloured propaganda, and emphasized the importance of profitability, of lively initiative on the part of the lower levels of the population and of constructive criticism. He declared himself in favour of a certain degree of democracy, especially with regard to the Sejm and the Provincial Colleges, but emphasized that the PZPR would continue to fulfil the function of providing leadership. The heart of his conception was the traditional devotion to the fundamental principle of socialism, that is, the abolition of the exploitation of one man by another; yet this declaration of faith moved away from the final goals of total communism, goals which had already disappeared from sight, and instead put the accent on the creation of a Welfare State organized primarily to secure social justice but sweetened by a sparing admixture of freedom.

Such a proclamation of an energetic policy aimed at the present seemed in fact unavoidable if an honest attempt was to be made to heal the structure of Polish society and to tend its particular spiritual traditions. The feeling of general misery went deep; the swift and comprehensive action of the intelligentsia, which now sought to emancipate itself completely, made this strikingly clear. What emerged above all from the wealth of publications and conversations which now sprang into life again was the confirmation of the underlying loss of confidence which the previous Governments had caused. The relaxation, now complete, of the iron grip of the Stalinist period revealed that the prevailing social order had certainly been consolidated by the exercise of naked power but had never acquired any real authority of its own or been legitimized by voluntary recognition. Since those weeks in October the carefully guarded ability of Polish society to survive alongside and under the State in unbroken spiritual resistance and intellectual integrity had shown itself to be more vigorous than ever. Up through the petrified structure of officially encouraged interpretations of Marxism there pushed a luxuriant growth of ideas which was soon written off by the Government as 'revisionism', although fundamentally it only represented the reinstatement of old established lines of Polish social thinking. The group centred round the weekly magazine *Kuznica* tried to see in Marx's philosophy that Platonic union of wisdom and power which had informed the republican ideal of the Polish enlightenment in the latter part of the eighteenth century; and the 'theses on socialism' advanced by the young philosopher Leszek Kolakowski – through an American indiscretion they swiftly became known – could be regarded more or less as a testimony to the continuing influence of Kantian and left wing Hegelian ideas. It was thus mainly the revolutionary ideas of Polish youth, ideas drawn from classical Polish thinking, which gave the 'spring in October' its dash and impetus.

Gomulka took note of this mood by at first making a somewhat reluctant alliance with the revisionist 'liberals'; contrary as this alliance was in itself to his own cut and dried, positivist mode of thought, it could not be avoided in face of the continuing strength of the Stalinist 'conservative' groups. At any rate, the alteration of course which he put into operation as soon as he had gained power was to strengthen the revisionist wing of his supporters. The most important change was the replacement of the War Minister, Rokossovsky, on 8 November 1956 by Gomulka's friend Marian Spychalski, for this removed the most striking symbol of Soviet domination. On 13 November, in addition to some non-party experts, another close colleague of Gomulka's entered the Government in the shape of the new Minister for Primary Education, Bienkowski. On 18 November yet another intimate friend, Loga-Sowinski, took charge of the already disintegrating trade unions in order to reorganize them. The direction of the 'State Commission for Economic Planning' was retained by Jedrychowski; alongside his board of control a liberal advisory committee came into existence in the form of an 'Economic Council' headed by the economist Oskar Lange. The particularly difficult job of Minister of Agriculture was taken over on 7 January 1957 by Edward Ochab, who had previously shown few liberal tendencies but had prepared the way for Gomulka and shared his sense of practical requirements.

The most pressing of the mundane tasks to which Gomulka had to address himself after the excitement of October was the reorganization of the PZPR, for when all was said and done it was intended that the party should continue to provide the nation's intellectual and social leadership. Gomulka could count on the support of the party's highest executive bodies, that is, the Polit-bureau and the secretariat, but not on that of the Central Committee – the PZPR's 'parliament' – or that of many of the subordinate committees, where the Stalinists banished from leading positions still wielded a good deal of influence. During the October revolution the PZPR had broken up into a number of different factions, and of these only Gomulka's direct supporters – the group led by Kliszko, Loga-Sowinski and Ochab – and the former PPS left wing under Cyrankiewicz and Rapacki seemed reliable. As a counterweight to the reluctantly accepted support of the 'liberals', who were led by the secretaries of the CC, Jerzy Morawski and Jerzy Albrecht, and mainly represented the younger, educated section of the party, Gomulka had to reckon with the obstinate opposition of the Stalinists, who re-grouped after the resignation of the compromised older leaders under the economic expert Eugeniusz Szyr and the hated Kazimierz Witaszewski (known as 'General Gaspipe'), and joined forces with the 'Natolin group', whose ideological basis was no longer very firm. The strongest section of the party turned out to be the 'Neutralists' or 'Centralists', who consisted mainly of the surviving members of the former KPP; they united round the CC secretary Roman Zambrowski to form the 'Pulawy group'. It was mainly through their help that in the first three years of his régime Gomulka was able to 'cleanse' the PZPR not only of Stalinist groups but also of declared revisionists, expelling altogether nearly 300,000 party members in the process. The elections at the long-postponed Third Congress of the PZPR (10–17 March 1959) brought him a safe majority in the Central Committee and enabled him to alter the party statistics in his own favour. The defeat of the Stalinist opposition also relieved Gomulka of the need to remain on friendly terms with the revisionist liberals, whose often unrealistic attempts at reform had already endangered ideological relations with the Soviet Union and had therefore frequently been censured. The economic crisis of autumn 1959, which was ascribed to the principles of economic revisionism, provided the desired opportunity to deprive the liberals of power. On 27 October 1959 Bienkowski had to leave the Ministry of Education, and on 29 October Morawski had to resign from the Politbureau and the secretariat of the PZPR; the process of forcing the liberals out of leading positions ended a year later with the resignation of the CC secretary Jerzy Albrecht, though it is true that on 16 November 1960 he was given the Ministry of Finance. However, at the Twenty-Second Congress of the CPSU (17–31 October 1961), which saw the final 'de-Stalinization' and the condemnation of the 'personality cult', the now over-powerful Pulawy group did not have to accept a thorough revision of the previously valid ideological and economic dogmas, and this in itself was a very desirable confirmation of its policy. Nevertheless, the Twenty-Second Congress shattered its supremacy, since Gomulka could now count on much stronger backing from the Soviet leaders and his plan for a gradual restriction of liberalism – which involved a slight increase in the power of the Natolin group – found support from Khrushchev. In addition, the consolidation of the PZPR and of the State after the Third Congress of the PZPR had favoured a new political group, most of whose leaders had served in the international brigades of the Spanish Civil War, the People's Army or the left-wing resistance movement in the Second World War and were therefore known collectively as the 'Partisans'. They grouped themselves, particularly after the Thirteenth Plenary Session of the PZPR (4–6 July 1963), round the CC secretaries Ryszard Strzelecki and Boleslaw Jaszczuk, who succeeded in forcing the two heads of the Pulawy group, Roman Zambrowski and Wladyslaw Matwin, out of the leading committees of the PZPR. Moreover, the Partisans held many important positions of

command in the army, the police, the security troops and the
frontier guards, since the Deputy Minister for Home Affairs,
Mieczyslaw Moczar, the Deputy Minister for War, Wojciech
Jaruzelski, and Generals Grzegorz Korczynski and Tadeusz
Pietrzak all belonged to this group. The Partisans were characterized by an almost military severity, even brutality, in their
mode of governing and by a decided hostility to discussion and
culture which was aimed particularly against liberals and centralists
and made the Thirteenth Plenary Session the climax of the process
of 'de-liberalization' which had been going on for some years.
In fact, the elections at the Fourth Congress of the PZPR, finally
arranged by Gomulka after long hesitation for 15–20 July 1964,
resulted in a substantial defeat for all the older groups in the
Central Committee, the almost complete exclusion of the liberals
and a relative majority for the Partisans, who now became the
strongest group. But access to the executive committees of the
PZPR – the real seats of power – was still barred to them; both in
the Politbureau and the secretariat Gomulka's direct supporters
retained a large majority. Thus the question whether the older
party leaders round Gomulka (they were almost all in their fifties
or sixties) had succeeded in checking the up-and-coming younger
generation remained open. On the other hand, it was by no means
clear how far the effort of the PZPR to transform itself from the
intellectually fertile but organizationally disjointed party of the
Polish October 'revolution' into a more rigidly organized, intellectually hardened organ of leadership was to be consistently
pursued.

As a result of the struggles between the various parties, Gomulka's attempt to strengthen the PZPR internally had in the previous
eight years certainly failed. In 1964 the PZPR's membership was
roughly 1,568,000, that is, about 5 per cent of the total population;
the party was thus really weaker numerically than at its foundation
in 1948, when it had possessed about 1,503,000 members, who at
that time constituted some 6 per cent of the country's inhabitants.
As in earlier periods of the party's history, the gains made since
October 1956 were counterbalanced by losses through indifference

or opposition and also by numerous expulsions, which quite often took place on account of moral failings; Gomulka himself stated at the Fourth Congress of the PZPR that many comrades 'had abused their authority for personal ends'. It was characteristic of the internal structure of the PZPR that in the sixteen years of its existence the proportion of workers among its members had sunk from three-fifths to two-fifths, and the proportion of peasants from 18 per cent to 11 per cent, while the intelligentsia had risen from 17 per cent to 44 per cent. This intelligentsia, which from now on gave its stamp to the PZPR, was recruited mainly from factory managers, technicians and engineers, officers and above all the lower ranks of the teaching profession; it thus provided a faithful reflection of the gradually growing *élite* of peasant or proletarian origin. This leadership structure in the PZPR brought with it a progressive intellectual impoverishment which corresponded perfectly, it is true, to Gomulka's own hostility to ideas. The rejection of far-reaching ideological thinking was dictated primarily by Gomulka's pragmatic conception of socialism, but he was also governed by the fear that any forward-looking ideology would involve either a relapse into Stalinism or a slide into revisionist ideas. Critical voices among the veterans of Polish socialism stigmatized this attitude, as the ideological debate at the end of 1959 and the beginning of 1960 showed, as 'a capitalistic ethic' and 'pure sociology', but their criticism made no headway. Gomulka, who was certainly better qualified than his ideological opponents to judge the effects of the advance of technology and automation, held fast to his honest, quite unrevolutionary concept of a peaceful, decent life for all the Poles entrusted to his care. To this was certainly added an instinctive, almost petty *bourgeois* distaste for any high-flown ideas. In his speech of 4 July 1963, which introduced the 'ideological cold spell' of the Thirteenth Plenary Session of the PZPR, he condemned revisionism as the 'chief danger' because it was usually accompanied by 'the rejection of Marxism in general'; so far as he was concerned, the value of practical Marxism was beyond question. On the other hand, when in April 1964 Chinese infiltration, which became more and more influential after the Twenty-Second Congress of the CPSU, led a group of old Stalinists round Kazi-mierz Mijal and Wiktor Klosiewicz to criticize his mode of govern-ing in the old revolutionary terms of the class struggle, he reacted just as sharply as Khrushchev. After the temporary arrest of these opponents he pronounced in his opening address at the Fourth Congress of the PZPR on 15 July 1964 the most severe judgement yet heard on the 'academic maintenance of the "purity" of theses' which had been 'put forward in another age and in different historical conditions', and went on to praise the socio-economic development of Marxism and its 'close relationship to life'.

This pragmatism was well suited to the rooted fear of all classes of any kind of 'ideology', and it had beneficial effects in the practical questions of welfare planning, but it was hardly calcu-lated to consolidate the PZPR's function of leading the country. The PZPR owed its position of power primarily to its internal link with the State and it therefore drew its strength from the classes who in any case controlled the State: in 1960 seven-tenths of all officers and a good fifth of all teachers were members, while only every eighth industrial worker and only every twenty-sixth peasant belonged to the party. The distribution of the membership of the PZPR within the nation explained how the Partisans' leading military positions outside the party had helped them to acquire their sectional power inside it. This unhealthy situation could not really be checked even by the temporary introduction of an 'in-ternal democracy', which assigned the choice of three-quarters of the candidates to the basic organizations of the PZPR. The resemblance of the party to a sort of State institution did little to attract young people to it, as was demonstrated by the small membership of the 'Union of Socialist Youth' (ZMS) and the 'Union of Rural Youth' (ZMW). Moreover, it was particularly the intellectual youth which rejected the PZPR: in 1960 only one in sixty-six of the students at all institutes of higher education belonged to it. The opinion polls taken among students in 1958 and 1961 reflected once again the PZPR's laxness in the realm of ideas, for they showed that most of those interrogated certainly approved of 'some form' of socialism, but that few could distinguish the nature of socialism from general notions of social justice. The intellectual dystrophy of educated youth and its hunger for a moral ideal continually provoked leading intellectuals of the PZPR such as Stefan Zolkiewski, who was for a time Minister of Higher Education, to walk the dangerous knife-edge between the permitted positivism and the forbidden revisionism until Gomulka intervened; the attempts of Adam Schaff, the party's chief ideologist, in preparation for the Twenty-Second Congress of the CPSU in 1961, to answer the pressing question of the meaning of life with speculations about a 'socialist humanism' were merely displays of dialectical fireworks which had no effect on the masses. Consequently the PZPR was able to give the nation outward form, but not to take over its spiritual leadership.

In these circumstances the institutions of the State – although Gomulka too wished them to remain functionally independent of the PZPR – were saddled with the burden of reacting on the latter. After taking over power Gomulka did not interfere with the arrangements prescribed by the constitution of 1952, but he did open the way to a limited measure of democracy. This was to benefit the local and regional people's councils and above all the Sejm, which remained from a constitutional point of view the sovereign representative assembly of the people. Thus the electoral law passed on 23 October 1956, like previous electoral regulations, still dictated the result of the elections in advance in so far as the lists of candidates ensured a majority for the PZPR; but the electorate at any rate had the chance to alter the order of candidates in each electoral district, to reject a few of them completely and thus to express its sympathies or antipathies. Such expressions of will were certainly restricted by the shattering impression made by the intervention of Soviet troops in friendly Hungary (1–9 November 1956), especially as Gomulka – after the Polish episcopate had recommended Catholics to vote – urgently requested the electorate on 15 January 1957, in an unmistakable reference to events in Hungary, not to strike out the PZPR candidates, as this would be as good as 'striking Poland off the map of Europe'. After all this the first elections to the Sejm under Gomulka could hardly bring any surprises: out of a total of 459 seats 238 went to the PZPR, 39 to the SD, 119 to the ZSL and 63 to independents (including 12 Catholics). The second elections, held four years later, lacked the spectacular element of an acute Soviet threat; on the other hand, the revised electoral decree of 22 December 1960 provided for a stricter limitation of the groups of candidates, particularly of independents. Thus these elections, which took place on the 16 April 1961, increased the PZPR's share of the seats to 256 out of 460, while the SD and ZSL were able more or less to maintain their strength thanks to a number of losses by the independent groups. In these second elections the voters were able to express their wishes still more clearly than four years before, even though the complete rejection of a regional chief was no longer possible as it had been in 1957. Among the groups of candidates for the 80 electoral districts only seven were able to maintain their places at the head of the list; these seven included Gomulka himself, Spychalski, the Minister of War, and Zawadzki, the President. Of the other leaders of the lists only 24 fell to last place; among them were four members of the PZPR Politbureau – Ochab, Jedrychowski, Zambrowski and Gierek – and the provincial secretaries of the PZPR in Warsaw, Cracow, Wroclaw (Breslau) and Lodz. At Wroclaw the Foreign Minister, Rapacki, who in himself was not unpopular, was forced out of first place by the energetic mayor, Iwaszkiewicz. At Cracow the first places were won by Jozef Radny, the leading SD politician, Stanislaw Stomma, the Catholic parliamentarian, and the historian Kazimierz Lepszy, pro-rector of the Jagellonian University, while the particularly unpopular prime minister Cyrankiewicz, who in 1957 had at least been able to achieve third place after two Catholic politicians, was forced from first place to last but one; the only thing that saved him from falling to last was the fact that his former colleague in the 'Cracow Left', Boleslaw Drobner, received the smallest total of votes given to any member of the Sejm. Even if these emphatic demonstrations could make no important changes in the composition of the Sejm, they did at least possess the weight of representative expressions of public opinion.

With the change in the mode of election came a change in the character of parliamentary activity, which had degenerated since 1952 into mere acclamation. When the new Sejm met for the first time on 20 February 1957 the members were once more given the right to unite in sectional groups; the smallest of these groups, the Catholic 'Znak' club, played a particularly lively part in the debates, since its members felt that they were the legitimate representatives of Catholic voters. Legislative work, which had previously come almost to a standstill as a result of the decrees issued by the Council of State, was now carried on in earnest, especially in the re-activated parliamentary committees. From 1952 to 1956 the Sejm had passed only eight laws; between 1957 and 1961 it passed a hundred and seventy-four. In addition, up to 1961 at any rate it was well-nigh unheard of in the history of parliaments in peoples' democracies that there should be real debates and votes cast not only against legislative proposals but even against the investiture of the Government. To this extent a kind of Parliament had come into existence which certainly lacked many of the freedoms of classical democracy but on the other hand was far more effective and serious than the Parliaments of authoritarian States in the Western world.

The Government formally re-united for the first time under Gomulka on 27 February 1957 consisted mainly of the men who had been prominent since the October revolution; the PZPR ministers, among whom only a few former Stalinists, such as the Deputy Prime Minister Zenon Nowak, were represented, held 25 of the 32 portfolios. The premiership went for the third time to Jozef Cyrankiewicz, who recommended himself as a reliable executant of the party's decisions by reason of his inexhaustible adaptability and his lack of popularity. During the next few years there were only small changes in this Cabinet and these were due to decisions of Gomulka's, though they were often also the result of factional differences on economic or cultural affairs inside the PZPR. Thus on 16 June 1959 Stefan Zolkiewski, the Minister for

Higher Education, resigned, and on 27 October 1959 Wladyslaw Bienkowski, the Minister for Primary Education, and Edward Ochab, the Minister for Agriculture, left the Government, all three making way for hitherto little-known experts. When Cyrankiewicz's fourth Government was formed on 18 May 1961 Jerzy Sztachelski gave up the delicate job of Minister in Charge of Church Affairs, a post for which he had apparently shown himself too compliant. Consequently the Government always retained the character of a Cabinet of experts, dependent in genuinely political questions on the directives of the leaders of the PZPR. At the same time as Cyrankiewicz's third Government was formed, on 27 February 1957, the collegiate State Praesidium, the 'Council of State', was reorganized; Gomulka himself took a seat in it, though otherwise he kept aloof from offices of state. As legislation now became the task of the Sejm once again, the Council of State reverted to the position of a body representing the majesty of the State. After the death of the Council's president, Zawadzki (7 August 1964), the Sejm elected, at Gomulka's suggestion, Edward Ochab to this highest office of state. The new President was indebted for his election to his unimpeachable personal integrity and also to the circumstance that the further plans of the Partisan group in the PZPR were thereby thwarted.

Thus in the eight years between the October revolution and the celebrations to mark the twentieth anniversary of the setting up of the Lublin Committee, the outbreak of the Warsaw rising, and hence the twenty-year existence of post-war Poland, the foundations had been laid of a mode of government which, for all its gloomier side, corresponded very well to the possibilities open to Poland at home and abroad. The transformation of the State into a classical democracy, a transformation expected by many Poles in the first flush of enthusiasm of those October days, could not possibly be accomplished, as was soon apparent to those with any insight, especially after the military suppression of the Hungarian revolt. Although on the surface the internal structure of the Polish People's Republic seemed to reflect the ideas of Gomulka and his supporters, fundamentally it was still a tried, tested and indispensable instrument of Soviet policy. To this extent Poland's geographical position, which had so often played an important part in the recent history of eastern Europe, had a more decisive effect on the shaping of the Polish State than any of Gomulka's ideas or actions. In these circumstances, once they had overcome their feeling of exhausted resignation, the Poles came to terms with the internal and external limitations on their political freedom without forfeiting a lively interest in politics or their keen sense of justice. Although the Polish spirit, to which any kind of domination is abhorrent, was constantly rubbing up against the thousand and one restrictions of everyday life, it was borne up by the feeling that, as in earlier periods, it had once again come forward as the champion of liberalism in the far east of Europe. In fact a middle way between objective conditions and subjective wishes, between the rigours of state socialism and the mildness of a democratic order, had now been found and taken. Consequently the inspiring idea of 'spring in October' gradually declined into the more homely notion of the 'Polish October', and therein lay a certain danger for the continuation of the 'individual Polish way'.

SOCIAL AND ECONOMIC CHANGES

The October revolution of 1956 disclosed the full extent of the radical mistakes in planning implicit in the economic policy hitherto pursued. Although the burdens of the Stalinist legacy had been slightly reduced since 1954, they were still pressing heavily on the productive capacity of the Polish economy. The universal nationalization or socialization which had overtaken all industries including farming now resulted in a critical decline in productivity and morale. This decline was caused partly by the swollen numbers of people engaged in administration and the increasing indifference of the workers to the quality of their work, but mainly by the profound physical exhaustion of the whole working population. At the same time, the unhealthy, almost megalomaniac concentration of all investment in the big basic industries had led to the decay of the medium-sized and smaller enterprises and to the near-extinction of crafts and trades. As a result the severe shortage of consumer goods now made itself felt as keenly as the hitherto consciously accepted neglect of the smaller towns and rural population. Finally, the quickly spreading chaos in the fabric of economic planning contrasted with the spontaneous take-over of power by the workers in many of the bigger factories, a process which found expression mainly in the creation of workers' councils. Consequently the general demand for higher wages and quicker improvement of the standard of living and state care coincided with a threatening low-water mark in production as a whole. Thus it looked as if the thaw in political conditions, hitherto so harsh, was going to bring with it a real economic catastrophe.

A particularly striking example of the depressed state of the Polish economy was provided by agriculture, which in 1957 with about 12,730,000 workers – roughly 45 per cent of the total population – still represented the most important industry. Round about 1949, after all holdings of a hundred and twenty-five acres or more had been broken up, the 'socialization of the village' had begun, which aimed not only at developing the big nationalized estates, but also at socializing private land. By 30 September 1956, 10,150 co-operative farms had been set up, but in spite of pressure from the Government they had succeeded in embracing only about a tenth of the land and of the people working on it. Even if the state farms are included in the reckoning, the 'socialist sector' of agriculture covered barely a quarter of the cultivable land. Moreover, although these enterprises had been treated as experimental areas for modern agricultural methods and given every assistance, their yield was far smaller in value than that of the private holdings. In the private sector of agriculture, thanks to the division of the land, the peasant-farming structure which had been predominant even before the Second World War had now become universal. What was downright dangerous was that the number of small self-sufficient peasant farms of under twelve acres producing almost no surplus at all had risen between 1950 and 1957 from 57·2 per cent to 63·4 per cent of all private farms;

of the rest, only those of over twenty-five acres, which formed 9·6 per cent of all farms of any sort, made a significant contribution to feeding the country. Thus the agrarian reforms completed eight years before had succeeded to some extent in assuaging the Polish peasantry's hunger for land, a hunger which had been pent up for at least five generations, but they had not benefited the national economy as a whole. In addition, the temporary satisfaction produced in the peasants by the demagogic agrarian policy of the earlier Governments had long given way, since the start of socialization, to deeply rooted fear and strong distrust. This mood found its most extreme expression in the wild, almost revolutionary dissolution of the co-operatives which began in October 1956 and finally left only eighteen hundred and three of them – a sixth of the original total – intact. Even these eighteen hundred were for the most part uneconomic. Thus the traditional peculiarities of the Polish agrarian structure, the long-standing disregard of agricultural needs and the collapse of the policy of collectivization led eventually to a situation in which the total yield of Polish agriculture was no longer sufficient to feed the nation. Before the Second World War Poland had been able to export large quantities of bread grains, but for the last eight years she had found herself compelled to import an ever-increasing amount of wheat without really being able to pay for these imports with industrial products. Thus the general economic collapse was accompanied by a serious shortage of food.

Gomulka saw clearly that the main requirement for economic recovery, apart from the reduction of investment and an increase in the production of consumer goods, was the relaxation of economic controls, which were far too rigid. On 1 January 1957 he therefore converted the State Commission for Economic Planning into the 'Cabinet Planning Commission', and at the same time limited its functions. However, his economic advisers were by no means unanimous about the precise nature and degree of the 'decentralization' or even 'liberalization' required. In addition to the Planning Commission under Stefan Jedrychowski there was a newly created 'Economic Council' under Oskar Lange, and this body favoured comprehensive changes in the organic structure of the national economy. The Council took the view that each factory should be run jointly by a State manager and an elected workers' council and should form a largely autonomous unit obliged to operate at a profit; in addition wages and prices should be reformed in such a way that they would no longer be instruments manipulated by the State but genuine reflections of real costs, as in a free economy. It was clear that economic planning of this sort, reminiscent as it was of Yugoslav models, would not only displease the more conservative communist political economists of Poland, but was also bound to be regarded as heretical in the other peoples' democracies. For this reason, it could hardly be put into effect without modification. Thus at first, up to the end of 1959, Polish economic policy was something of a compromise. This became quite clear from the fate of the workers' councils, the very heart of factory autonomy. The councils themselves had been legalized by the hastily passed law of 19 November 1956; but at the same time, by the wording of this law and also by the nominal continuance of the trade unions, rescued by Gomulka, they had been pushed out of managing factories and left simply with the right of co-decision. The 'law concerning workers' self-government', adopted on 20 December 1959, completely deprived the workers' councils of any power at all, since from now onwards they had to share even the right of co-decision with other industrial bodies. This meant the victory for the next few years of central economic direction and the continuance of wage- and price-fixing by the State. The ideas of the Economic Council were at first fully implemented only in the realms of handicraft, commerce and retail trade, where by 1960 there was a noticeable resurgence of private enterprise to the detriment of the co-operatives. In addition, the provincial councils received permission to undertake a sixth of state investment themselves or at any rate to control it; these projects were chiefly concerned with social questions, particularly housing. All other domains remained part of the rigidly organized state economic apparatus. Oskar Lange gave repeated warnings of the dangers of once again carrying centralization to excess. He had the satisfaction of seeing some of his theses approved by the Twenty-Second Congress of the CPSU (17-30 October 1961) and in the end, a year later, openly accepted by the Soviet economist J. J. Liberman. But Lange lost influence precisely because his views gained ground in the peoples' democracies of eastern Europe. Finally, in 1963, his Economic Council disappeared completely from the list of Polish official institutions. Nevertheless, in spite of its equivocal character, the new economic policy was able to show undeniable successes. By about 1960 it had succeeded, in spite of some severe reverses, in overcoming the inherited economic disorganization, balancing the hitherto unco-ordinated individual branches of production and making good the most serious deficiencies in consumer goods. Between 1956 and 1960 industrial production rose by some 59 per cent, partly because the huge investments of the Stalinist era were now also beginning to show a profit. Owing to the state manipulation of wages and prices the rise in real income was smaller than the official figures might have led one to expect; nevertheless between 1956 and 1960 it could be estimated at about 29 per cent. With the perceptible improvement in the standard of living the national economic policy gradually began to inspire a modest degree of confidence again, as was made clear by the rise in savings; between 1956 and 1962 there was a tenfold increase in deposits. Yet in 1962-3 the wages of Polish workers still represented some of the lowest incomes in Europe. House-building, too, in spite of praiseworthy efforts, lagged so far behind needs that in 1962 there was still a deficiency of about 1,320,000 dwellings, a good 19 per cent of the total required. It became apparent once again that Poland, as a notoriously poor land, without any reserves of its own or sufficient foreign aid, had a great deal of leeway to make up in comparison with those European countries which had long been industrialized. In addition, the national economy had been so deeply shaken by the destruction of the Second World War that a high rate of investment was still unavoidable. To that extent only a very slow improvement in the standard of living could be expected, and consequently plans for 1963–4 envisaged only the modest yearly rise of 5 per cent.

The economic successes were due mainly to the achievements of Polish agriculture. Agricultural policy was based on the resolutions adopted by both the Central Committee of the PZPR and the Executive Committee of the ZSL on 8 January 1957; these resolutions governed the activities of the Minister for Agriculture, Ochab. In accordance with these decisions the Government gave up the idea of pursuing the discredited 'socialization of the village' and turned its main attention to encouraging private agriculture. The co-operative farms were limited to the reduced proportion of 1 per cent of the peasantry and of the usable land; the state farms were on the whole left as they were, but in fact between 1957 and 1960 their acreage fell from 13·4 per cent to 11·9 per cent of the usable land. Thus about 85 per cent of all agricultural land remained in the hands of private owners; according to the census of 10 June 1957 it embraced about 3,632,800 farms. With the basic agrarian laws of 13 July 1957 the Sejm met the wishes of the Polish peasants to own their own land by finally declaring the land distributed at the time of the agrarian reform private property; in addition, it was made legal to own up to thirty-seven acres (15 hectares). Finally these laws reduced the amount of produce which had to be handed over to the State by about 31 per cent, and small farms of under five acres were relieved of the obligation altogether. These measures brought a swift rise in agricultural productivity, but it was not sufficient to prevent serious shortages of food. On 27 October 1959 one of these food crises led to Ochab's resignation; his successor at the Ministry of Agriculture was Mieczyslaw Jagielski, the son of a small farmer. Gomulka did not entirely abandon the socialization of agriculture. In conformity with the long-standing Polish tradition of a highly developed system of agricultural co-operatives he sought to achieve socialization through the conception of the 'Agricultural Circles' (KR), an idea which he first enunciated in his speech of 19 March 1959. At the first congress of the KR (3–5 September 1959) statutes were drawn up according to which these circles were to be organized with help from the State as legal, public bodies for common agricultural production, the land itself, however, being left in private ownership. The United States Government seemed to give these plans its tacit approval; at any rate, on 30 September 1959 the American Secretary of Agriculture said in Warsaw that these circles were 'not the worst way' to raise agricultural production.[1] Although Polish farmers remained distrustful of the agricultural circles, the machinery stations and the State agronomists, they showed their gratitude for the legal confirmation of their own positions as private owners by making great efforts; they produced several good harvests, including the record one of autumn 1961, the best in the whole modern history of Poland. In view of these successes, at the Twenty-Second Congress of the CPSU Gomulka obtained Khrushchev's permission to complete the gradual socialization of Polish agriculture 'without nationalizing the land'. Nevertheless, Polish agricultural production continued to lag behind that of the countries of the European Economic Community, and also behind that of Russia and the German Democratic Republic; it was still necessary to import wheat and cattle fodder, mainly from the USA, Canada and Russia. The main reason for this was neither bad farming nor weaknesses in distribution, but the still extremely old-fashioned methods prevailing in Polish agriculture. The low degree of mechanization – in 1962 there was only one tractor to every two villages – was accompanied by the traditional, and sometimes exaggerated, Polish fondness for keeping horses, and above all by a serious lack of artificial fertilizers, which was partly due to the compulsory export of fertilizer factories to Russia. But the decisive factor was the extension of the traditional system of smallholdings. Between 1957 and 1960 the total number of farms of all kinds declined, mainly because of emigration into the towns and into the former German territories, but the proportion represented by tiny farms of under five acres rose from 30·8 per cent to 32·6 per cent. The main reason for this rise was the old

---

[1] The Soviet Minister of Agriculture also gave them his blessing somewhat later.

Polish custom, followed for at least four hundred years, of splitting up holdings. This progressive fragmentation of property could not really be balanced by the forced establishment of the agricultural circles. According to the reports of the Second Congress of the KR (29–30 May 1963) there were at that time about 30,000 circles with some 1,150,000 members; but more precise inquiry disclosed that of these only 21,133 had been 'active'. The farmers remained distrustful of the agricultural circles, especially as the Government was trying gradually to convert them from mere co-operatives into communal enterprises. Since the Government refrained from making membership of the circles compulsory, the great majority of farmers clung to private enterprise, and thus also to division of land among a farmer's heirs. On 25 June 1963, the Sejm therefore passed a law forbidding the division of holdings of less than twenty acres and prohibiting the leaving of land to people not connected with farming. This harsh interference with old peasant customs obviously sprang from Gomulka's wish to strengthen the medium-sized farms and thus gradually to become independent of wheat imports. It is true that Gomulka's measures also affected the small farms, which in the meantime had changed over to cattle-raising and thus produced the bulk of the valuable exports of meat. On the whole, the historical structure of Polish agriculture and the tough way in which the individual farmer clung to his property continued to prove stronger than the Government's very cautious and tentative attempts to nationalize land ownership and agricultural production. As Gomulka was very much aware of this situation and, thanks to his sober, unorthodox and pragmatic mode of thought, took it fully into account, Poland remained the only country in the Communist bloc which in fact retained private ownership of the land.

The Government's agricultural policy was indissolubly bound up with the inherited rural over-population of the country. This over-population was the most important cause of the proliferation of smallholdings and the fragmentation of property, that is, of 'rural poverty in the shape of a superfluity of fields'. The start made with industrial development in the Stalinist era had not yet acquired sufficient momentum to exert any noticeable effect on the agrarian structure; between 1952 and 1956, 450,000 people at the most had moved from the country into the towns. Apparently the land distributions of the barely completed agrarian reform had had more attraction than the life of a factory worker. Thus according to the rural census of 10 June 1957 the provinces of Little Poland and Upper Silesia, which had long been known to be over-populated, still showed an unhealthy concentration of people living on the land; in spite of a good deal of emigration since 1950 the farming population in the regions of Katowice, Cracow, and Rzeszow and the neighbouring districts still far exceeded the critical figure of eighty persons to every 250 acres of land available for agriculture. To the north this over-population gradually became less pronounced. Thus in spite of all the demographic changes brought about by the war and the post-war period the breaking up of these over-populated rural regions by the creation of jobs in non-agricultural professions and the corresponding re-training involved still formed the most important social problem. None of the previous Governments had been able to solve it.

The best possibility of reducing this rural over-population was offered by the former German territories, officially known as the 'recovered territories'; here, according to the figures of 10 June 1957, there were, on an average, only forty-four persons to every 250 acres of agricultural land. The population of these areas, which in 1950 had amounted to about 5,900,000 persons, did in fact grow, according to the census of 6 December 1960, to some 7,800,000, or nearly 81 per cent of the size of the population under German sovereignty (according to the last German census of 31 May 1939). The material conditions and psychological atmosphere in these new settlements improved considerably under Gomulka's régime. The most important factors were the legal recognition of the right to own land, care for the land itself and the small towns, and the encouragement given to house-building. These factors all helped to increase the inhabitants' confidence in the permanence and legitimacy of their new holdings. Moreover, as a result of the favourable age-structure of the new arrivals, the natural increase in population was much greater here than in the rest of Poland. By the end of 1960 there were nearly 2,810,000 children who had been born and grown up there, in addition to about 900,000 children of the original inhabitants, so that those with roots in the western territories formed half the total child population. The Polish Government did not fail to use these figures in support of the Polish right to these territories. At the same time, the economic integration of the territories into Poland moved swiftly towards completion. According to estimates made in 1960 these regions, which embraced 33·08 per cent of the area of Poland and 26·04 per cent of the population, accounted for about 27·9 per cent (in value) of the total industrial production and nearly 33·9 per cent of the agricultural land. Thus the former German territories played a decisive part not only in reducing the rural over-population but also in the development of industry. The need for Poland to retain these areas permanently was thus adequately demonstrated. According to official forecasts, by 1965 their population would equal the population under German sovereignty.

The demographic and economic integration of the former German territories formed only a part of the general process of social transformation, which from 1956 onwards was particularly evident in the urbanization of Poland. Before the Second World War Poland had been a predominantly agricultural country in which the rural population outnumbered the urban population by seven to three; but the 1950 census showed that 39 per cent of the population was now living in the towns. By 1960 the figure had risen to 48·1 per cent, and in 1963 about half the population (some 15,000,000 people) consisted of town-dwellers. Before the war Poland had possessed fourteen large towns; she now possessed twenty-two. This enormous increase in the urban population was due mainly to the massive emigration from the countryside, which between 1957 and 1963 embraced at least 2,200,000 persons; in 1962 alone about 360,000 people moved into the towns. This flight from the land brought a huge increase in non-agricultural occupations. According to figures quoted by Gomulka on 14 March 1963, the number of people engaged in agriculture dropped by about 250,000 between 1956 and 1963, while the number of those engaged in other occupations rose by about 1,400,000. Thus under Gomulka the Polish nation changed – for good, it seemed – from a predominantly agricultural country into an industrial country. Gomulka's social policy had clearly succeeded in finally solving the four-hundred-year-old problem of rural over-population.

It is true that this task required the concentration of all the country's economic strength on the creation of new industrial areas; from 1960 to 1963 alone the number of people employed in industry rose by about 1,026,000, or 11·4 per cent of the total employed population. Between 1961 and 1963 nationalized industry absorbed about 785,000 new workers – some 50,000 more than had been foreseen in the plans. All this meant considerable new investment, and this in turn had to be paid for with a very modest general standard of living. Thus it was certainly true that the fruits of the Polish workers' efforts were reduced not only by the country's poverty but also by the phenomenon inseparable from a centrally controlled economy, namely the locking-up of huge sums of money over a long period, either in projects always costing more than the original estimates, or else as a result of the big foreign trade obligations incurred within the framework of a socialist state; nevertheless, the average standard of living, though low, still came as a blessing to those sections of the population which for generations had lived in scarcely imaginable poverty.

But all the sacrifices made to create new centres of employment were in danger of being nullified by the huge growth in population to which Poland owed her inexhaustible strength. Between 1950 and 1962 the population of Poland rose by some 5,683,000 or 22·3 per cent; in 1962, with about 30,691,000 inhabitants, Poland had a population only slightly smaller than that of the pre-war republic, which was larger in area, at the time of the 1931 census. The comprehensive health service had succeeded in keeping down the death-rate – from 1960 to 1963 it stood at 7·5 per cent per year – to the lowest figure in any country of eastern Europe. At the same time the birth-rate was higher than in almost any other

European State; up to 1957, with figures of 27 to 31 births per thousand of the population, it was even higher than it had been in Poland from 1936 to 1938. Only by 1963 had it fallen to 19 births per thousand. Thus even in 1963 Poland displayed the greatest annual increase in population in the whole of Europe (apart from the Soviet Union), and this in spite of all administrative efforts to secure a substantial reduction in the birth-rate. Up to 1963 this natural increase was not too great a burden on the labour market, for from 1960 to 1963 young people formed only about 18 per cent of those coming into employment for the first time; apparently the reserves of labour from agriculture still provided the bulk of the increase in the number of persons employed. But by 1963 the capacity of the Polish economy to keep creating new jobs – not all of them essential from an economic point of view – had reached its extreme limit. This was all the more crucial since the former German territories were now almost fully settled and openings on the land were gradually disappearing. The Fourteenth Planning Session of the Central Committee of the PZPR (29–30 November 1963) was therefore compelled to put into operation 'Plan R', already drawn up by Jedrychowski's Planning Commission, which involved a large number of dismissals. Thus by 1964 unemployment had made itself distinctly felt again, although a certain amount of labour was re-absorbed by agriculture and sole supporters of families were still spared. By 1965 probably about 500,000 people were without work. On 13 March 1964, during the discussion of the new plan for 1966–1970, Gomulka himself confirmed that in this five-year period, which would include the 'bulge' years for Polish youth, nearly 3,260,000 young people would be coming on to the labour market. In view of the fact that over-manning in industry and the beginning of automation would certainly involve further economies in manpower, this meant a hardly supportable burden on the national economy. The planned number of new jobs mentioned by Gomulka – about 1,500,000 – might be sufficient for the urban youth, but certainly not for the rural youth. Consequently, if Poland did not receive substantial aid from abroad, an increase in unemployment – if only a fairly slow one – or the reappearance of rural over-population could be expected. By 1964, thanks to the huge growth in her population, Poland was challenging Spain for the position of sixth most highly populated country in Europe, but she had to pay for this distinction with these exceptionally difficult social problems. The transformation of the country into a fully industrialized state, a process which in the countries of western Europe had been completed many decades earlier, required sacrifices from the Polish nation which were all the greater because they had to be demanded of a people which had been worn to the bone in the quite recent past.

THE SCOPE AND LIMITS OF POLISH FOREIGN POLICY

Gomulka's accession to power brought no fundamental changes in Polish foreign policy. For Gomulka, as for Pilsudski – this was the only point on which the two statesmen's ideas coincided – the sovereignty of Poland was an essential postulate of socialism. However, the situation in October 1956 left no possibility open but the unconditional continuance of the existing treaties of alliance with the Soviet Union. Both the outward circumstances and Gomulka's own conviction led inescapably to this conclusion. It was quite impossible for Poland to break away even partially from the communist bloc because of the dominating position occupied by the twenty motorized or armoured Soviet divisions in East Germany; their readiness for action had formed a sombre background to the events of the October revolution. Gomulka accordingly took over Poland's obligations in the politico-military system of the Warsaw Pact, which had been signed on 14 May 1955 and, as a counterbalance to NATO, bound together the countries of eastern Europe, previously allied unilaterally to the Soviet Union, in a collective alliance. The internal organization of the pact had been completed on 27–28 January 1956 by the inclusion of the East German army – in precise correspondence with the gradual incorporation of West Germany in NATO – and by the creation of a unified military command. Finally, the lesson of the Hungarian revolt showed that it was precisely the denunciation of the Warsaw treaties by Nagy's Government (1 November 1956) that had been the decisive factor in provoking the Soviet military intervention in Hungary, an operation with which the Western Governments made no attempt to interfere. In view of all this, Gomulka confined himself to putting Poland's relations with the Soviet Union on a more advantageous basis within the framework of the existing treaties and in accordance with a special Soviet declaration of 30 October 1956. At his discussions in Moscow (15–18 November 1956) he confirmed Poland's obligations under the Warsaw Pact and in return obtained the remission of old debts, the promise of the repatriation of a number of Poles who in many cases had been in Soviet custody since 1939, and renewed guarantees of the inviolability of the Oder-Neisse line. The economic tribute which Poland had been paying to Russia under the name of 'trade treaties' and which had particularly incensed Polish opinion was replaced not only by genuine treaties but also by considerable economic assistance from the Soviet Union. Probably the most important result of the discussions was the agreement about the stationing of Soviet troops in Poland, which abolished the extra-territorial rights enjoyed by the occupation forces and guaranteed fresh respect for Polish sovereignty. On 17 December 1956 a military agreement on this subject was signed; it was followed by similar arrangements between the Soviet Union and other eastern European States. Poland thus came nearer to enjoying the status of an equal partner of the Soviet Union. By the revision of the military treaties and the recall of Rokossovsky and most of the Russian military advisers the Polish armed forces were freed from a number of bonds which had previously cramped their internal structure. In the course of the next few years they were transformed into a well-equipped modern army, with a peace-time strength of 500,000 men, possessing fourteen armoured or motorized divisions, rocket weapons and a tactical air force. It is true that their reliability in operations against the armies of western Europe remained to be seen, although the influence of the generals belonging to the partisan faction, under the formal command of the War

Minister, Spychalski, now promoted to marshal, grew steadily, and ideological indoctrination was carried out energetically.

In face of the internal consolidation of the Warsaw Pact system, a task which was looked after by the periodic sessions of the advisory political committee, Poland's freedom of action in her dealings with states outside the eastern bloc was extremely limited. The cardinal question in foreign policy remained the assertion of Polish sovereignty over the 'recovered territories', that is, the ex-German regions, including the free city of Danzig, now under Polish administration. The swiftly progressing 'Polonization' of these territories and their importance to the national economy were in themselves reasons which could be used to good effect, especially as since 1956 hundreds of thousands of 'recognized Germans' and 'autochthonous' inhabitants had emigrated and to that extent there was no longer any real German minority problem. Nevertheless, both Government and nation felt worried about the ownership of these territories, since the Polish claim to them still rested on the Potsdam decisions with their vague and often contradictory statements. The official Polish case, which was based partly on the 'fundamentally Slav character' of the disputed regions, partly on the theory of a 'historical nationality' that had existed for nine centuries and partly on the interpretation of the Potsdam Conference as a 'preliminary peace', had still failed to secure international recognition in the West. The Governments of the USA, Great Britain and France certainly let it be seen on numerous occasions that in fact they recognized the Oder-Neisse line as the western frontier of Poland, but out of regard for the Government of West Germany they never made an unambiguous, legally binding pronouncement on the frontier question. Up to autumn 1958 Gomulka therefore tried cautiously to achieve a lessening of tension with West Germany and the establishment of diplomatic relations. The compulsory re-arming of West Germany in the framework of NATO strengthened Polish fears of a West German revisionist policy, which was compared, in accordance with the traditional attitude of the Poles towards foreign affairs, with the Weimar Republic's efforts to have the frontier revised and even with the partitions of Poland. Even the plan for an atom-free zone in central Europe, which was first unfolded at the United Nations by the Foreign Minister, Rapacki, on 2 October 1957 and has never since been absent from the deliberations of European Cabinets, was indirectly connected with the frontier question. Mainly because of her obligations to her allies, but also because of the 'Hallstein Doctrine' and of the interest in the Oder-Neisse territories shown by certain groups or associations inside Germany, the West German Government felt that it could not respond to the Polish approaches, although it was well aware of the gravity of Polish fears. Political relations between Bonn and Warsaw subsequently cooled off to a state of icy correctness, even though trade between the two countries assumed considerable proportions. West Germany took no part in the wide development of cultural relations with Poland undertaken by other Western countries. This political stalemate was not even broken by the trade treaty between West Germany and Poland which was signed on 7 March 1963 and which resulted in the establishment of a West German trade mission in Warsaw. Meanwhile, however, the persistent West German claim to the former German territories had sunk, in face of the complete ethnic and economic integration of these regions in the Polish State, to a mere diplomatic bargaining counter without any real political significance. Nevertheless, the Poles' deeply rooted mistrust of German 'revisionism' did not disappear, and therefore on the frontier question the nation – and even the Poles in exile, who were at loggerheads with the Warsaw régime – were at one with the Government. To this extent the alliance with the Soviet Union – the only power which promised reliable guarantees for the Polish western frontier – was also approved by the non-communist and even the openly anti-Government section of the Polish nation. Thus the continuance of the West German legal claim to the Oder-Neisse territories formed the strongest foundation of the Polish alliance with the Soviet Union, a stronger one than any political or military consideration adduced by the Governments in Warsaw and Moscow.

Poland under Gomulka (1956–1965)

This situation alone was sufficient to strengthen Poland's loyalty to her alliance with the USSR. This loyalty came into play in the rivalry between the Soviet Union and China, which was already perceptible, though still glossed over, at the Twentieth Congress of the CPSU in February 1956. In pushing through the changes of October 1956, Gomulka had been able to make use of the Chinese Government's support against Khruschev, and this seemed justified at the time, since in those days Chinese communism was reckoned to be more liberal than the Soviet brand. During the course of the next few years, however, as Soviet practice and his own drew nearer to each other, and further and further away from the more rigid Chinese conception of communism, Gomulka ranged himself more and more unequivocally on the side of Khrushchev. The Soviet leader's first state visit to Poland (14–23 July 1959) was arranged as a symbol of this collaboration. When, in April 1960, with the first Chinese attack on Khrushchev's policy of co-existence – which for its part gave new value to the Rapacki plan – and the withdrawal of Soviet economic aid to China, the split in the communist camp became obvious, Gomulka's support for Khrushchev acquired fundamental significance. In return for its constantly pro-Soviet policy the Polish Government was able to maintain a limited number of economic and cultural contacts with Western countries, above all with the USA. How interested the Polish nation was in such contacts – far more so than the official attitude of the Government indicated – had already been shown by the spontaneous demonstrations on the occasion of the visit of the American Vice-President, Richard Nixon, on 2 August 1959. The growing bitterness of the Sino-Soviet dispute, especially after the Twenty-Second Congress of the CPSU in October 1961, encouraged 'polycentralism' in the communist world and thus considerably increased the importance of Poland as an ally of the USSR. The semi-independence of Polish foreign policy from that of the Soviet became particularly clear in the discussions on the tasks of the 'Council for Mutual Economic Assistance' (Comecon), a supra-national organization which had been set up as long ago as 25 April 1949 as a counterweight to the west European economic union, but up to the time of the ratification of its statutes on 13 April 1960 had never become fully effective. From September 1960 onwards Khrushchev, pointing to the example of the European Economic Community (EEC), sought to turn Comecon into a supra-national planning authority with common investments, common property and complete co-ordination of the economic plans of the individual member states. However, he was unable to overcome the resistance of the Rumanian and Polish Governments; even before this Gomulka had sharply criticized the minimal usefulness of Comecon to the economic development of Poland and the burdening of the national economy with long-term foreign investments. Therefore although a number of common economic enterprises were founded, and a Comecon clearing bank, the Bank of Socialist Countries, started operations in October 1963, the economic sovereignty of the individual countries was left fundamentally intact. To this extent, the supra-national economic integration of the countries of eastern Europe was delayed like that of the EEC, and through very similar motives on the part of the countries concerned. But Poland's close economic links with the Soviet Union, and the politico-economic affinities of the governmental structure to that of her neighbour, which in the last analysis formed the most effective practical basis for a common foreign policy, did not alter in the slightest degree. Thus although Khrushchev's unexpected fall on 14–15 October 1964 cast a certain gloom over relations between Poland and the Soviet Union it could not produce any real change in the factors determining Polish foreign policy.

THE LIMITED FREEDOM OF CHURCH AND CULTURAL LIFE

Gomulka regarded the revision of the relations between Church and State as one of his most pressing tasks. He considered it senseless 'to try to alter mentality and religious convictions forcibly by administrative measures', as earlier Governments had attempted to do, and he recognized clearly that Catholicism was 'deeply rooted' in the 'majority' of Poles. At the same time he

believed, quite correctly, that he could assume a genuine appreciation of the need for national solidarity in the Catholic clergy.
In fact the imprisoned cardinal primate, Wyszynski, had often
observed that the Catholic faith contributed to Polish unity and
that the priesthood was an 'emanation of the nation'. In addition,
since the Second World War, during which, as Bishop of Wlocla-
wek, he had lost almost half his clergy as a result of the National
Socialist occupation policy, Wyszynski entertained a positive
dislike of Germany which could only be helpful to Gomulka.
Thus although Gomulka always emphasized the ideological
opposition of his socialism to Catholicism a politically conditioned
modus co-operandi lay ready to his hand, especially as the help of
the ecclesiastical authorities in rebuilding the shattered fabric of
the State was very welcome. Therefore on 28 October 1956 he
gave Wyszynski permission to return from custody in the
monastery of Komancza to his archiepiscopal throne. The cardinal
accepted Gomulka's offer, in order to be able to ensure, as
'spiritual father and shepherd', the maximum of spiritual effective-
ness for the Church entrusted to his charge; he completely
rejected the entanglement in political activity to which the
Hungarian primate, Cardinal Mindszenty, fell a prey at this time.
Thus the negotiations between Sztachelski, the Government's
plenipotentiary for ecclesiastical affairs, and the Polish episcopate
were enabled to result in a purposeful co-operation which was
just as free from the taint of ecclesiastical 'collaboration' as from
any fundamental renunciation by the Government of atheistic
principles. The Polish episcopate was guided by the realistic
perception that any attempt to carry the October revolution further would provoke a reaction not only from their own Government but also from the Soviet Union – as the violent repression
of the Hungarian revolt showed – and thus seriously endanger
the activity of the Church. The basis of the new undertaking was
the release of all bishops and priests still in custody, including
those convicted by courts of law, and a limited degree of freedom
of action for Catholic politicians, journalists and publicists. On 7
December 1956 an agreement was signed which did not, it is true,

restore the Church to its former position in Poland, but did guarantee her free and unfettered pastoral activity in all domains of public life, including the army, hospitals and prisons. Religious instruction was again allowed in all schools if parents decided in favour of it – and more than 95 per cent of parents did. Finally the Government agreed to the removal of the 'vicars capitular' who had been appointed by the State and had been officiating in the former German territories since 1951; Wyszynski, who himself assumed the title of Apostolic Administrator for these regions, installed four titular bishops as vicars-general and appointed a *Coadjutor sedi datus* for Danzig. The rebuilding of a spiritually integrated ecclesiastical organization was completed by the substitution of loyal clerics for priests who had compromised themselves before the October revolution.

The Catholic Church in Poland had thus achieved a recognition of her spiritual position which was to continue undiminished in the next few years. The episcopate utilized the thousandth anniversary of the conversion of Poland to embark in 1957 on a nine-year course of spiritual exercises and big pilgrimages or missions designed to deepen still further the Catholic stamp on the Polish national character. In the temporal realm of public life, too, Catholic circles were able to exert a modest degree of influence, as was shown by the fearless activity of the parliamentary club *Znak* and the freedom enjoyed by the Catholic Press. But more impressive still was the development of the Church's organization. By 1962 the number of secular clergy had risen from the pre-war figure of 12,940 (1939) to about 16,000, and that of the regular clergy from 23,050 (1937) to some 37,000. The number of theological students, whose training was catered for by twenty-four higher seminaries, the Catholic University of Lublin and the Theological College of Warsaw, stood constantly at about 4,000. Instead of the 7,251 Catholic churches and chapels of pre-war Poland there were now 10,881, including about 3,300 churches in the Oder-Neisse territories – most of them former Evangelical churches – and at least 500 newly-built houses of God. This increase in ecclesiastical institutions corresponded more or less to the growth of the Catholic population in comparison with the pre-war figure. Between 1957 and 1964 Catholics formed about 97 per cent of the total population, and of these, in 1963–4, roughly nine-tenths – about twenty-seven million people – could be regarded as practising Catholics. Further evidence of Catholicism's deep roots in the Polish nation was provided by the circumstance that although the Church had forfeited most of her property, raised no kind of tax or tithe and was thus forced to depend on voluntary contributions taxed by the State, she always had adequate financial means at her disposal. Thus the external damage suffered in the period of persecution before Gomulka was made good in a surprisingly short time.

As for the Government, it could not avoid respecting the integrity of the Church as an institution, since it had no effective spiritual weapon with which to oppose it. The Church's influence on intellectual life was for the time being so great that even a few opportunists joined her ranks. The *Pax* organization, which had lost its dominating position in Catholic publishing, became more and more like an ordinary business concern. At times the small non-Catholic churches suffered from Catholic intolerance, and in 1957 the leaders of the Evangelical-Lutheran Church made bitter complaints about the 'Twentieth Century Counter-Reformation.' Furthermore, there were often commotions and clashes between Church personnel and the police, mainly in connection with Church buildings which had not been approved by the State authorities, but also as a result of the dissemination of ecclesiastical literature which had not been passed by the censorship. In face of these continually renewed proofs of the wide scope of ecclesiastical influence, efforts by the party leadership to propagate atheism had little success. The 'League of Atheists and Freethinkers' formed a diminishing minority even among intellectuals and its officials remained fewer in number than the clerics of one single deanery. Therefore even members of the PZPR were allowed to be practising Catholics. The Government consequently resorted to administrative measures in the realm of taxes and educational policy to check ecclesiastical influence. In the summer and autumn of 1960 it quietly had most schools converted into 'secular schools' and religious instruction removed from their timetables, while the school law of 1 July 1961 elevated the 'scientific outlook' to the status of guiding principle of education and prevented religious instruction completely. To combat this move the Church very soon created a comprehensive network of 'catechism centres', at which religious instruction was given by her own teachers; the Government was unable to enforce the state control over such instruction originally required by law. Still more serious than the school conflict was the dispute about birth control, which the State encouraged in view of the swift growth of the population, while the leaders of the Church, in accordance with Catholic moral teaching, rejected it. Nevertheless, these continual clashes were not sufficient to put the agreement of 1956 in any serious danger. In fact, in critical situations both the State and the Church authorities sought to avoid an open break; a good example of this was the confidential meeting between Gomulka and Wyszynski on 14 January 1960. In spite of the continuance of the Government policy of small pin-pricks and of corresponding protests from the Church, both sides observed their tacit truce. The Government confined itself to awaiting the results of 'practical materialism' through the gradual construction of a Welfare State, although it knew from the questionnaires circulated among students in 1958 and 1961 that this process of laicization and secularization would take a very long time even among the intelligentsia. The bishops for their part openly acknowledged that the real spiritual strength of Polish Catholicism still lay in fideism and traditionalism. This was particularly evident in the new working class of peasant origin. The critical, intellectual sharpness of modern Catholic theology could make little impression on the tranquil, pastoral tone of Polish religious teaching. Thus the realization that neither State nor Church was strong enough to conduct an uncompromising struggle created the conditions for a kind of co-existence which was always practised watchfully and contentiously, but never in such a way as to make reconciliation impossible.

Poland under Gomulka (1956–1965)

In its cultural policy, as in its policy towards the Church, the Government sought to find a middle way between the wishes of the nation and the needs of practical socialism. The longing expressed in the excitement of October for universal intellectual freedom had to be forgotten during the course of 1957, but most of the newly founded or revived publications, clubs and circles were able to enjoy a certain degree of independence and limited intellectual contacts with the Western countries so long as the liberal faction still possessed some influence in the Central Committee of the PZPR. When the liberals lost power at the end of 1959 the limitations on literary and academic activity became more perceptible. The Government had already suppressed 'revisionist' views such as those of the left-wing intellectual periodical *Po Prostu*, but this had not prevented the continual upsurge of revisionist ideas, and the State now began to take general measures against the freedom to publish. The main signs of this were a number of reprimands for the authors' association, the manipulation of the censorship and pressure on the political debating clubs to stick to unpolitical themes. The regimentation affected even such well-known exponents of intellectual Marxism as Kotarbinski, at that time president of the Academy of Sciences, and his pupil Kolakowski, although in themselves they were welcome as intellectual opponents of the Catholic Church. On 5 February 1962 the last of the independent political discussion circles, the 'Crooked Circle' in Cracow, was closed, and this in spite of the tacit protection given to it by a leading Marxist thinker like Adam Schaff. Just at this time more and more influence in the Central Committee of the PZPR was being acquired by the anti-cultural Partisan faction, which contained the principal supporters of the 'ideological freeze-up' of the Thirteenth Plenary Session in July 1963. Obviously Gomulka himself shared the view that learning and literature only had the right to exist if they provided direct, practical support for the construction of a socialist society.

The Polish intelligentsia, which had a clear and sensitive appreciation of Poland's political needs, was in itself quite ready to come to terms with the sober positivism of Gomulka's cultural policy, so long as it could be ascribed to Poland's external political ties. But when it became clearer and clearer that the party leaders were shackling intellectual creativity on their own initiative, the intellectuals began to offer resistance. After numerous individual protests, on 14 March 1964 a group of thirty-four writers and scholars – among them were such world-renowned names as the writers Jerzy Andrzejewski, Maria Dabrowska and Antoni Slonimski, the philosophers Tatarkiewicz and Kotarbinski, the physicist Leopold Infeld, the mathematician Waclaw Sierpinski, and the literary historian Julian Krzyzanowski – signed a complaint to the Prime Minister, Cyrankiewicz, in which they demanded in curt, sober and almost threatening words 'a change in Polish cultural policy in the spirit of the rights guaranteed by the constitution of the Polish State'. Gomulka, who was extremely irritated at this letter, found himself compelled to give way when large groups of students and printing workers announced their solidarity with the protest. Above all, governmental attempts at repression of thirty-four signatories aroused world opinion more than at any time since the activities of Polish intellectuals in the First World War. The Government was all the more inclined to compromise by the thought of the thousand-year existence of Polish culture and above all by the celebrations of the six-hundredth anniversary of the Jagellonian University (12 May 1964), which, over and above their internal significance, were calculated to increase Poland's credit abroad.

Thus it became clear, especially from the unyielding attitude of the Polish intelligentsia, that the big historical breaks of the last few decades had not seriously endangered the continuity of Polish culture. A good half of those in leading positions still bore old names well known in Polish cultural history. Notwithstanding the enormous changes which had transformed the outward aspects of Polish society, the Poles were still in essence a nation whose culture, as in the past, formed a bridge between East and West. The decisive factor in the moulding of Polish life and thought was still nationalism, united now to a higher degree than ever before with the Catholic faith. Within the framework of this all-embracing national faith, the individual Pole was still able to find in the traditional values of regard for one's fellow beings, old-fashioned aristocratic modes of behaviour, respect for intellectual and artistic achievements and the unconditional sanctity of the law, powers of resistance which quite often endowed him with a positive immunity to all political influences. Thus for the majority of the nation even the pressing question of the nature and practical shape of socialism had taken the form not of the realization of an abstract economic pattern but rather of the creation of a society based on social justice. All these phenomena lead the historian to the fairly firm conclusion that, although it is impossible to predict the future course of Polish history, Polish society has shown that it knows how to adapt to the present many aspects of the old, free, happy Poland of the past.

SELECT BIBLIOGRAPHY & INDEX

Select Bibliography

Akten zur Deutschen Auswärtigen Politik 1918–1945, Series D, Vol. V, Baden-Baden 1953

W. ANDERS, *An Army in Exile*, London 1949

Badania nad okupacja niemiecka w Polsce (Researches into the German Occupation of Poland), Posen 1946

O. FORST DE BATTAGLIA, *Zwischeneuropa*, Vol. I, Frankfurt 1954

J. BECK, *Dernier Rapport, La Politique polonaise 1926–1939*, Neuchâtel 1951

Biuletyn Glownej Komisji Badania Zbrodni Hitlerowskich w Polsce (Bulletin of the Commission for the Investigation of Hitler's Crimes in Poland), Warsaw 1946

A. BORKIEWICZ, *Powstanie warszawskie 1944* (The Warsaw Rising of 1944), Warsaw 1957

T. BOR-KOMOROWSKI, *The Secret Army*, London 1951

R. BREYER, *Das Deutsche Reich und Polen 1932–1937*, Würzburg 1955

The Cambridge History of Poland (1697–1935), Cambridge 1941

J. CHALASINKI and J. ULATOWSKI, *Przeszlosc i przyzlossc inteligencji polskiej* (Past and Future of the Polish Intelligentsia), Rome 1947

W. CONZE, *Polnische Nation und Deutsche Politik*, Cologne 1958

Deutschland und Polen, Beiträge zu ihren geschichtlichen Beziehungen, ed. A. Brackmann, Munich and Berlin 1933

R. DMOWSKI, *Pisma* (Writings), Vols I–IX, Czestochowa 1938–9

R. DMOWSKI, *Polityka polska i odbudowanie panstwa* (Polish Politics and the Reconstruction of the State), Hanover 1947 (3rd edition)

Documenta occupationis Teutonicae, Vols I–VI, Posen 1945–1958

Documents on Polish-Soviet Relations 1939–1946 (General Sikorski Historical Institute), London 1961

M. K. DZIEWANOWSKI, *The Communist Party of Poland*, Cambridge (Mass.) 1958

Select Bibliography

S. FILASIEWICZ, *La Question polonaise pendant la guerre mondiale, Recuei des actes diplomatiques, traités et documents concernant la Pologne,* Paris 1920

W. GOMULKA, *Przemowienia* (Speeches), Warsaw 1957

O. HALECKI, *A History of Poland,* London 1955

O. HALECKI, *Borderlands of Western Civilization: A History of East Central Europe,* New York 1952

R. HISCOCKS, *Poland, Bridge for the Abyss?,* London 1963

J. KIRCHMAYER, *Powstanie warszawskie* (The Warsaw Rising), Warsaw 1959

W. KOMARNICKI, *Ustroj panstwowy Polski wspolczesnej* (The Constitution of Contemporary Poland), Wilna 1936–7

T. KOMARNICKI, *Rebirth of the Polish Republic,* London 1957

Konstytucja i podstawowe akty ustawodawcze Polskiej Rzeczypospolitej Ludowej (Constitution and Basic Laws of the People's Republic of Poland), Warsaw 1954

S. KOT, *Listy z Rosji do Gen. Sikorskiego* (Letters from Russia to General Sikorski), London 1955

KPP w obronie niepodleglosci Polski (The Communist Party of Poland and the Defence of Poland's Independence), Warsaw 1953

H. LAEUEN, *Polnischen Tragödie,* Stuttgart 1955

R. MACHRAY, *The Poland of Pilsudski,* London 1936

S. MACKIEWICZ, *Historja Polski od 11 listopada 1918 r. do 17 wrzesnia 1939 r.* (History of Poland from 11 November 1918 to 17 September 1939), London 1941.

J. MALARA and L. REY, *La Pologne d'une occupation à l'autre (1944 bis 1952),* Paris 1952

S. MIKOLAJCZYK, *The Rape of Poland,* New York 1948

Najnowsze Dzieje Polski (Recent History of Poland), Vol. I, Warsaw 1957

Niemcy i Polska, Dyskusja z powodu ksiazki 'Deutschland und Polen' (Discussion arising out of the Book 'Germany and Poland'), Lemberg (Lwow), 1934

Osteuropa-Handbuch, Polen, ed by W. MARKERT, Cologne 1959

J. PILSUDSKI, *Pisma zbiorowe* (Collected Works), Vols I–X, Warsaw 1937–8

W. POBOG-MALINOWSKI, *Najnowsza historia polityczna Polski, 1864–1945* (Recent Political History of Poland, 1864–1945), Vols II and III, London 1956 and 1960

Polen und das Minderheitenproblem, ed by S. J. PAPROCKI, Warsaw 1935

Polish–Soviet Relations 1918–1943 (official documents), Washington *c.* 1943

Polskie Sily zbrojne w drugiej wojnie swiatowej (The Polish Armed Forces in the Second World War), London 1950

A. PROCHNIK, *Pierwsze pietnastolecie Polski niepodleglej* (The First Fifteen Years of Independent Poland), Warsaw 1957

Quellen zur Entstehung der Oder-Neisse-Linie, ed by G. RHODE and W. WAGNER, Stuttgart 1956

W. RECKE, *Die polnische Frage als Problem der europäischen Politik,* Berlin 1927

W. J. ROSE, *The Rise of Polish Democracy,* London 1944

H. ROOS, *Polen und Europa,* Tübingen 1957

H. SETON-WATSON, *Eastern Europe between the Wars 1918–1941,* New York 1946

L. SIKORSKI, *La Campagne polono-russe de 1920,* Paris 1928

W. STUDNICKI, *Das östliche Polen,* Kitzingen 1953

J. SZEMBEK, *Journal 1933–1939,* Paris 1952

W. WAGNER, *Die Entstehung der Oder-Neisse-Linie,* Stuttgart 1957

W. WIELHORSKI, *Polska a Litwa* (Poland and Lithuania), London 1947

W. WITOS, *Wybor pism i mow* (Selection of Writings and Speeches), Lemberg (Lwow) 1939

L. ZELIGOWSKI, *Wojna w r. 1920* (The War of 1920), Warsaw 1930

A. ZÓLTOWSKI, *Border of Europe, A Study of the Polish Eastern Provinces,* London 1950

Index

Index

A NOTE ON THE TYPE

THE TEXT of this book was set in *Garamond,* a modern rendering of the type first cut in the sixteenth century by CLAUDE GARAMOND (1510-1561). He was a pupil of Geoffroy Tory and is believed to have based his letters on the Venetian models, although he introduced a number of important differences, and it is to him we owe the letter which we know as Old Style. He gave to his letters a certain elegance and a feeling of movement which won for their creator an immediate reputation and the patronage of the French King, Francis I.

Printed by Halliday Lithograph Corp.,
West Hanover, Massachusetts
Bound by The Book Press, Brattleboro, Vermont